Praise for Rose Rosetree's Face Readings

"I decided to send her a picture of myself . . . with the caveat that my wife would 'check' her report for accuracy. 'She's got your number,' was my wife's simple response."
—*The Catholic Standard*

"Rose Rosetree can spot a potential fibber a mile away. Or, in this case, 2,400 miles away."
—*Las Vegas Sun*

Governor John Engler and Mayor Terry McKane "were highly skeptical [but] both men said they found Rosetree's readings uncannily true."
—*Lansing State Journal*

"She doesn't immediately seek feedback on her accuracy. She sits back, confident that she's at least partly on target. When she does ask, it's with a flat sense of curiosity, like someone peering out of a rain-splattered window to check on a storm's progress."
—*The Washington Times*

"It's like she's known you forever . . . but that's crazy, because you just met. Still, she has described you perfectly, and not just your surface traits."
—*The Washington Post*

"Is face reading some flaky fad for the '90s? Absolutely not."
—*Redbook*

"You can't judge a book by its cover; but according to Rose Rosetree, author of *The Power of Face Reading,* you can learn all about a country star by their face."
—*Country Weekly*

More Praise for Rose Rosetree

"All over America, singles are finding that face reading is far more reliable than computer dating. Rose Rosetree is the acknowledged expert and has evolved her own system from the ancient Chinese system of physiognomy."
  —*Daily Mail* (United Kingdom)

"You haven't been reading my face, you've been checking with my Mum."
  —John Maytham (Capetalk Radio, Capetown, So. Africa)

"As Rose Rosetree says, 'The truth of what we are shows in our faces and each face, in its distinctive way, is perfectly beautiful.'"
  —*Style* (Hong Kong)

Rosetree's "unconventional look at the presidential candidates' features reveals much."
  —*The World & I*

"Rosetree's goal is to demolish societal standards which separate so-called good looks from bad. All facial features have meaning and value, she declares, regardless of their popularity or apparent lack of appeal."
  —*Aloha Magazine*

"Rosetree is a renowned aura and face reader...even skeptics will enjoy it if they are open-minded."
  —Napra Review

"Rosetree's motto is 'God don't make no junk.' For her, every facial feature tells a story. So, if you want an edge in knowing if he's Mr. Right or Mr. Way-Wrong, if he's fling material or worth a long-term investment, don't just read between the lines—read his face."
  —*Flare (Canada)*

Wrinkles Are God's Makeup

How you can find
meaning in your
evolving face

Rose Rosetree

Women's Intuition Worldwide

Wrinkles Are God's Make-up:
How You Can Find Meaning in Your Evolving Face

Copyright© 2003 by Rose Rosetree
Cover Design© 2003 by Women's Intuition Worldwide, LLC
Cover Designer: George Foster, Foster & Foster, Inc., www.fostercovers.com
Book Designer: Eda Warren, Desktop Publishing Services, Inc., www.gotraining.com
Editor: Mitch Weber; Photo Consultant: Anthony Sullivan, Account Executive, Getty Images

Face Reading is taught exclusively for entertainment and spiritual growth. The author and publisher disclaim responsibility for any decisions that readers may make based on the contents of this book.

10 9 8 7 6 5 4 3 2 1
Library of Congress Catalog Number: 2002109934
Publisher's Cataloging-in-Publication

(Provided by Quality Books, Inc.)

Rosetree, Rose.
    Wrinkles are God's makeup : how you can find meaning
in your evolving face / Rose Rosetree. — 1st ed.

        p. cm.
        Includes bibliographical references and index.
        ISBN 0-9651145-7-0 Printed in Canada by Westcan Printing Group

        1. Physiognomy. 2. Face—Social aspects.
3. Surgery, Plastic—Popular works. 4. Aging —Social
aspects. 5. Biometric identification. 6. Spiritual
life. I. Title.

BF859.R67 2003   138
                    QBI02-701900

Please direct all correspondence and inquiries to:
Women's Intuition Worldwide, LLC
116 Hillsdale Drive, P.O. Box 1605, Sterling, VA 20167-1605
Tel: 703-404-4357; fax: 413-677-1659
E-mail: Rosetree@Starpower.net

Website and online supplement: www.rose-rosetree.com

Dedication

In ten thousand places
I have seen Your faces
troubled, seeking, scattered, tossed
like so many autumn leaves.
When will Your grace show me Your Face?

Beauty of expression
lights up your creation.
Joy, compassion, newness
shine like so many perfume flowers.
When will I see That smell smile at me?

Your love, I am certain
Takes the bow each curtain.
Serious performers,
we're just so many dancing bears.
Wasn't my part to give You my heart?

— Rose Rosetree, Boston, 1969

Online Supplement

Enjoy extra face readings, photos and links to enrich your experience of this book.

Find it all at the author's website, http://www.rose-rosetree.com.

Click on the link to the Online Supplement.

Send questions or comments to Rosetree@Starpower.net.

Contents

Online Supplement at http://www.rose-rosetree.com includes:

- Bonus Chapter: Integrity Counts (This chapter features brief Integrity Readings of all U.S. presidents for whom photographs are available)
- Transformation Reading of the Author
- Transformation Readings of more U.S. Presidents
- Villains Gallery (Brief Integrity Readings of five notorious faces)
- Glossary of Nasty Names for Face Parts (Humor)

List of Photographs

All photos used in this book have been supplied by the Library of Congress, with the following exceptions: Author's personal photo collection, Rose Rosetree (2002 photo by Jan Kawamoto Jamil); Baruch/Getty Images, Golda Meir; Fotos International/Courtesy: Getty Images, Maya Angelou; Franklin D. Roosevelt Library, FDR and Eleanor Roosevelt; Getty Images, George W. Bush, Indira Gandhi in 1966, Ang Lee, Colin Powell in 2001 and 2002, Robert Redford, Oprah Winfrey; Hulton/Archive by Getty Images, Laura Bush, Lady Diana,Princess of Wales, Indira Gandhi in 1981, Thurgood Marshall, Marilyn Monroe, Colin Powell in 2002, Mother Teresa, Margaret Thatcher; National Archives at College Park, Richard Nixon; Ronald Reagan Presidential Library, Ronald Reagan

Foreword

Even I wasn't prepared for the impact of this book, and I've been involved in face reading since 1992.

As a businessman, I've found it enormously helpful for dealing with clients and hiring staff. And although I won't claim that face reading is the only reason for my success, I count it as a major reason why my small business has gone on to gross more than $10 million a year.

Similarly, I'd credit face reading for helping my business to survive the disastrous dot.com bubble mania of the late 1990's. Just one example is the time I hired Rose Rosetree to consult on a proposed business merger that, in retrospect, would have been a serious mistake.

I'm hardly the only executive to have discovered the value of the subset of biometrics known as physiognomy. The 3,000-year-old art is emerging as a hot new industry. Amid increasing globalization of the marketplace, concerns about terrorism and economic uncertainties, it makes sense to delve deeper into what can be learned about the human face.

Biometric facial recognition systems worth millions of dollars are now being installed worldwide. My fascination with this technology caused me to develop ReadingFaces.com, a unique tool that allows the best of the growing ranks of America's professional physiognomists to reach the desktops of business professionals the world over, via the Web.

All this experience notwithstanding, I wasn't prepared for Rose Rosetree's new book. She has convinced me to examine something I never used to question— how faces change over time. Assuming that faces turn a generic version of "old" now strikes me as pathetically simplistic. And about as helpful as thinking that French fries, baked potatoes and hash browns are all the same food.

There's enormous meaning in how faces age, if only we'll pay attention. Now that Rose has pointed my eyes and heart in the right direction, I'm amazed at how much more there is to so-called "facial aging." To see what she means about these changes being "God's makeup," skip ahead to the Transformation Readings. The one on Lady Diana shocked me most. How many times have you seen her face? I figured I knew everything about how she looked, but was I ever wrong!

It's that way with all the detailed face readings. You also might want to browse in this book by turning to the Integrity Reading of President Nixon, with its dramatic finish. If I hadn't seen it with my own eyes, I wouldn't have believed it. Rose's interpretation of Nixon's face is typical of her work—so accurate it would be scary, if it wasn't for her heart-centered approach. And this separates her from her peers. She stands alone as the world's best.

Rose's compassion comes in handy for the how-to part of this book. You'll learn how to examine what shows in the mirror, compare it to old pictures in your photo album and interpret how you have changed. Because Rose's writing is so entertaining, accessible and witty, it can take a while for the seriousness of her message to sink in. But eventually you get it. Absolutely everything about how your face changes is meaningful.

For a baby boomer like myself, this message couldn't come at a better time. Thanks to this book, I'll look differently at myself, my wife and my friends. If I hear that any of them is heading for the cosmetic surgeon's, even for a little shot of Botox, I'm going to urge him or her to read this book first. Rosetree really does offer a true second opinion.

Until I read this book, I didn't realize how much brainwashing I'd received when it comes to faces. Not only about aging, either. Stereotypes about race and weight run so deep, they come automatically. We can't make ourselves blind to ways that society has taught us to see, but we can supplement the foolishness with something more valuable.

I believe this book can profoundly change how we see people. The implications are enormously exciting for communication, management, relationships and the real bottom line—what you see in the mirror. Is looking older really so bad? What if it turned out to be one of the best things that ever happened to you? Whether you're 30 or 90, this book can change your life.

Charles McDonald
CEO, American Business Network
Omaha, Nebraska
January 2003

1. Wrinkles Are God's Makeup

Wrinkles are God's makeup. The rest of a face has meaning, too. This book will show you how to read it. We'll use techniques of **face reading**, an inquiry that is especially useful for exploring how people evolve over time.

Wrinkles are only the most obvious part. Ever look at an old friend and notice the changes that *don't* involve wrinkles? Maybe your friend has developed new cheek proportions, eye angles and nostril shapes. A face can evolve in dozens of ways. To a face reader, these are subtler forms of God's makeup.

You may be especially interested in changes to one face in particular: that aging stranger who stares back at you from the mirror. Changes aren't usually welcome. TV has taught us that faces are valued to the degree that they're young and conventionally attractive. And who would you rather be in life, a glamorous superstar or a forgettable character actor?

Given the social programming, it's understandable if you scrutinize your face anxiously for signs of decay. Fear you're ancient at 30, 40 or 50? Hey, if you want to know from ancient, you're going to love face reading. It's at least 3,000 years old.

Face readers from history include Aristotle, Plato, Hippocrates, Darwin, Lincoln and Dickens. Whether they're famous for being face readers or not, all **physiognomists** (pronounced fizzy-OG-nuh-mists) have an advantage in life. Instead of being limited to interpreting facial expressions, they can look through physical faces themselves to see the soul.

This book uses a distinctive, trademarked system of physiognomy that I've taught to thousands of people since 1986. Face Reading Secrets® is an update of ancient Chinese *siang mien*, designed to bring compassion as well as insight. Face part by face part, I'll show you how to use this system to gain insight into a soul's preferences in areas like power, work, money, communication and intimacy.

Face Reading, Not Face Judging

At a formal dinner party in London, one of my physiognomy students was asked by the gentleman sitting next to her what she did for a living. When Teresa Dane told him that she read faces, the gent removed his tie and unbuttoned his starchy shirt. Then he pulled it up over his face so he could hide!

Such is the terror that can be aroused by the very idea of face reading. But keep in mind, my system is not face *judging*. Just the opposite. Physiognomy reveals how people are complex, both strong and weak, and always very individual. No face reading worth the name can be done in two minutes. You wouldn't trust anybody to figure *you* out that fast, would you?

Even *observing* the physical face takes time. It's crude to instantly assess any physical feature as "big" or "small," "attractive" or "ugly." Each feature contains many categories to investigate.

Take noses, for instance. Not that I'd inflict a complete nose reading on you so early in the book, but there are plenty of categories. Many of them, when present to an extreme degree, could result in an entire nose wrongly being called "big."

What do I mean by **categories?** They're sets of attributes with two or more variations. Each facial feature, like a nose, includes many categories, each one worth reading because it gives information about something specific, like tips for career success (pun intended).

Each variation within a category is called **face data**.

What about face data could be more important than size? It's the meaning, of course. Each way that a nose might be big or small *means* something. For instance, you'll read in Chapter Eight about four different nostril shapes—and, believe me, once you know what they reveal, you'll definitely want to read them.

In Face Reading Secrets, each category of face data tells you about a talent or soul-level preference. Also included is a warning about a potential challenge or life lesson. Thus, face readers first identify data, then interpret it.

In this book we'll emphasize how faces evolve. *The Power of Face Reading*, a companion work, delves into the full range of implications for more bits of face data than we will cover here; I recommend it as supplementary reading either before or after this book.

What's a Big Nose?

Every adult human nose could be described in terms of the following 16 categories, each of which contains one option that could give the impression of that dreaded thing, a "big nose." Categories plus one option are shown in the following list. For example, under the **Nose length** category, options for face data are **short**, **moderate** and **long**. The option listed here is **long**, because some people consider a long nose a "big nose."

From the front:
1. Nose length: long
2. Width at the bridge: big
3. Relative nose tip size: chunky
4. Degree of chiseling at the tip: very strong (emphasizes a large tip)
5. Presence or absence of the nose bonus: present
6. Width just before the tip: big
7. Size of nose tip roots (flanges): large
8. Nostril shape: round
9. Nostril size: small
10. Nose angling (does the nose veer toward the right or the left?): either right or left, depending on other asymmetries
11. Nose lines or wrinkles: the mark of Divine discontent

In profile:
12. Shape at the bridge of the nose: arched
13. Thrust (how far the nose sticks out): big
14. Profile shape halfway down: arched
15. Profile shape before the tip: arched
16. Nose tip angle: down-turned

Peek a boo

As you read, some of your most fascinating discoveries will concern parts of your face you never noticed before. I've seen this happen repeatedly with my readers, clients and students. How come? Since they mostly looked for expression, they mostly saw eyes and smiles. Even there, a great deal of data was missed. How often does a non-face reader notice things like eyelid thickness, under-eye curve, lip proportions or mouth puckers?

Hardly ever! That's understandable. Why notice unless it is meaningful? But, as you'll see, there's an alphabet of data on your face, easy to spot once you become skilled at the facial form of literacy.

Literacy isn't too strong a word, by the way. Before you gained regular literacy, could you tell a "d" from a "b" or a "p" from a "q"? Back then, they were all lollipop letters. Poor thing, you couldn't tell a *dog* from a *bog*. By now, it's second nature for you to distinguish the shapes of letters. Eventually reading became easy for you, effortless even, and so rewarding that you couldn't spend a single day without it.

Face reading, likewise, can become delightfully indispensable. It's especially helpful if you're concerned about looking old. And clearly, that is a concern. Cosmetic surgery is rampaging through America like forest fires during a drought. Over the past five years, both men and women dramatically increased their rates for vanity procedures; for seniors, cosmetic surgery rates tripled.

People who don't read faces focus on the dreaded "signs of aging": sags, bags and wrinkles. Ironically, the most significant signs of aging—or evolution—are often missed completely. Every part of your face evolves over time. These changes can inspire you, once you learn what they mean. Rather than dreading the onset of wrinkles, why not learn to see what is right, even *perfect,* about them?

Perfect? Isn't that word a bit extreme?

Hey, who said that?

Us, the class.

And you thought you were alone with your own mind when reading this book....
Surprise! I've invited assorted members of our Wrinkles Are God's Makeup Class to join us and pepper the proceedings with questions.

Why not? Since 1971, I've taught classes in personal development. Hired as a face reader by corporations and party planners, I've read faces of the rich and powerful in our nation's capital, given hundreds of media interviews internationally. And regardless of where on earth the faces are from, the readings turn out to be accurate. When my students learn to use my system, their readings are accurate, too.

Questions are essential for the learning process. So I've invited virtual classmates to join you and me in the experience of this book. They'll pose questions like ones that real students have asked. You and I (and they) are all in this together. Famous faces are here as well.

Those of you who use the Internet can find extras photos if you'll click on the link to our **Online Supplement** at http://www.rose-rosetree.com. Among the goodies are links to photos, supporting references to faces not pictured in this book.

Wrinkles are God's makeup? Makeup is supposed to improve your appearance. Let me tell you, the wrinkles Mr. Mirror shows me don't make me gorgeous. How can you call that stuff makeup?

Usually makeup accentuates what you want to show others. Want your eyes to look bigger? You'll use products like mascara. But what if God, also, has something to emphasize? **Wrinkles** show highlights of the soul's journey through a lifetime. Face reading enables you to interpret that journey in depth and detail.

How about the rest of the face, the parts that aren't wrinkles?

Every part of the face reflects the soul. So when face parts change, they mirror the soul's evolution. That's why changes aside from wrinkles count as God's makeup, too.

But eyes are the only part that mirrors the soul. That's what I've always heard, anyway. Isn't there truth to that?

So what does that make the rest of your face, chopped liver? Decide for yourself, as you learn to read the alphabet of spiritual symbols commonly known as "the face."

2. The Truth About Your Face

Until they learn about face reading, most people believe that faces are determined by heredity. But determinism relates to only one thing about faces: What you believe about them will determine how you see them.

Unless you actively choose your beliefs, guess who'll choose them for you? As Deep Throat could have said about investigative reporting *above* the throat, "Follow the money."

The whole force of America's consumer culture, driven by no motive loftier than greed, programs you to believe in a highly debatable "truth"—that all natural changes to your face are bad. Then, guess what? Advertisers can sell you a cure, in the form of cosmetics, vanity surgery and so forth. When you look good, you'll feel good, and nothing in life's more important than that, right?

Wrong, actually. Character matters, not to mention finding a personal mission in life, seeking a closer connection to God, honoring family, making friends, choosing ethical actions, taking care of your physical and psychological health, earning and spending money wisely, helping to protect the environment, building community, educating yourself as a voter, plus a few other little things you could do in your spare time, such as alleviating the war, disease, ignorance and hunger that run rampant all over the globe.

Short of passing a federal law that makes it mandatory to pursue vanity as life's top priority, today's social pressure couldn't be worse. Here's just one example of our vanity culture. As I write this, Amazon.com, the online bookstore, lists 437 titles on cosmetic surgery. Every one of those titles is pro-surgery. What does that say about us?

Despite our vanity culture, you're free to choose what you believe and value. Face reading can make what you see in the mirror a story about meaning, rather than vanity. From this perspective, every face reveals secrets of the soul.

The soul connection

Here is the key to interpreting change as a physiognomist:

Each human soul expresses its uniqueness through physical face data.

Soul and face are, respectively, inner and outer aspects of human life. They're linked through a **reciprocal relationship.** If you change one, the other will change. This happens because God writes the human face as a sacred and symbolic spiritual alphabet.

Soul means the unique, immortal piece of God energy that takes form as a human being. Your soul has likes and dislikes about all areas of life, including how you solve problems best and the work choices that thrill you. Will you manage to discover these deep preferences? To honor them is to live with soul. You become increasingly authentic, awake, natural, at ease when alone, effective with others.

Learning to express your soul takes time, of course. Appropriately, in the tradition of physiognomy, there's no point to reading a face until its owner is at least 18 years old. It takes that long for your soul to form a human identity. Even physically, it takes that long for your face to jell.

Once you're an adult, your face continues to express your soul. And souls live on earth to **evolve**. We learn life lessons, making choices that set in motion future lessons. As this happens, your face records the story.

Usually facial changes start from the inside out. The inner person evolves a new way to handle an aspect of human life, such as intimacy or communication. Then, due to the reciprocal relationship between soul and face, the change physically out-pictures. Alterations like this develop gradually. Think of couples you've known who've grown closer over the years and have come to look alike.

Does face change ever happen backwards? If you change your physical face, will you change the inner person?
That's the side effect of cosmetic surgery. It rapidly changes the inner person in ways that correspond to the physical alteration. Face reading can help you to view in advance, or understand in retrospect, how a particular surgery procedure im-

pacts the soul. I've devoted all of Chapter Ten to this fascinating, practical and thoroughly counter-culture topic.

Since eyebrow plucking is so easy to do, doesn't that disprove the notion that face change has meaning?

Actually, most of the key categories for eyebrows *can't* be altered by plucking. Plucking primarily changes the distribution of hair, and this can be altered in one direction only, from more to less. We'll explore the significance more deeply in the next chapter.

What do eyebrows mean in face reading, anyway?

Each part of the face carries an overall significance. Eyebrows reveal thinking patterns. So it's appropriate that they can be changed faster than other parts of the face related to decision making, communication or work.

Different eyebrow characteristics have specific meanings, too. Whenever you'd like a shortcut to learning about a particular part of the face, such as eyebrow shape, look it up in Index II: Face Data.

How to use this book

I've packed this book with everything you need to start reading the soul's journey. Chapters present face data in order of how quickly it changes. Interspersed, you'll find sample readings.

Transformation Readings are a specialized form of face reading that you will learn to do by comparing photographs taken at different times in a person's life.

As we get started, here are some suggestions to ensure your success:

- Locate a mirror, the bigger the better. Keep it nearby as you go through descriptions of face data in different chapters. (Don't use the mirror in your car. Face reading is a full-time job!)
- Use your mirror properly. Face readers don't look down at people. Or look up at them. Look on the level to see the truth.
- Which side of the face is left, which is right? Mirrors reverse your image, so what shows on the *right* side of your reflection in a mirror

corresponds to the *right* side of your face.

- How about faces not seen through a mirror? Whether you're seeing faces in person or as photos, you must *cross over* from your right to find the other person's right. Think of it as if you're preparing to shake hands. (Otherwise you'll get stuck in the confusing thought that what you see as the left side of *his* face is actually to *your* right—enough to make a poor face reader feel dyslexic.)
- How can you progress from learning about face reading to doing your own Transformation Readings? After you've read through this book the first time, go to your family photo album and pull out photos taken at five-year intervals. With your well developed face reader's eye, go through the book again, only this time focus on what in the photos has physically changed. Ideally, you'll use head shots taken from a straight angle.
- Digital cameras have become so affordable, it's easier than ever to collect quality head shots of people you'd like to read—including yourself. Why not capture the changes your face goes through over the course of a day, a month or a year?
- For more than twice the fun, find a face reading buddy. Go through this book together and do Transformation Readings on each other. (Often it's easier to be objective about a face when it doesn't belong to you.)
- Remember the motto of Face Reading Secrets. It holds true no matter how much your face changes over time: *God don't make no junk.*

Which Side Is Which?

Mirrors reverse our images, so the right side that you see in the glass corresponds to the right side of your face. In all other cases, you must *cross over* from your right to find the other person's right, as if preparing to shake hands. This applies to seeing faces in person, screening Internet images of potential dates, watching actors in movies or examining faces in photos.

But what if someone reverses a print image? With today's technology, that's easy to do. If you suspect an image has been flipped, it's not hard to check. Find several other photos of the same person, pictures not taken at the same photo shoot. (If it's a celebrity, you can easily find many samples over the Internet.)

Use differences between left and right as reference points. Even though faces change over time, you should be able to find enough consistent asymmetries to help you distinguish one side from the other.

Asymmetries are differences between the right and left sides of a face. For instance, the next chapter shows a photo of the Rev. Martin Luther King. His right eyebrow and eye are higher than the left. His nose angles toward the left, while his chin tilts toward the right. You'll find asymmetries in every adult face, especially if that person is at least 40 years old. To date, I've found only one exception, Cher.

3. Instant Alterations

Mirror, mirror on the wall, which parts of your face change fastest of them all? This chapter will give you the answers, as we begin to explore specific face data, what it means and how it can evolve over time.

Juggling projects

The world's fastest diet has got to be slimming your eyebrows. Once you understand the consequences, however, you may not be terribly eager to go on this particular reducing regimen.

The Data

Browfulness is the relevant category. Having a lot of eyebrow hair counts as **full**, as with William Henry Harrison. Small browfulness translates as **thin**; you'll find it on Calvin Coolidge. **Moderate** browfulness consists of just the amount you'd expect. Check it out on Dr. Martin Luther King, Jr.

The Meaning

Full eyebrows represent an intellectual gift. If you have them, you can easily juggle many projects at once. The corresponding life lesson? It's learning to trust things that seem "too" simple. A complicated plan will instinctively seem more appealing than a straightforward one, even if the latter might work better.

Thin brows go with the single-minded pursuit of one goal at a time, be it a job, a relationship or a cause. Compare this to the admirable single-mindedness

President Calvin Coolidge

President William Henry Harrison

Dr. Martin Luther King, Jr.

to the famous loyalty of dogs, who serve one master at a time, mustering a degree of commitment unequaled by other animals.

What's your life lesson, if you have this gift? It's being willing to focus on one major project at a time. The thinner your brows, the more you need to set—and stick to—priorities. Otherwise you risk losing your effectiveness.

Moderate browfulness means that you're effective regardless of how many projects you juggle. What's your life lesson? It's just a minor problem, something that can happen whenever a person has face data that is attractively average. Nothing to worry about really, it's merely this:

A lack of tolerance for the rest of humanity.

You mean that perfection could make me a snob?
Frankly, yes.

When you have a gift that makes life relatively easy for you, it's tempting to judge everyone else as inferior. Such is the case with moderate browfulness. If it's a snap for you to juggle projects, you may wonder (however politely) what's going on with those weirdos around you. Why do some of them complicate everything? Why do others oversimplify?

For the ultimate tolerance lesson, keep reading faces. Unless you're as facially moderate as Ronald Reagan (more about him in Chapter Five), you're guaranteed to find many areas of life where *you* could be considered the strange one.

Change

Quick change of browfulness works in one direction only, from more to less. Women, in particular, are under social pressure to thin their brows. Fortunately this pressure has lessened considerably since the 1930's, when most American actresses wore near-identical eyebrows: skimpy and curvy. Today, women aren't so pressured to trim their eyebrows—and, with it, their intellectual functioning. Of course, they are pressured in other ways: to juggle work outside the home, caring for children and/or aging parents, plus doing most of the household chores in their "spare time."

So listen up, postmodern woman or man. If God gave you big browfulness, appreciate the gift. And consider keeping it.

Handling details

Distribution of hair in eyebrows reveals how creativity flows when a person handles details. Read one brow at a time because both sides may not be alike. Start at the top of your nose. Then follow the amount of hair all the way through to the end. How is that hair distributed?

The Data

A **starter** brow, as with Martin Luther King, has most of the hair near the start. An **ender** has the opposite, as with William Henry Harrison. For **even** distribution of hair, consider the prudent set worn by Calvin Coolidge.

The Meaning

Starter eyebrows go with creativity for starting new projects. The life lesson? Handling those "stupid little details." Although you can force yourself to do this, it drains your energy. Usually you're better off either delegating to others, redefining your scope of work so it takes better advantage of your talents or (when you can get away with it) lowering your standards.

Enders, by contrast, belong to people who revel in follow-up. Deeper into a project, you'll find that more remains to be done. It's great to have such creativity as an implementer; your only catch is perfectionism, which may needlessly delay your completion of the project.

Even brows show ability to progress through a task from start to finish, easily handling all the details. Your life lesson? Back comes that silly little problem, a lack of tolerance for the rest of humanity. Since details are such a snap for you, what's wrong with people who zip through details too fast? And what's with those foolish folks who knot themselves into a corner?

Change

If your eyebrows have ample browfulness, you can pluck starters into enders, or change evens into starters. Hey, you can do just about everything but turn a silk eyebrow purse into a sow's ear. Beware, though. Alterations may sabotage the form of creativity that suits your soul. Any major alteration can be done only at the expense of your browfulness. That represents a loss of intellectual power.

As an extreme example, there's the Alzheimer's look. Some seniors who have lost their mental acuity have also lost significant clumps of their eyebrows.

But surely, in young people, eyebrows grow back, don't they?

Not necessarily. Many people have told me that after they over-plucked once, the hair never grew back. So before you go wild with the tweezers, be prepared to live with the consequences; long-term absence of brows may impinge on your brain power.

So you're adamantly opposed to plucking eyebrows?

Of course not. Just know what you're choosing.

Actually I do recommend eyebrow plucking in one case, if you have a **unibrow**. That's where eyebrow hair grows in the space above your nose, connecting the two other eyebrow segments. The meaning is a mind that doesn't turn off, resulting in problems like insomnia and anxiety. By all means, trim that third brow. Everyone needs a third eye, but not a third eyebrow.

Can't eyebrows grow extra hair, too?

Those seemingly spontaneous quirks correspond to inner change. I've noticed this happening to me during the quarter century that I've been involved with face reading. Most notably, lots of ender hair grew in when I self-published *The Power of Face Reading*. This was the first book I ever typeset and, with the enthusiasm typical of someone with extreme starter brows, I figured it would take me only a couple of months to do it.

Wrong! Learning Adobe PageMaker took more than six months, a relative eternity punctuated by lamentations and frequent calls to Adobe's help desk. Even under ideal circumstances, typesetting is detail intensive. By the time the job was done, I'd grown a huge number of ender brow hairs. Eyebrow plucking is known to be painful. Who guessed that growing new eyebrow hair could hurt even more!

Passions of the mind

Only God knows everything, the rest of us must specialize. Which sort of information does a person handle best? The answer shows in **eyebrow shape.**

The Data

Look at shape alone. That's the only tricky part of learning to see this category. Sometimes new face readers get sidetracked into distribution of hair, browfulness or other variables. Here you're paying attention to each eyebrow's overall shape.

You'll find just three varieties: **Straight**, like the ramrod brows of Franklin Pierce; **curved**— check out those arches on John Quincy Adams; and **angled,** meaning that an eyebrow is shaped with a hinge place where the hair changes direction, such as the angled eyebrow shape on Lyndon Johnson.

Angled brows are the hardest eyebrow shape to see. The angle could connect a straight part to another straight part, a straight part to a curve, or two different segments of curve. For instance:

- Johnson's angled left brow shows a *very* long straight bit of brow hinged to a short straight bit.
- William Henry Harrison's angled right brow shows a curved bit of brow hinged to a straight one; both are about equal in length.
- Ronald Reagan's angled brows are straight toward the nose, curved toward the ears, hinged deeply.
- Our three comparison photos of Colin Powell in Chapter Six show that the angle in his eyebrows grew progressively deeper over a three-year period.

The Meaning

Straight eyebrows go with curiosity about facts and concepts. The straighter your brows, the more single-minded your fascination with ideas. For instance, after attending a Fourth of July celebration, you might give the following report:

"I had several informative conversations. The highlight of the party was learning a new application for some software I never had much use for before."

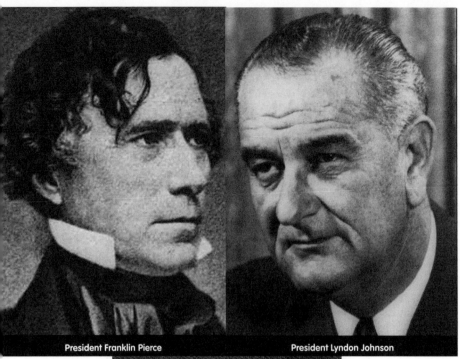

President Franklin Pierce

President Lyndon Johnson

President John Quincy Adams

Profitable though information gathering can be, it may be hard to figure out how to overcome your potential challenge: coming across as excessively cerebral.

Who would mind this the most? It's the folks with **curved** eyebrows, who are specialists in understanding emotions. The deeper the curve in your brows, the more intense your involvement in the world of feelings. So after that same Fourth of July party, your report might go like this:

"When the party began, my feelings were hurt by a friend, but later we had a pretty good conversation where she described some problems she's been having. Now I like her better."

Sensitivity that shows in curved eyebrows is wonderful, except for the potential challenge: going overboard with emotions, something less likely to be an issue for people with angled brows.

Angled eyebrows symbolize changing the direction of thought. You constantly evaluate things. If expected to waste your time or resources, you'll take action to change whatever situations don't meet your standards.

And the deeper your eyebrow angle, the more you're apt to relish conflict as part of the process. People with subtler angles use subtler means to change how things are being done, while those of you with deep angles won't be indirect or devious. You'll come right out and shake up the joint.

After that aforementioned July Fourth party, you might sum up your evening like this: "Mr. Q. was there, dropping hints about his political beliefs, which I couldn't disagree with more. Finally I called him on it and we cleared the air. There's nothing like a good honest argument!"

The potential challenge with angled brows is that others may sense the presence of your Inner Critic and feel intimidated.

How about this weird thing I've got, angles like little birds' nests?

When triangles of hair fill in the brow angles, it's a special case of **macho management eyebrows.** You revel in confrontation, even more than the people with *very* angled eyebrows who don't have that extra bit of hair.

Novelist Salmon Rushdie has the macho management trait. Unfortunately he tangled with the person who had the most extreme version of it I've ever seen, the late, and not widely lamented, Ayatollah Khomeini. This religious leader was, in fact, so ideologically macho that he offered a large reward to murder Rushdie. Hunting down a novelist who writes in a foreign language and doesn't even live in your country, now that's a pretty extreme form of literary criticism!

Remember, when this book refers to people who aren't pictured, you can see their photos via the Online Supplement. There's even a special Villains Gallery where you'll find other men with *very* extreme versions of macho management eyebrows: Adolph Hitler, The Unabomber, Muammar Al Qadhafi and Saddam Hussein.

Change

Depending on the original shape of your brows, you may be able to thin them in a way that alters their shape. Just don't overestimate your ability to change brows... or underestimate the consequences, should you succeed.

No amount of plucking could give you John Quincy Adams' poetically visionary eyebrows: *very* curved, even and up-angled. Nor could tweezers grant you LBJ's set of full, even, *very* angled and, therefore, mega-wheeler-dealer eyebrows.

Whatever shape changes are feasible for you to make, they'll affect you inwardly in corresponding ways. So be careful what you wish for, when it comes to your eyebrows. You will surely get it.

What if you were to tattoo on a different eyebrow shape? Could that change your thinking permanently?

Yes, so make that change with care. Base it on more than your aesthetic preference for a fashionable eyebrow look. Read your entire face, searching for deep patterns. Make sure that your proposed new brows will harmonize with your soul.

How about the changes made with cosmetics? Do they have consequences too?

Maya Angelou

President Thomas Jefferson

President Rutherford Hayes

To a lesser degree, yes. The consequences depart when the makeup goes off... unless you become famous for a particular look. Witness the example of Leonard Nimoy, who played Mr. Spock on "Star Trek." The actor's real eyebrows are curved. But the TV character's brows were famously up-angled and straight. They were perfect for a character whose half-Vulcan heritage made him a futuristically thinking information gatherer, with life lessons around the lack of human feeling.

Nimoy's drastic eyebrow makeover helped him to play his role, but it also affected his life. His book, *I Am Not Spock*, was a flop. In the public's mind at least, the straight-browed Nimoy persona had more credibility than the real man.

Even if you don't contemplate a career in show biz, there's a lesson here. Any role you play with cosmetics can take on a life of its own.

Intimacy revealed

Singles, newlyweds, romantics of all ages, did you know that **eyelid thickness** can reveal secrets that affect your love life? Reading this particular bit of data can turn you into an intimacy detective. To start, observe the rim of flesh that frames your upper eye—the place where those who wear cosmetics apply the eyelid-enhancing makeup called "eyeshadow." (Read eyelid thickness only on faces that have a double eyelid fold. See sidebar on the next page.)

The Data

While **full eyelid thickness** can be flaunted effectively with an eyeshadow color like bright green, the cosmetics are wasted on someone whose eyelid thickness is **small** or **not visible at all.** Both George Washington and Thomas Jefferson had huge eyelid thickness. Rutherford Hayes had small eyelid thickness, whereas Franklin Pierce had none; Maya Angelou shows one eye with each, right and left, respectively.

The Meaning

Full eyelids suggest an intense intimacy style. Personal boundaries stretch to include others, and not only for romance. Should you have full eyelids, you may have noticed that:

Eyelid Fold

Eyelid thickness is simplest to interpret in conjunction with eyelid fold. Most of my students have a little trouble at first with the concept of eyelid fold, but all it takes is one Aha! to see it easily for the rest of your life.

Start at your subject's brow bone and follow the contour to the eyelashes. A double eyelid fold has a crease beneath the brow bone, giving the illusion of two attached eyelids, while a single eyelid fold drops down from the brow bone all in one piece. The clearest way to see the difference is to ask your subject to close his eyes. Or close just one of them if the subject you're scrutinizing is *you*! All photos in this book show people with double eyelid folds except for film director Ang Lee, who has a single eyelid fold. Either type of eyelid fold, double or single, is a soul signature trait, unlikely to change during your lifetime.

Eyelid fold reveals your expectation about being socially connected to other people. A single eyelid fold means that, deep down, you consider yourself interconnected with family members and society at large. In cultures where most people have this soul signature trait, consideration is a way of life.

By contrast, a double eyelid fold means that, deep down, you believe that you're separate from others—as in having a constitutional right to *my* life, *my* liberty and the pursuit of *my* happiness. But just how socially independent is the eyelid wearer? Interesting nuances will show in the related category of eyelid thickness.

Ang Lee | President George Washington

- Emotional intimacy is what you expect, so people who need more distance may disappoint you.
- Superficial relationships strike you as a waste of time. You want to get close! (Note: This may contrast with your style as a communicator. See "Mouth, lipfulness" in Index II.)
- You can relate to the lyrics of Country Western music—songs about otherwise tough people for whom intimacy is life's be-all and end-all. Alas, many of these songs are also anthems of co-dependence. And therein lies the challenge with full eyelids.

By contrast, **small** eyelid thickness goes with tighter personal boundaries. With this face data, your sense of personal identity is strong. No matter how deeply you love your main squeeze, you need your own emotional space, your own room, your own life. Obviously, your expectations for relationships couldn't be more different from those of people with full eyelids.

Your gift is self-sufficiency. The downside? Your strong need for personal space may be misinterpreted as aloofness.

No eyelid thickness counts as a *very* extreme version of small eyelid thickness. The exception is when it goes with a single eyelid fold.

How do you interpret eyelid fold along with eyelid thickness?

People with double eyelid fold are the most likely to show variation in the amount of eyelid thickness. Even if your eyelids are as full as George Washington's, and thus you get very close to others, it's still in a context of believing that you're independent. Compare that to people who have a single eyelid fold. Even without eyelid thickness, they feel socially connected. It could be psychologically challenging to add a feeling of being even more connected.

But can't people have this face data anyway?

Sure. In fact, you'll find it in the photo of film director Ang Lee. Look carefully at his left eyelid.

Although his right eye shows a single fold with no eyelid thickness, his left eye has both a single eyelid fold and an even rim of extra eyelid thickness. I call this a **double whammy.** If your soul has chosen this combo, life will give you boundary lessons galore. As if it weren't enough to constantly feel connected to others, you'll often find yourself yearning for even greater intimacy.

In the Orient, isn't it a popular form of cosmetic surgery to add this extra bit of eyelid?

Yes, since supposedly this is a more Western look. Unfortunately, the surgery carries inner consequences that may be very challenging. I wish everyone considering this vanity procedure would learn in advance about the inner significance. Double-strength drive for closeness can bring great spiritual beauty, but the potential challenge is equally great.

Due to intermarriage, isn't there a growing number of Asian-Americans who have a single eyelid fold plus pretty big eyelid thickness?

That's true, but for these people the double whammy develops naturally, as a soul signature trait. To me, this means that before incarnating, the soul has prepared to specialize in learning about personal boundaries. Compare that to buying a look from a vanity surgeon, having no clue about the spiritual and psychological side effects, then suddenly having to live with the consequences.

Change

Non-surgically, how fast can eyelid thickness change? All it takes is one good cry. Some of us have tested this in our own personal crying laboratories! Instantly (though temporarily) and with no conscious effort, eyelid thickness can go from nonexistent to huge, or just the opposite. To a face reader, this is one very clear way that the soul speaks through the eyes.

Don't old people usually develop droopy eyelids?

Only the old people who become very dependent on their significant others, Thurgood Marshall being an example. At least as many seniors do the opposite— as with the diminishing eyelid thickness of Eleanor Roosevelt. (You'll see both examples in Chapter Five.)

That's why I say, forget the ageist stereotypes. Change in either direction is common. What matters is who develops what.

Incidentally, as long as you're questioning reality, how about reconsidering the use of words like "droopy" for faces? Vanity surgeons push words like this to shame people into signing up as customers.

My advice is, turn back to our photo of Thomas Jefferson. If "droopy" is the best word that you can summon up for him, it's time to read a thesaurus. Better yet, a history book!

Hidden suspicion

Crossed arms and a scowl ought to tell you something. But what if you want to read deeper? Lower eyelid curve reveals more than expression or body language. Subtle changes to the lower half of the eye usually occur unconsciously—but you can still read them on purpose.

How can an instant change to someone's eye shape not be considered expression?

I define **expression** as a conscious face change, done by moving voluntary muscles. By contrast, structural changes to the face are primarily **involuntary**; they happen when involuntary muscles move unconsciously, due to the mind-body connection. One example is lower eyelid curve An unconscious emotional link changes its physical shape. Though you can narrow your eyes purposely (which is expression), usually you don't know when you're doing it. In fact, many non-face-readers are clueless that this part of the face even exists, let alone that it can change, or that the changes have meaning. So you're gonna have fun with this one!

The Data

Focus on the lower half of the eye, where a woman might apply mascara to the tiny set of lower lashes. Curved lower lids form half circles—for an example, go back to that picture of Thomas Jefferson. Straight lower lids, like those of writer Maya Angelou, form a ruler-like line. To see eyelids with moderately curved lower eyelids, move ahead to page 119 and the third photo of Colin Powell, Photo C.

The Meaning

Curved lower eyelids indicate childlike openness to people, which deepens your knowledge. It comes at a price, of course. Your challenge is emotional vulnerability. Most adults don't open themselves up so fast or so far, except with people they already know well. Should you take rejection personally, you'll often get hurt.

Straight lower eyelids relate to self-protection, whether you're shy, selective or downright judgmental. Manners may hide your emotional distance from strangers. But whether or not your behavior gives clues about your inner wariness, strangers are going to have to earn your trust. And precious few will. For them, your loyalty is magnificent, which is the gift that goes with this face data.

Moderately curved lower eyelids indicate balanced openness in dealing with strangers. Will you trust them? Somewhat. Lucky you! Your only challenge in the openness department is a lack of tolerance for the rest of humanity, the people you may secretly label as snobs and gushers.

Change

At any time in your life, you'll have a **default setting** for lower eyelid curve, the degree to which you generally keep it either straight or rounded. This shape reflects

The Social Mask

Does your personality change radically in social situations? Probably. The evidence shows right on your face. However, you won't see it when posing in front of a mirror. For a true view, you need someone to follow you around in real life, snapping candid pictures.

Each of us plays many social roles: The work one, the romantic one, the one when you're playing with your kid, etc. For each of these roles, you have at least one habitual way to hold your face. I call this **the social mask.** It's the version of yourself that you try to show others, and your face reflects the impression you would like to make.

Imagine someone taking your picture when you first enter the scene (any scene) and say "Hello." Count that as one social mask. Not everyone manages to keep the mask on consistently for the whole visit. (Skilled actors are the exception; they work hard to stay "in character.")

Generally, social masks stay on tightest during "Hello" and "Goodbye." It's easiest to start noticing this on people other than yourself. Compare a stranger's "Hello" face to the more normal face that shows up several minutes later. Often a face will show considerable change.

To read the social mask in detail, pay attention to a variety of physical face data. There may be changes to eyebrow height, eyebrow shape, lower eyelid curve, cheek padding, cheek proportions, powerline dimples, nose angling, lipfulness, smile depth, Priority Areas and wrinkles. Oy vey, that's a lot of face! All of it has meaning within the system of Face Reading Secrets.

your habitual degree of openness—or the reverse. That's why I read it as a Wariness Index.

Fascinating but true, this part of your face also shifts as a minute-by-minute **trust indicator.** Within seconds of talking to someone, it's possible to go from straight to deeply curved or vice versa.

Next time you talk with someone face-to-face, have fun reading the trust indicator. You'll find it surprisingly revealing.

For additional insight, take one more step backwards into detached observation. Notice how much **mobility** the person has in this part of the face.

Watching presidential press conferences, for instance, I've noticed that George W. Bush shows little variation in this part of his face. Lower eyelid curve stays straight. **Little mobility** brings the advantage of a consistent personal style.

When the shape of that unwavering eyelid curve is straight, as with the elder Bush, an additional meaning is limited emotional range. By contrast, the president between the Bushes, Bill Clinton, routinely moves from full curve to straight. **Extreme mobility,** like his, suggests that he opens up to strangers but has also learned to protect himself from snubs. Potential challenge? It's having to deal with those snubs.

An unintended consequence of some cosmetic surgery is complete **loss of mobility** in lower eyelid curve. Even a mere "lift" can turn a face into a rigid social mask, e.g., See the before-and-after photos of Robert Redford in Chapter Ten.

Seeing through smiles

Smiles reveal how personality shifts when presenting the self socially.

Hey, don't you mean expression? I thought face reading wasn't about expression.

Here are some definitions to clarify the distinction between reading smiles emotionally (as an expression reader) vs. structurally and symbolically (as a face reader).

We've already considered that **expression** means intentionally moving the face to project emotions, such as friendliness. All that the smiler has learned by way of social skills can go into that conscious intention.

Beats Saying "Cheese"

Here's how to observe your smile as a face reader:

- Hoist up the mirror and observe the structure of your lips when you don't smile. Remember, always look at faces from a straight angle, right on the level.

- Put your mirror down. Give the most natural smile you can— switch it on and off a few times until you manage to produce a smile that feels like your everyday smile.

- Freeze. Bring the mirror up to your face, on the level. What's different about your mouth, compared to the way it looked in repose?

You may have to repeat Steps 1-3 a few times until you can see the structural changes.

Expression includes nuances of behavior related to **social status.** Has the smiler gone to finishing school, or the equivalent? People with more wealth or position learn to wear tight social masks, minimizing their facial gestures.

Expressiveness means how much emotion shows through the facial mask. Ethnic background includes cultural training about expressiveness. For instance, first generation Italians and Latinos are more expressive than newly arrived Chinese and Germans. And extroverts smile more than introverts.

Power dynamics add another overlay of meaning about the emotional content of smiles. It's well known that people with less status smile more. Unconsciously they defer to those with more clout.

All these considerations help you to evaluate smiles as expression. They tell you a great deal about temperament and upbringing. By contrast, face reading attempts to deconstruct the soul:

- What is the structure of your mouth when your face is in repose? That conveys information about who you are in private.

- How does that mouth structure change when you switch on a smile? That shows who you are in public behind your social mask.

Smiling can alter your lip proportions, mouth length and lipfulness—all discussed in Chapter Eight, which analyzes longer-term mouth changes. If you're an experienced face reader, you know these categories already, so go ahead and interpret all the ways that your smile changes your lips.

If you're a new face reader, however, I'd recommend that for now you simply observe the structural changes. This will develop your eye for face data. Put off interpretation until you've read Chapter Eight.

Either way, I know you'll have fun with the following category.

Emotional generosity

Smile depth means how much smiles open up. Symbolically, that's a big deal. (Did you ever consider that smiling is the only socially acceptable way to show complete strangers the inside of your body!)

Corresponding to the physical act of opening up, your smile depth symbolizes emotional generosity. How willing are you to reveal your inner depths?

The Data

To read this category on yourself, don't start off by grinning into a mirror. Instead, keep it nearby. Pretend that you're smiling at a friend. Freeze. Now hoist up your mirror and look.

How much of your mouth's inside shows? **Lips only, gums exposed,** and **semi-toothy** are the main smile styles; the last one has an exquisite variation, the **tooth framer,** where lips open exactly wide enough to show all the teeth, but no gums. Occasionally you'll find a smile with **lower teeth bared,** which reveals the bottom set of teeth instead of the uppers.

America's early presidents were far too formal for much smile depth. Blame the lack of modern dentistry. Or acribe it to prescience. Later research on power dynamics would reveal that smiling can be interpreted as a sign of weakness. Whatever their reason, most presidents and their wives specialized in lips-only smiles; they didn't unbend enough even to curve their mouths.

Twentieth century presidents opened up more, but the reserved smiles on their portraits may surprise you. (Library of Congress portraits are used in this book, except for Mr. and Mrs. George W. Bush, for whom they weren't available at this writing.)

Bet you can't guess which American president was the first to show teeth in his official portrait. Not JFK or LBJ, it was that touchy-feely guy, Richard Nixon.

Now guess this. Of all those relatively open smilers since Nixon, how many did the least open version, the tooth framer?

You're right if you guessed *every one* so far. The only exception is George Bush, Sr. While the right side of his face obeyed presidential protocol when he posed and gave up the standard tooth framer, his left side daringly delivered the first American presidential portrait with **gums exposed**.

Regarding first ladies, Pat Nixon was the first to smile with anything bigger than lips only. She managed a faint **semi-toothy**. The rest have posed exclusively with tooth framers. For an example of **lower teeth bared**, see the final photo of Nixon in Chapter Eleven.

The Meaning

A **lips-only** smile expresses self-satisfaction—that's in contrast to reaching out to others. If your favorite smile is lips only, perhaps you live in a state of inexpressible bliss. More likely, the meaning is lack of emotional involvement in relationships. Of course, it's also possible that you're a president or other person of outrageously high social status, which explains why you choose not to open up emotionally.

What if you're just ashamed of your teeth?

A face reader uses other face data to tell. Regardless of shame about teeth, a genuine smile shows eyes that crinkle or twinkle. It won't be lips only. By contrast, a smile that's just for show will merely curve the lips. For example, compare Agnew and Nixon in their "handshake" photo in Chapter Eleven.

But don't most TV stars smile with closed lips? I think it looks more sophisticated.

Apparent sophistication is one advantage. A **lips-only smile** can make the wearer appear contented, attractive, maybe even stunningly confident. Mostly, however, this smile relates to a life lesson, because the lack of smile depth shows that, emotionally, the smiler has chosen to give others the absolute minimum.

Sometimes we forget that TV and movies are illusion packaged as reality. In two dimensions, the lips-only smile appears less fraudulent than it looks in three dimensions. Face readers, knowing this, are far ahead of the general screen-watching public.

My prediction: You'll know that the majority of Americans have become face readers when, by popular demand, actors quit the phony mugging.

At the extreme opposite of withholding inner depth from relationships, consider those smilers whose **gums show**. Facially it's as though they're saying, "You want the inner me? Sure, how's this? Hey, want more? Would it help if I show you the inside of my cheeks and my eye sockets?"

If they could smile that big, they would. Opening up to display the maximum amount of gum tissue reveals generosity. Sound like you? When you hear about a friend's problem, is your first reaction, "How can I help?" Is your second reaction, "What more can I do?" Long before this, the lips-only smiler has asked herself, "What's in it for me?" By contrast, you give unconditionally. The challenge is being generous to a fault. The remedy? Balance.

Semi-toothy smiles can be guarded or gracious or both. You give of yourself—but only up to a point. The giving is measured, even calculated. And chances are, your smile is also slow, rather than spontaneous. The social mask is being worn very deliberately.

The **tooth framer** smile indicates rare balance in setting personal boundaries, especially about giving emotionally. Undoubtedly, if you smile in this way, you've worked hard to arrive at those fine-tuned emotional boundaries. Is it a coincidence that, when politicians smile, they do tooth framers so often? I doubt it.

Maya Angelou's photo, shown earlier in this chapter, displays a touching variation. Although her smile depth is the tooth framer at the edges of her lips, right at the center her upper lip pulls downward toward the front teeth.

I interpret that as intense self-protectiveness; after all, front teeth symbolize the ego. The suggestion is that Angelou opens emotionally to others, with hard-won personal boundaries, yet she still hasn't managed to release all the pain of her childhood years. Angelou's memoirs recount events so traumatic that she spent six years as a voluntary mute. That courageous smile is a bit of God's makeup designed to move the heart of any face reader.

Smiles with **lower teeth bared** reveal exceptional tenacity. No official presidential portrait yet exemplifies this, thank God, but you can see this data on the rare photos of Saddam Hussein that show him smiling. Another example is Muammar Al Qadhafi.

Change

Experimenting with smile styles is easy and instant, with a significance that's equally fleeting. But *changing* your habitual smile style isn't so easy. In order for a change to look and feel natural, it must come from inside, which can take years to develop. Read about these changes when you examine other long-term changes to lips in Chapter Eight.

They may not be what you'd expect. But you're already learning that face reading is full of surprises. For many people who study face reading, the biggest surprise is its potential for spiritual depth.

Although you can approach physiognomy simply as a practical way to read people—and this book will help you to fulfill that goal—face reading can also help you to become aware of a person's **Thou-ness,** a way of being that's different from your own core individuality. Experiencing Thou-ness, you can make contact with another person's soul.

Thus, you can learn to read people in a way that approaches the depth and compassion with which *you* would like to be read. Secrets for doing this begin in our next chapter.

4. Become a Spiritual Talent Scout

To a spiritual seeker, life abounds with symbols. Qualities of God's presence show in the beauty of new snow, the perfect structure of a flower. The secret to reading these symbols is taking the time to slow down and gently question where the spiritual message might be for you.

Once you ask, receiving an answer won't necessarily take a long time. In a heartbeat, God can come around the corner to meet you. Some discoveries take longer than others, but there's joy even in the waiting.

This chapter explains how you can grow spiritually by exploring multi-layered truths about faces, a search that has the side effect of awakening deeper perception. My techniques help you to delve into a face's spiritual symbols, layer by layer. In the process, you're learning nothing less than how to be a **spiritual talent scout**, someone who aims to find a deep, compassionate level of truth about each individual.

Spiritual doesn't necessarily mean **religious.** Matching Bible verses or other belief principles to daily life, practicing rituals (however beautiful), joining a community of believers—all these facets of religion can have great value. Ironically, though, being sure of "the answers" doesn't guarantee new knowledge of God.

Spirituality means asking "the questions," inviting God's presence by thirsting for it, in the here and now. Rather than requiring a set creed, spirituality demands that we approach life as innocent beginners, curious to discover truth that is not yet known. Unencumbered and spontaneous, we're more likely to be given deeper experience of Divinity.

This chapter presents **Talent Scout Rules** that aim you toward a spiritual experience of wrinkles as God's makeup, along with the rest of the ways faces change. These rules help you to see new things, elusive things you wouldn't otherwise notice, even if that face is already familiar. To show how that's possible, in

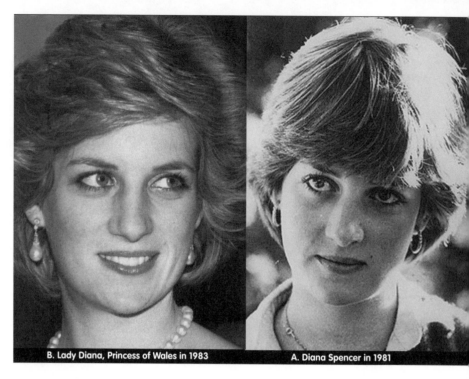

B. Lady Diana, Princess of Wales in 1983   A. Diana Spencer in 1981

this chapter I'll use the example of Lady Diana, Princess of Wales, the most photographed woman in the world. Photo A shows her at the time of her engagement to Prince Charles of England; Photo B shows how much she changed in only two years.

If you're an experienced face reader, you'll be familiar with the data I analyze, items like "cheek proportions." If not, please don't be intimidated by the terminology. For any face concepts you're burning to master immediately, you can consult Index II; for the rest, I recommend that you absorb what you can in context and wait until later in the book for the technicalities to be explained more fully.

Intention

Talent Scout Rule #1 is:

Slow down and set a worthy intention.

Stereotypes and judgments come easy. Too easy. They tell precious little about the person on whom they're being projected. As an advanced face reader you'll do the opposite of making quick judgments. It's a different game entirely, not Pin the Tail on the Donkey but Meet a Unique Human Being.

To shift into this spiritually-oriented game, it helps to prepare yourself at the start. Before you read anyone's face, take a deep breath, center yourself in the present and ask your spiritual source to open you up to the highest truth available. (More detailed instructions for using intention spiritually can be found in my book *Empowered by Empathy,* pages 115-125.)

- Before reading Diana, I set aside all that I had heard or read about her. That could be considered afterwards. As a spiritual talent scout, I would encounter her pictures as though I knew nothing about her.
- Then I set the following intention: "Inner Teacher, help me to see a deeper truth about Diana through her face."

Refine your vision

Your next step as a spiritual talent scout is to ask yourself what on a face is, physically, most extreme. In the words of Talent Scout Rule #2:

Very = Very

For at least 3,000 years, face readers have paid attention to the *verys*. The more extreme a particular bit of face data, the more extreme the inner meaning.

As you already appreciate, face readers don't just see facial features, like ears and noses. Each feature contains many categories, such as ear angles and nose length. Within each category, there are at least two contrasting traits, or bits of data, such as in-angled ears vs. out-angled ears.

Talent Scout Rule #2 invites you to refine your perception within a trait. Is an in-angled ear just somewhat in-angled? Or does it look as though it's fastened to the head with chewing gum? That would be a *very*!

Notice the *verys* to add nuance to your interpretations. For example, the young Diana Spencer had only two *verys*:

- **Lower eyelid curve,** beneath both eyes, was 10 on a scale from 1-10. This suggests extreme openness to the strangers in her life.
- Her Priority Area with the greatest length was eyebrow-to-nose tip. This was far greater than the other two areas, hairline-to-eyebrow or nose tip-to-chin. Having **Priority Area II** so large suggests that, contrary to

her reputation as the diffident "Shy Di," this young woman was intensely ambitious.

- Having so few *verys* on a face is unusual—a sign of beauty. By contrast, consider Abe Lincoln, pictured and described at length in the next chapter. Even when young, he had at least 10 *verys*. When older, he developed even more.

Read without forcing

The Very = Very rule can help you to refine your insights. So can the flip side, Talent Scout Rule #3:

Barely there = Don't bother

When face data is the opposite of *very*—so barely discernable that it's hard to shove it into a face category—don't bother with it.

And this is your fancy way to justify laziness, right?

In this case, laziness counts as a virtue. It's counter-productive to struggle or squint over a physical trait so iffy that its very existence is questionable. The inner correlate of barely-there data won't be strong, either. Therefore, effortless face reading is more likely to be accurate.

- **Cheek proportions** can be read for insight into leadership style. In Photo A, it's hard to read Diana's cheek proportions (i.e., no part of her face is clearly widest). Yet in Photo B, her face is definitely widest at the cheeks. The meaning? Power style wasn't greatly developed for Diana when she first became engaged to Prince Charles. But she came to have the power style of someone who loved the limelight and was eager to act like a leader.

What else don't you read?

As a spiritual talent scout in training, there's plenty more besides iffy traits that you need not bother to read.

How about the most important thing in faces, heredity? Science tells us that faces are a combination of our genes and the luck of the draw, nothing more.

Science is correct, except it only tells half the story. Science explores material life. How about spiritual life?

Regarding faces, consider the possibility that the spiritual side drives the material side. You have an inner set of preferences about how to be human, a soul. This evolves over time, depending on your thoughts, values and behavior. Physically, your soul is expressed through face data. So that's a reason for faces to change, other than heredity.

But don't certain traits run in families?

Sure. So do diseases—and a spiritual perspective tells us that inner patterns of imbalance are the underlying cause of recurring physical traits, as well as diseases.

How can you prove that inner patterns, rather than heredity, cause people to develop their facial characteristics?

If you look with an open mind, you'll prove it to yourself. How many people do you know who aren't physically related but still look alike? That's because their inner patterns are similar. For instance, consider:

- Compatible couples who draw closer over the years, often coming to resemble each other—not just their facial expressions but their physical face data.
- Adopted children who bond with a parent can grow up to physically look like that parent.
- Blended families (ones that really blend) provide many examples of people from different gene pools who wind up developing similar face data.
- And the exception that proves the rule: Twins. If heredity explains everything, how come identical twins look increasingly different from each other as they mature? It's common for me to point out significant physical differences, then interpret them accurately.

Hey, how about people who look like their dogs?

Funny though that sounds, it also makes spiritual sense. Pets serve their owners spiritually, sharing their psychological quirks and sometimes even their diseases.

Not only will pets take on the strongest physical resemblance of which their bodies are capable, they'll also take on illnesses that relate to spiritual difficulties of their owners. The best authorities to verify this idea would be animal communicators, psychics who telepathically converse with dogs and other pets. Beatrice Lydecker, author of *What the Animals Tell Me,* had this to say when I asked what she noticed about the connection between pets and their owners:

"I have talked to animals who tell me about diseases but, according to their vet, don't have them. But the symptoms are starting to develop. I then look to the owners to find out what they are experiencing. Usually they have that same problem.

"The closer the bond of the animal with the person, the more this happens. It's called empathy pains."

Celebrate free will

Regardless of whether you're scrutinizing the family goldfish or your uncle, be sure to use Talent Scout Rule #4:

Aim to see an individual.

Expecting faces to be mostly about family resemblance is enormously limiting. In small towns, people gossip in ways that suggest that all family members think or act alike, e.g., "Isn't that just like a Jones? They never have any gumption." or "Those Smiths, always putting on airs; they'll never come to any good."

Go back far enough in your own family tree and you'll find people who lived in small towns. Gossip like that is one reason why, most likely, your ancestors got the heck out of their small town as fast as they could!

Many people today believe that individuals express family tendencies. If you're going to follow that model, might I suggest that you do it thoroughly. Buy into the full set of related concepts:

- Your career should be that of your father.
- Your marriage should be dictated by parental choice.
- Family honor must be defended, even to the death.

- Unquestioned sacrifice for your family should be your life priority.
- Your personal happiness doesn't matter, so long as the family prospers.

Unless you'd like to live according to that complete set of family values, I'd recommend that you follow Rule #4.

Racing to conclusions

How about race? That's got to be an important part of what shows in faces. It's sure the first thing I see.

Long before you considered the art of reading faces for meaning, you've had extensive training in how to stereotype people, and not just by race. You've learned to judge the face owner according to beauty, social status, age and weight. By the time you've finished this book, I hope you'll have put all these limiting stereotypes in their place: history, not reality.

You mean that I've got to pretend to be color blind? That idea has always seemed so phony to me.

I recommend paying attention to what really shows in a face, which is far more than color. Most people are so busy seeing color, they notice maybe five percent of what an individual's face really looks like. Think I'm joking? Turn to Index II at the back of this book and count how many of the facial categories you've never noticed before.

Racial stereotyping creates tunnel vision; there's a limit to the spiritual information that can be gained by scrutinizing the color of skin and eyes, or deconstructing hair texture.

Forget color when you read faces, not to be blind but to see things of greater value to a spiritual talent scout. When you read an individual rather than playing Stereotype Lotto, it's so much richer. You'll be shocked, shocked!

Sure, many Americans of African origin have full lips, but so do Americans with ancestors from other parts of the world. And many Americans with dark complexions have white, red or yellow in their genealogical paintboxes.

Intermarriage is such a fast-growing trend that, in your lifetime, America will have no one majority "race." Even now it's inappropriate to think in terms of ethnic purity. For more people than you might suppose, ethnic origin is a complex puzzle.

I'm proud of my heritage, including my race. What's wrong with that?

Nothing, unless pride turns into prejudice. In today's world—even more so, tomorrow's world—the best way to tell about a person's racial heritage is to ask. That's also how you'll get to hear the wonderful family stories that can go with taking pride in one's roots. Don't feel comfortable asking? Then chances are you don't know the person well enough for her ethnicity to be any of your business.

Thus the Talent Scout Rule #5:

Set aside all stereotypes, race included.

But what if you're just plain curious about race?

Go out and get a Ph.D. in physical anthropology. Or you could try something even more daring. Become the first person on your block to switch from *race* reading to *face* reading.

- When Britain's heir to the throne, Prince Charles, announced his engagement to Diana Spencer, staunch royalists questioned if her blood was sufficiently blue. How best to compare her with Charles, by the whiteness of her skin or the narrowness of her nose? Face reading doesn't give the answer but genealogy does. Upon consulting the royal couple's family trees it became clear that Diana was *more* ethnically British than Prince Charles. Oops!

What spiritual talent scouts can find

Spirituality that's valid bears fruit in the practical world, so the knowledge you gain from faces ought to help you with real-life situations.

To make this possible, my system informs you about **personal style.** This means an individual's comfort zone in areas of life like handling details, dealing with power and spending money.

Judgment need not be involved in matters of personal style. Yet most people make assumptions about style that run even deeper than racial stereotypes. We expect others to behave "Just like me," assuming that what comes naturally for us is the one and only way to behave.

As if! The expectation doesn't just cause disappointment. We'll overlook what people *do* have to offer. As a spiritual talent scout, you'll find greater joy in relationships when you can make room in your heart for human variety.

How can you open your heart? Talent Scout Rule #6 can help:

Read another's face with as much care as if it were your own.

Each human soul, just as it is right now, contains the potential for a glorious life. Rule #6, combined with the facts of face reading, can help you shift into deeper appreciation of that potential.

This makes it possible for you to live in the world of **namaste** (pronounced naah-maah-STAY), a Sanskrit word that means "The God within me salutes the God within you."

- Comparing the two photos of Diana, do you notice that she developed **nose grooves**? Here's a perfect example of the use of Rule #6. If you saw these vertical lines appear on either side of your nose tip, would you think, "Phooey, those lines just wreck the perfection of my queenly visage?" Or would you prefer to interpret them as meaningful?

In my system of Face Reading Secrets, the appearance of nose grooves is about feeling financially unsupported by family. Think how that might relate to Diana.

Before her marriage, she was accustomed to generous support; the family fortunes came to her without strings attached. After the marriage with Charles became troubled, her sense of security shifted. Did Diana feel that money came to her grudgingly? She had to perform, slim down, follow protocol.

Even then, her face suggests that she didn't feel her support flowed freely enough. I'm willing to bet that her famously extravagant wardrobe purchases were more about rebellion than the love of shopping.

Note that personal style with finance, as shown in nose data, is never about specific amounts of cash. (If face reading could divulge exact sums, we'd have had to charge just a little more for this book!) Wealthy though Diana had been before her marriage to Charles, she became even richer; what evolved on her face, however, didn't correspond to her objective financial status. Instead, her face reflected subjective worries about her marriage, including lack of support.

Facing up to asymmetry

Another refinement to your work as a talent scout comes when you appreciate **asymmetry,** the difference between the left and right sides of a face. Many of us have no idea, at first, how much difference can show in these lengthwise segments.

Face reading systems vary in how they interpret asymmetry. In Face Reading Secrets, we view the **right side of the face** as a source of information about the public self, a.k.a., your masculine energy. What kind of first impression do you give? How do you come across in the workplace?

By contrast, the **left side of the face** reveals the private self, a.k.a. your feminine energy. What are you like in your long-term relationships? How do you handle family and close friends?

Is the right side of a photo the same as the right side of the page?

No. Admittedly, this can be confusing at first. Remember to treat the person whose image you're viewing as though the full person were there and you were about to shake hands. Cross over in your mind to reach for that person's right side.

How about your own face in a mirror?

That's the only exception. Thanks to our reversing mirrors, the right side of your reflection shows on the same side as the right half of your face. Makes it easier to comb your hair! As a face reader you'll soon learn to allow for the difference between your own reflected image and that of everyone else you examine.

- The most significant asymmetry that developed for Diana concerns the amount of curve in her lower eyelids. You've already had a chance to see that, in Photo A, her eyes scored 10 (for maximum curve) on my **Wariness Index.** By Photo B, only Diana's right eye kept that curve. Her left eye turned into a 1, as straight as could be.

The meaning? In public, Diana remained open and vulnerable. But in her personal life, keeping the secret of her unhappy marriage to Prince Charles, Diana became highly wary—loyal to those who proved themselves trustworthy but suspicious of everyone else.

Faint asymmetries in youth often become more exaggerated over time. Our choices and destiny converge to shape the soul, which then outpictures facially.

- You'll have to look very carefully at the earlier photo of Di to observe that her nose angled slightly toward the right. To see it, start with the later photo, where her **nose angling** had become more pronounced.

The meaning? Like many influential figures (including ones you'll read about later in this book), Diana's public life became far more important to her than her personal life.

Asymmetry happens! In fact, asymmetry happens so often that it's the single most universal way for faces to change over time. Even when wrinkles don't develop, asymmetry does. How come? Life hands us disappointments, pressures and pleasures. We respond by evolving different styles of behavior in public and private. Hence Talent Scout Rule #7:

Seek the spiritual meaning of asymmetry.

Baby pictures and photos of seniors are worlds apart. For an adventure in family history, find both types in your family album. Compare the degree of symmetry. Most infants show a breathtaking similarity between the left and right sides of the face. By contrast, you may *never* find an eighty-something face with perfect symmetry. I haven't.

If you think you're pretty good at finding asymmetry now, wait until you have gone through this book. **The I Method,** explained on the next page, can fine-tune your face reader's eye.

Usually non-face readers miss asymmetry completely… starting with ourselves. When we look in the mirror, that's our blind spot: We tend to favor one side, our "good" side, the one we consider more attractive.

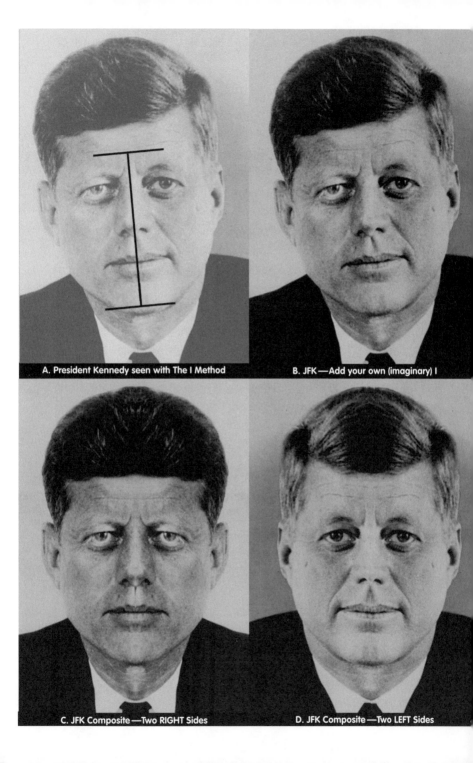

A. President Kennedy seen with The I Method

B. JFK —Add your own (imaginary) I

C. JFK Composite —Two RIGHT Sides

D. JFK Composite —Two LEFT Sides

Develop Your I for Asymmetry

To enhance your face reading skills, develop your eye for asymmetry with the I Method. To get you started, here are four special photos:

- Photo A shows how to use the I Method. For a visual aid, I've placed a capital letter "I" down the middle of the nose, at the bridge.
- Photo B gives you a regular head shot of President Kennedy. This time, use your imagination to compare both sides. Draw that imaginary "I" down the middle of his nose. Lengthen the "I" until it cuts the face in two. Now compare the two lengths, eyebrow to eyebrow, ear to ear, etc.
- Photo C is a composite picture, showing just the right sides of Kennedy's face; the right side was copied, then flipped and put back together with the real right side. (Note: Don't try this at home —unless you're using a photo. In that case, you may be able to do it with computer software. A low-tech version is to take a rectangular mirror and position its edge over a photo. Place the mirror along the down stroke of the imaginary "I." This will be at right angles to the photo. Then, if you tilt your head, you'll see a full face made from one half reflection, one half photo.)
- Photo D is a composite picture, showing two left sides of Kennedy's face.

Usually the I Method is done without the benefit of these composite photos. So you won't see dramatic contrast, like that between photos C and D. But you still can gain information that has dramatic impact.

Go on to use the I Method to read the subtle clues of asymmetry everywhere from TV and newspaper photos to real-life visits with strangers and friends. Less obvious than wrinkles but no less important for that, facial asymmetry is one of the most informative types of God's makeup.

Actors and models do this even more than the rest of us. Entire scenes can be staged specifically to show a star from that "good" side.

- Nearly every photo you'll see of Diana, dating from her marriage to Charles, emphasizes the right side of her face. This makes it harder to spot her growing facial asymmetry.

As a spiritual talent scout, you'll be more concerned with the truth than with flattering camera angles. In fact, you will learn to see right through those photographer's tricks.

Asymmetry isn't something to hide. It's evidence of a soul's evolution. Through relationships and work, people move through lessons that leave their mark. Every asymmetry on a face holds many meanings. Besides its specific significance, each asymmetry deepens a person's human complexity. Take your face as an example.

- There's good news: Each asymmetry means that your repertoire of personal style includes more than one choice from a given category. That means you'll be able to understand the styles of more people, based on your personal experience.
- Then comes the bad news: You increase the opportunities to give yourself a hard time. No matter which way you choose to act in a given situation, another part of you knows very well how to act differently. Reading your own facial asymmetries can help you to reframe these conflicts. It's healthy to have differences between your public and private selves. Face reading helps you to understand this aspect of human complexity.

Exquisite scouting

Did you know that someone (an angel, perhaps) has singled out one or two parts of each face to show the soul's most special gifts? Hence Talent Scout Rule #8:

Look for a face's area of greatest refinement.

Some faces have tougher features than others, signifying resilience. More delicate faces, overall, show more sensitivity. Either way, a part of each face is **chiseled,** being physically shaped in a way that is delicate or refined compared with the rest of that face.

How can you tell what's chiseled? Hold the intention to find it. Look calmly and quietly at a face. One or more bits of face data will jump out at you. The meaning? For you, this face data is chiseled.

Finding this is more subjective than other aspects of face reading. So when you look at the photos of Diana, you might find something different from what I find. Whatever you consider chiseled is valid for your face reading.

Interpret it in a way that's helpful for the person whose face you read. Even if you don't have the chance to tell that person what you admire, what you find will uplift *you*. (This holds especially true for any chiseling you find on your own face.)

- Go ahead and look at the young photo of Diana, then at the older one. What stands out for you?

For me, it's the crisp contour of her chin. The crispness stayed although the shape of Diana's chin bottom actually changed (highly unusual though it is for this part of the face to change shape). Look carefully and you'll see that her chin bottom went from a curve to a well-honed angle.

The meaning? Diana's will was uncommonly strong. The change to her chiseled chin shape suggests that she went from making choices based on pleasing people to choosing what would keep her in control of her life and relationships. Biographically, we know that Diana used her iron will to starve herself into anorexia. She also developed strong self-interest after dealing with an unfaithful husband and a queenly mother-in-law who despised her.

Pain drives most face changes. Some of the deepest long-term pain shows at the level of the chin. Having chiseling at this part of her face suggests to me that, when taking on her life contract, Diana was given a boost to her personal strength. She knew she'd need it.

- Another example of chiseling is the lip definition on the Rev. Martin Luther King, Jr. In the photo on the next page, see how his lips are accentuated by a fleshy ridge, like a natural lip liner? If you have this data, your standards for communication are high, and you may be exceptionally articulate as a speaker. The only challenge lies in being your own harshest critic.

Dr. Martin Luther King, Jr.   President John Tyler

Where wrinkles fit in

Another way you'll see faces differently as a spiritual talent scout is by reading wrinkles in context. Sure, anyone can *notice* wrinkles, and we're especially prone to do so if our personal collection is sizeable. But often people look for one or two types of wrinkle as a basis for making sweeping character judgments:

- "Laugh lines," those horizontal marks off the outer eye corners, supposedly mean having a sense of humor. Thus, they show "a good person."
- "Frown lines," any vertical lines near or between the eyebrows, supposedly mean that a person frowns all the time. Thus, they show "a bad person."

Not exactly, friends. Wrinkle enthusiasts would be wise to use Talent Scout Rule #9:
Read wrinkles in context.

In practice, make that *contexts*. Three different contexts can help you:

First, you pay attention to the part of a face where the wrinkle develops. **Wrinkle location** matters more than a newbie might think. Examine how a wrinkle is shaped and where, exactly, it's located.

- Lady Diana acquired a double set of powerline dimples on the left side of her face. They suggest that, in her personal life, she developed the form of charm related to humility.

A second context for wrinkles involves **comparing wrinkles to other face changes.** Begin by considering what changed structurally. Then examine the lines and furrows and gauge which type of change was more prevalent. Often the non-wrinkle changes are more significant than the wrinkles. Now there's a context that it takes a face reader to notice!

- No quick illustrations can be offered here, but you'll find plenty of examples in the next chapter—all five of Chapter Five's Transformation Readings, in fact.

A third context involves relating wrinkles to **highly individual traits,** those *verys* we've already discussed. Again, examples follow in Chapter Five.

Dare to read the soul

Some face data won't change, the soul signature traits. Before incarnating, the soul sets up a contract for the basic rules in that particular game of life. Who will be the parents? In what neighborhood? Under which socio-economic conditions? What will be the main challenges and strengths for that soul?

If you're curious about life contracts, including the core issues that come up for a person again and again, you'll pay particular attention to soul signature traits. This book emphasizes the other side of the coin, how a soul evolves, as seen in the next chapter's Transformation Readings. As a spiritual talent scout, however, you should be aware that additional techniques are available expressly for learning more about souls and their life contracts:

- A **Soul Reading** compares photos taken at different times, emphasizing what *doesn't* change. Interpret these bits of face data, using the system of Face Reading Secrets, and you'll find patterns—multiple layers about themes like loneliness, control and vulnerability.

Presidential Wrinkle Research

To put wrinkles in context, let's interpret a cheek wrinkle that took longer to evolve than Diana's, the one on President John Tyler: On both sides of his face, he grew long wrinkles, running from cheekbone to chin.

For a location context, use the start and end points of Tyler's wrinkle. Cheeks are about power while chins are about ethics. Next, relate the wrinkles to his very high cheekbones, which mean a preference for uncompromising action based on principle.

Thus, the meaning of Tyler's distinctive pair of wrinkles is that he chose uncompromising action based on principle, a choice for which he paid inwardly. The coin of this realm is deep suffering; and the resulting winkles could be considered his sales receipt.

To further deepen your reading, supplement insights about wrinkles by asking for information about your subject's life story—whether from history books or by asking questions directly to the person for whom you're doing the reading. If John Tyler were here with us, we might ask, "Can you remember an action you took, based on conviction, for which the consequences were especially painful?"

Time and again, in my real-life face readings, clients have answered similar questions with a great big "Yes!" Often wrinkles and scars appear right after a trauma. And the significance of that trauma corresponds exactly with what it means in face reading.

- Another type of face reading related to the study of the soul is a **Past Life Influence Reading.** Lee Stone, a past life regression therapist (www.leestone.net/PastLives.html), has developed a technique for entering into an altered state of consciousness, then investigating different physical features to learn which lessons from *previous* incarnations are most important for *this* lifetime.

- My favorite way to supplement research into souls is an **Aura Reading**, which can reveal both gifts of the soul and the pain that temporarily obstructs the expression of those gifts. With practice, auras can be read from photos as easily as faces; they'll reveal how even the relatively fixed face data can be inwardly modified.

Here's an example that shows how aura reading can pick up where face reading leaves off. A certain sexual wattage is an important aspect of a soul's original set-up. Facially, it shows in the degree of **philtrum definition**. (See page 168.)

The given amount of sex appeal can be used in various ways, shaped by personal choice over time. For specifics, supplement physiognomy by reading the part of the aura about sexuality. You'll find fascinating contrasts. Some people develop a great deal more sexual magnetism than their philtrum definition would suggest, while others who began with great innate sexiness have squelched it; the contrast is apparent aurically long before it out-pictures onto an altered philtrum.

- Lady Diana had only moderate philtrum definition. Reading her aura in Photo A, I found that although her sexiness was also moderate, it had a joyful, earthy quality. By Photo B, her philtrum hadn't changed. Yet the sexual part of her aura was stunningly different, far bigger and more powerful, yet disconnected from body awareness (not unusual with anorexia). Her charisma grew enormously, gaining a more calculated seductiveness.

When I read clients professionally, I check both the face and the aura. Where they give different data, I favor what shows in auras. That's how reliable a tool it is for spiritual talent scouting. But whether or not you read auras yet, face data is immensely revealing. Once you've become fluent at seeing the data and interpreting it, you really can read people like a book. And that includes a great deal about their spiritual lives.

Free will

Celebrate the power of free will with Spiritual Talent Scout's Rule #10:

Facial change = Free will in action

Simple as this rule seems, when the full meaning dawns on you, it's mind boggling. Much of our social programming trains us to believe in illusions; many of these illusions are pursued so actively that we don't notice face data at all.

A stranger may stand inches away from you, yet look right past you, her eyes vacant and mouth busy, gabbing away on a mobile phone. If she does notice you, she'll scrutinize your coloring, your makeup, your slenderness or your outfit. She'll deconstruct your hairstyle—do anything but make contact with your face.

It takes a special person, a spiritual talent scout, to be willing to do that, or to dare explore the mystery of another human soul.

Even when faces are seen clearly and face changes are noticed, social programming trains us to interpret all data in terms of illusions. My personal favorite is the invocation of gravity as supreme facial cause, as if the downward force could really apply especially to one face part more than another. I've heard people use gravity to "explain" changes to eyebrows, eyes, noses, cheeks, lips *or* chins—with all the rest of the face mysteriously unaffected.

As a face reader, you're allowing your perception to make direct contact with reality. What on a face physically changes? You're way ahead, talent scoutwise, when you realize that people evolve… and the evidence shows in their faces.

- You've already read that Lady Diana developed **nose angling** towards the right, signifying the growth of ambition. In addition, her **nose padding** decreased, reflecting a change in work style. This highly unusual face change suggests that Diana lost her team-player mentality and, within the confines of palace life, struck out on her own. In the light of her biography, doesn't this make sense?

Come on, Diana slimmed down a lot. Couldn't she just have lost weight around her nose?

If noses were involved in weight loss, all the yo-yo dieters in America would have their nose padding go in and out like accordions. Can you imagine the scene at work, when your dieting co-workers go back on the job after vacations, and every-one checks out everyone else's nose width?

Trust me, that wouldn't be a very productive form of face reading. You'll see very few instances of nose padding alterations that happen non-surgically. Re-garding Diana's nose padding, it makes sense that the physical change reflected her growing independence as a public figure.

Unanswered questions

Many people read faces just for fun, and that's fine. As far as I'm concerned, it's some of the biggest fun around. But this chapter has introduced you to the spiri-tual depths.

In the Mormon religion, there's a beautiful tradition that restricts entering the main sanctuary to members. Tourists are given another building to visit. Every religion has its mystical aspect, a holy of holies that can be entered only when the aspirant is no longer a newbie… and has shown enough curiosity and sincerity to earn admission.

Although face reading isn't a religion, it similarly includes an esoteric aspect Not apparent to beginning face readers, it's a delectable invitation to those who hunger for more truth. You can become an accomplished face reader, yet have no desire to become a spiritual talent scout. Or you can become both. It's up to you.

What if you just want to tell good from evil?

That question is important enough to deserve a thorough answer. You'll find it in the final chapter of this book. Turn to it now if you like. But I recommend that you explore good and evil later, rather than sooner, because it will require your greatest skill as a spiritual talent scout.

The next chapter presents detailed Transformation Readings. None will give you a black-and-white answer to questions of good and evil. But they can help you adjust your eyes to spiritual life's many shades of gray. In a face reader's holy of holies, years can be spent adjusting to that light, an education that is both subtle and powerful. Then, when you least expect it, you may start to see flashes of gold.

The 10 Talent Scout Rules

1. Slow down and set a worthy intention

2. Very = Very

3. Barely there = Don't bother

4. Aim to see an individual

5. Set aside all stereotypes, race included

6. Read another's face with as much care as if it were your own

7. Seek the spiritual meaning of asymmetry

8. Look for a face's area of greatest refinement

9. Read wrinkles in context

10. Facial change = Free will in action

5. Five Famous Faces

Five Transformation Readings in this chapter use my system of Face Reading Secrets to compare photos taken years apart.

Ronald Reagan, Thurgood Marshall, Indira Gandhi, Abraham Lincoln and Eleanor Roosevelt are especially fascinating subjects. If you're already familiar with these major historical figures, you may be amazed at how a Transformation Reading can deepen your knowledge of them.

But the main purpose of sharing these readings is simply to demonstrate some samples of Transformation Readings. By now you've learned some of the ways that faces change; more details await you here. You will see how dramatically faces can change—in ways you never thought faces *could* change—and how facial patterns emerge that are related to inner evolution.

Although some people find these detailed readings enormously entertaining, others may find them intimidating. Please don't. There are many ways for you to have fun with this chapter's offerings. Here are some if the possibilities:

- Play detective. Before each reading, see how many face changes you can find on your own. Compare Photos A and B. Make a list of your observations. Interpret away! Then compare your readings with mine. (If you find something interesting that I neglected to mention, please write to me at Rosetree@starpower.net. I'd love to hear your interpretations.)
- Stretch yourself. If you're already an experienced face reader, you'll be familiar with the many technical terms of physiognomy. But have you emphasized how a face evolves over time? These Transformation Readings may inspire you to do more sophisticated talent scout work.
- Go at your own pace. If you're a less experienced face reader, you may be stumped initially by the large number of technical terms, explained here

only in summary. Use Index II as your resource. Flip back and forth between the face data pictured here and the referenced pages in the book, where the data is defined in detail. Although this kind of investigation takes a bit of work, your skills as a face reader will improve enormously.

- Lighten up! If you're new to physiognomy, you don't have to research what you don't understand in context. You may prefer to skip this chapter altogether and return to it when you read this book the second time around. But before you skip, *be sure to read the section on Eye Height Asymmetry, page 77.* This information will serve you well in all your face readings.

- Here's the boldest idea of all. Use this chapter as an apprenticeship exercise for doing your own Transformation Readings. Here's how:

1. Choose a sample reading to use as a model. (For simplicity, pick the shortest of the readings here, the one of Lincoln.)

2. Choose your own pair of before-and-after photos of someone you know well. This person will be the subject of *your* Transformation Reading.

3. Give your insights *gravitas* by choosing a quiet, dignified setting for your work, where you won't have distractions or interruptions, and you keep by your side either a pen and paper or a recording device, like a cassette tape recorder.

4. Scan through your chosen model reading from this chapter (e.g., Lincoln's). Notice that it includes three major sections: the early face, what changes, and the wrinkles. (Sometimes a Transformation Reading includes additional sections; disregard them to simplify this apprenticeship exercise.)

5. As you scan each major section of the model reading, do the same sort of reading on your photos. Record it. Repeat until you've gone through all three sections: the early face, what changes, and the wrinkles.

6. After you're done, review your reading and fine-tune it. At this point, if you wish, you may choose to share it with other people.

7. After you've done a few of these readings, they'll come easier, and you'll be in a position to give them to others as gifts. Eventually, you may even decide to do readings like these professionally.

A. Ronald Reagan in 1940

B. President Ronald Reagan in 1980

Ronald Reagan
A handsome advocate for conservative values

- As a Hollywood actor, Ronald Reagan appeared in 53 movies. One about a football player earned him the nickname "The Gipper."
- As President, he attacked big government, cutting taxes and domestic social programs.
- His widespread popularity was undiminished by the Iran-contra scandal and unprecedented deficit spending.
- Famously optimistic, he was known as the Great Communicator.
- President from 1981-1989.

The most beloved Republican president of the 20th century is arguably our handsomest president ever. What's especially significant is that none of these handsomeness-related traits changed over the years.

The early face

Research into beauty has shown that, technically, attractiveness means moderation—being the quintessential man (or woman) in the street. Reagan is blessed with moderate eye set, moderate nose width, moderate nose length, moderate mouth length, moderate chin length, moderate chin curve, moderate chin thrust and a beautifully proportioned ratio of face length to face width.

Other handsomeness traits include how Reagan's eye length and eye width equal the dimensions of his nose tip. In addition, his ear length matches the length of his nose from bridge to tip.

Every face shows a power style. Surprisingly, Reagan barely squeaks into the leaderlike category; you must look hard to tell that his cheeks are the widest part of his face. (Contrast that to Lincoln's hugely prominent cheekbones.) Reagan's are generously padded, signifying support from others. His confidently understated style of leadership resembles an accomplished horse trainer who can, when he rides, go easy on the reins.

"Handsome is as handsome does." This old saying about handsomeness means that actions matter more than good looks. For Reagan, however, face readers could adapt the meaning of this saying to "Handsome is, *so* handsome does." In other words, when someone has physical good looks, his actions are especially likely to be rated as handsome, or popular.

Why? For each bit of face data that is average, there's the greatest number of people with similar data, folks who can understand the corresponding personal style because they have it, too.

Oddballs like Lincoln are harder for the man in the street to understand. As reported in *The Washington Post,* Lincoln was vilified during his lifetime as a "liar, thief, braggard, buffoon, usurper, despot, monster, scoundrel, perjurer, robber, swindler, tyrant, fiend, butcher and Ignoramus Abe. And those were just the insults from the North."

By contrast, Reagan seemed Teflon-coated against criticism. His soul couldn't have chosen anything more perfect to ensure popularity: his handsomeness (i.e., physical averageness) symbolizes a moderate personal style in a variety of areas:

- His **moderate eye set** signifies a relatively easygoing style for solving problems.

Remember, technical terms in this chapter can be found in Index II.
Explanations follow later in this book.

- **Moderate nose width** means ease in working with others: being neither a loner nor open to criticism as an excessive delegator.
- **Moderate nose length** translates into a flexible work style.
- **Moderate mouth length** suggests a gift for appealing to the largest possible number of people without having his honesty questioned.
- **Moderate chin length** signifies courage without undue risk taking.
- **Moderate chin curve** helps others to identify with his rationale for policy decisions.
- **Moderate chin thrust** brings an appearance of healthy aggression kept within reasonable bounds.
- The well-proportioned ratio of **face length to face width** represents a soul-signature gift for influencing others with apparent effortlessness.
- **Equal proportions of eyes, ears and nose** help Reagan to achieve his reputation as the "Great Communicator."
- Of course, it also helps that Reagan has the lower lip proportions that physiognomist Lailan Young has dubbed **"blarney lips."** He's a natural at persuasiveness.
- Finally Reagan's faintly **leaderlike power style** corresponds to attracting attention without seeming overbearing.

Reagan's secret weapons

The Star Wars president has plenty of weapons to draw on to ensure popularity. Facially, this corresponds to the data on his face that *isn't* moderate.

A **right eye higher than the left** indicates a social style that values male authority over female intuition, a value traditionally shared by the majority of the American people (and one reason we've never yet had a female president).

Paralleling Reagan's preference for form over feeling, consider the proportions within his ear structure. **Outer ear circles** are larger than the inner ear circles. This symbolizes unconsciously trusting facts over feelings.

Not only does Reagan have **low ear position,** his left ear is *very* low. This relates to deliberation as a decision maker, especially in his personal life. Lucky

Sensory Preference

Research into learning styles (including Neuro Linguistic Programming) shows that most individuals have a deep inner preference for being either visual, auditory or kinesthetic. One of the more abstract techniques of physiognomy is to link these preferences to the relative size of features within a face.

Although it's not the most accurate component of face reading, you'll find that big-eyed folk are often visual, those with large ears are auditory, while people with noses largest are kinesthetic. Having equal proportions among these features, as with Reagan, is extremely rare. It means being able to receive information, and receive it powerfully, through all three modalities. Reading faces for sensory preference was discussed in my first physiognomy book, *I Can Read Your Face*, p. 227-235.

guy! A quick speed of intelligence is tough for presidents because the corresponding challenge is impulsiveness. (Bill Clinton's *very* high ears may have represented his biggest personal liability in office.)

Reagan's deliberate low-eared instincts help to counterbalance his **lowbrows,** symbols of spontaneous speech. His **angled, full eyebrows** relate to a managerial mind set, able to oversee many projects simultaneously.

Reagan also has an **undefined philtrum,** which probably didn't help his movie career. Lack of sex appeal may explain why he was relegated to B movies, since highly sculpted philtrums are practically a job requirement for leading men and ladies. Other Republicans with presidential aspirations have had far more sex appeal, shown facially. That includes Reagan's Director of Policy Development, later a leader of the Christian Coalition, Gary Bauer.

But sexiness plays differently in movies and politics. Our only contemporary presidents with highly sculpted philtrums have been Kennedy and Clinton, both of whom have had problems with handling their highly-tuned sexuality. Thus, history suggests that, as far as presidential faces go, overall handsomeness is safer than raw sex appeal.

Remember, technical terms in this chapter can be found in Index II.
Explanations follow later in this book.

The biggest surprise in Reagan's face is his **long canine tooth** on the right. This signifies highly effective (and usually hidden) aggression. In his public life, Reagan was unstoppable.

If the young Reagan asked for a face reading, he'd be complimented on his potential for popularity and success. Perhaps, though, he might be invited to develop more of an inner life.

To prosperous Americans, his administration represents a refreshingly straight-talking rescue of the free enterprise system; those who fault him as President will cite his insensitivity towards the poor and the environment. You need look no further than your own high school homecoming king and queen to realize that people with popularity often look down on life's apparent "losers."

Haven't you known beautiful people like Reagan back when you were in high school? Later some are hit by hard knocks, forcing them to evolve in ways that show on the face. By contrast, Reagan leads a charmed life until his post-presidential encounter with Alzheimer's. Even if you don't know the details of Reagan's success story, you can infer it from all the non-changing elements of his face.

What changes

Reagan's uncommonly youthful appearance reminds us that sometimes life can be easy. America's oldest president has enjoyed a wildly successful career, a stable marriage to an adoring second wife, wealth beyond his childhood dreams and recognition in his own lifetime verging on hagiography. So, what's there to change?

In fact, three of the ways his face changes are so common, they could be considered standard issue for an American president:

Reagan's **out-angled right ear** becomes in-angled, meaning increased skill at social conformity in public life.

His relatively **thin lips** grow slightly thinner. Thin lips are an asset in office because they correspond to reserve about self-disclosure. How likely is it that Reagan would have given a Clinton-style interview about his preference for boxers or briefs? Fat chance when Reagan was governor, even less likely when he was president.

The final predictable change is the straightening of Reagan's **lower eyelid curve.** His youthful photo shows relative straightness in his public (right) eye but deep curve in his left eye. Later, both sides of his face develop ruler-straight lower eyelid curve, corresponding to extreme wariness of strangers.

In the realm of *surprising* changes, Reagan smashes two stereotypes about aging. This seems appropriate, considering that his very election to the presidency, at age 69, broke through a glass ceiling of ageism.

Do you believe that **earlobes** automatically grow with age? Then pay close attention to Reagan's right earlobe. Although his left earlobe, corresponding to the President's private life, doesn't change significantly, his right earlobe shrinks, losing nearly half its length. This suggests that, through the years, Reagan has become less aware of his physical surroundings but, perhaps, more interested in metaphysics. Maybe he's been listening to his wife's astrology readings!

Do you expect **nose tips** to automatically grow over the years? Then scrutinize Reagan again. He keeps his moderately sized, round nostrils. (They're indicative of moderate inclination toward spending coupled with resourceful management of debt.) But his nose tip does change…by growing *smaller*! This suggests diminished concern about saving money, of interest to political observers who point out the increase, under Reagan, of the national debt.

Smiles differ from photo to photo, of course, but it's particularly interesting to observe Reagan's mouth in Photo B, the portrait taken at his ranch (the place where, presumably, he feels most free to be himself). Notice the *very* **crooked smile,** angled towards the right. It signifies speech directed toward the public, not necessarily backed up by private belief; the advantage of this style is charming persuasiveness, the drawback is lying. A comparison of Photos A and B suggests that, over time, the degree of crookedness in Reagan's smile increased considerably.

The wrinkles

The pattern of Reagan's wrinkles was set in his early years. By Photo A, taken at age 29, he's developed most of what will show for the rest of his life.

Powerline dimples on his cheeks (related to charm) serve the Gipper well. A **suffering line** on the right side of his youthful face scores the area from nose

Remember, technical terms in this chapter can be found in Index II.
Explanations follow later in this book.

to mouth. Because it's on the right side only, the line suggests an awareness of pain that will be useful in his career. It's unusual to not also have the personal version (on the left side), and Reagan adds this later. Even for such a relentless optimist, public service can be an education in suffering.

Eye extenders add to Reagan's charm from a young age. These symbols of convivially reaching out to others increase through the years. Reagan never develops the complimentary eye wrinkle, eye deepeners that symbolize the inward striving for wisdom. He does, however, develop a fascinating evolution of the eye extenders on his left, where the wrinkles extend so far they range over to his cheek. As part of this process, Reagan has facially traded in the deep powerline dimple on his left cheek. Bet you didn't think such deep wrinkles could entirely disappear, but take a good look!

This corresponds to a power shift in his personal life. Reagan's wrinkle revolution suggests an early strength at charmingly implementing his own ideas; later he comes to rely on the advice of close friends, translating their ideas into action. Idealists might be appalled that a leader could use his influence to fulfill ideas that originate from other people. But ask anyone experienced in government, business, even grass-roots community organizing. Teamwork is the mature and pragmatic way to go. Indisputably Reagan's bent for cooperation strengthened his rule.

The most interesting wrinkle development for Reagan is his **mark of devotion** (visible in Photo B only), where an anger flag at his left eyebrow has moved upwards to his third eye, signifying anger sublimated into service.

Reagan wasn't just one of America's most popular presidents, he was one of the most deeply social men ever to live in the White House. A powerful consensus builder, he was so skillful that even his political enemies had to admire his gift for leadership. Reagan did in office exactly what he set out to do; his personality came across as relaxed, confident and dependably conservative.

One of Reagan's most endearing and reassuring qualities is that he never seemed to change. This certainly is confirmed by his Transformation Reading. Faces of presidents usually change extra rapidly, due to the pressure of high public office. Yet so little change was inscribed on Reagan's face, his eight years in the White House could just as easily have been spent relaxing at his ranch. Reagan fulfilled his destiny in a way that made him a hero to all Republicans. He was handsome, with all the best that implies, from beginning to end.

A. Thurgood Marshall in 1957

B. Supreme Court Thurgood Justice Marshall in 1970

Thurgood Marshall
A brilliant mind dedicated to social equality

- Built his legal career by vigorously defending the rights of African-Americans against racial discrimination. From 1940-1961, was Legal Director of the NAACP.
- During World War II, opened doors for African-American soldiers to become officers in the U.S. Military.
- Planned and pursued a long-term strategy to eradicate segregation in public schools.
- Won the Supreme Court case of Brown v. The Board of Education, which declared illegal the segregation of public schools.
- Supreme Court Justice from 1967-1991.

Although deservedly famous for his contributions as a Supreme Court Justice, Marshall's face shows gifts that could help him excel in any intellectually demanding profession. Even more extraordinary is the way those gifts evolve.

Remember, technical terms in this chapter can be found in Index II.
Explanations follow later in this book.

The early face

In Photo A, a **far-set right eye** pairs with a **close-set left eye.** This asymmetry suggests that, when working, Marshall has a broad vision, using imagination and creativity to solve problems. Yet in his personal life he can be a meticulous craftsman, careful to get details right. When dealing with work that is personally important to him, Marshall can, of course, combine both kinds of vision. (Indeed, the combination of visionary and craftsman comes to characterize his career.)

Deeply-angled eyebrows suggest a mind that takes nothing at surface value. Marshall's face also shows the special creativity of starter brows, the inclination to innovate. Beyond that, his full eyebrows reveal the capacity to juggle many projects at once.

These eyebrows deserve your scrutiny. If you look closely at the muscles directly above them, you'll see that Marshall has developed **eyebrow bulges**, related to intellectual forcefulness.

If a man is destined to change the world, he must have a way to communicate powerfully. Marshall's mouth is **short**, corresponding to a gift for sincerity. This indicates that he chooses his words for truth value, rather than popularity value.

Like many with an important role to play on the world's stage, Marshall's **nose angles toward the right,** just at the bridge.

You may notice, too, his **down-turned nose tip,** indicating a gift for career management: planning the steps for his advancement, then sticking to his plan.

Given his **small nose padding,** from bridge to tip, the young attorney brings independence to his work. He's self-motivated, less concerned with pleasing others than with achieving what he sets out to do. And that is to restore opportunity to a population that has advanced shockingly little, socially and economically, since the days of Civil War reconstruction. Born in Baltimore, just below the Mason-Dixon Line, Marshall shows the independent work style symbolized by a **narrow nose bridge.**

His **moderate lower eyelid curve,** a 5 on the scale from 1 to 10, symbolizes an easy balance between openness to people and self-protection.

Other assets in Marshall's youthful face will change in meaningful ways. Pay attention to what will change after Photo A:

- The rare trait of **high ears** relates to a quick mind. Combined with the other intellectual gifts already mentioned, Marshall can think circles around those who oppose his ideas.
- His **survivor power style,** signaled by a diamond-shaped face, suggests an ability to keep going, even when the going gets tough.
- And his moderately **out-angled ears** reveal that, although not intimidated by society's rules, he's still not as far-out as a young Prince Charles or a Ross Perot; Marshall can play the game, he'll just play it with an edge.

If the young Thurgood Marshall were to request a face reading, I'd say that I expect great things from him, given his intellectual brilliance and drive. But I'd warn him to take care of himself. And to please change that mustache!

The **mustache depth,** obliterating his upper lip, is a problem since Marshall's mouth already has **moderate lipfulness** (relating to small self-disclosure) and is **proportionally small** in comparison to his eyes and ears.

The combination relates to a challenge with bottled-up speech, the habit of saying far less than he could. Considering this man's mind, work ethic and integrity, he'll be sure to have an impact on his profession. But will he speak up enough on his own behalf?

When Marshall was named to the Supreme Court, 13 years after Photo A, I would have warned him about personal problems ahead. Two challenges, related to some of his talents, could make his job extremely frustrating on a personal level.

First, his **independent work style,** related to his narrow nose and out-angled ears, might make it personally agonizing for him to spend the rest of his professional life at a highly conservative workplace where all decisions will have to be made by majority vote. (No wonder he'll later shine at writing dissents.)

Five Famous Faces **71**
Remember, technical terms in this chapter can be found in Index II.
Explanations follow later in this book.

Second, does the poor man have any idea what he's getting into, bringing **high ears** into the Supreme Court? I'm not being entirely facetious here. As someone else who has high ears, I can attest to the challenges that go with this trait: impatience when people dawdle, frustration with lack of closure. People with high ears don't merely have the ability to decide quickly. It's a need. We can't stand having matters remain unresolved for months or years without our having the power to speed things up.

What changes

You won't find many Supreme Court justices with high ears and, in this respect— probably after enormous frustration—Marshall has adapted beautifully to his new corporate culture. His ears settle down to a **middle position.** They also become more **in-angled,** suggesting that he comes to care more about fitting in socially.

Undoubtedly, when you compare Photos A and B, ears are not the main change that you notice. Marshall has **gained weight,** a lot of it. And some of that weight shows above the neck. But here's an experiment that may surprise you. Compare the *left* side of his face in Photos A and B. The amount of **extra cheek padding** in either photograph isn't great, despite the weight gain.

In face reading, the meaning is clear. In his private life, Thurgood Marshall doesn't feel strongly supported by others.

Next, compare the *right* sides of his face in Photos A and B. You'll notice that what changes most in Marshall's face isn't weight-related at all. Check out his jaw width. Marshall's **right jaw** has gone from very narrow to very wide. That's bone and muscle, not flab.

So, what's involved, if not chubbiness? In public, TM has learned to hold his ground and hold it resolutely. A tripled jaw width has been earned through monumental tenacity and, no doubt, enormous inner pain. Being a pioneer sounds wonderful if you're in heaven, planning a life contract. But imagine what it's like, here on earth, becoming a target for the collective fury of the segregationist south. Marshall has truly earned that glorious bit of God's makeup.

Cheek proportions are also changed by Marshall's new jaw asymmetry. On the right, corresponding to his personal life, he gains the **polite power style**—an even face width from forehead to jaw. This relates to getting things done without calling much attention to himself. On the left, corresponding to his public role, Marshall's jaws become the widest part of his face; that's the **pacifist power style** of someone who cares deeply about getting along with others.

Anger is the potential challenge with this face data, where periods of conciliation are punctuated by bursts of concentrated, pent-up rage. Marshall is, in fact, remembered for some of his blustery asides, as when a death penalty argument came before the Court. When Justice Rehnquist complained that an inmate's appeals had cost the state too much money, Marshall interrupted, "It would have been cheaper to shoot him right after he was arrested, wouldn't it?"

The theme of getting along with others, despite his controversial public role, also outpictures in changes to Marshall's **eyelid thickness.** When young, his right eye has no eyelid thickness while the left eye shows a small, even rim. This combination points to independence in social relationships, particularly work relationships. When older, his face changes so that both sides show *very* large eyelid thickness. This suggests he has come to depend on close relationships.

Thankfully he changes his mustache depth into a **lip framer,** related to speaking up for himself—a wise choice indeed.

These social changes are highly significant, but Marshall has changed intellectually, too, in ways that could be considered even more extraordinary. He develops **far-set eyebrows,** a rare configuration indicative of a deeply reflective mind with far-ranging ideas.

Brow height also changes drastically. Middlebrows turn into *very* extreme highbrows, signaling a strategic advantage for circumspect communication. This justice can keep his own counsel and wait to express his ideas until the timing is right.

Eye angles shift, reflecting a change in TM's outlook. Photo A shows both eyes to be *very* up-angled, symbolizing idealism. Apparently that has been knocked out of him fast! His right eye becomes only slightly up-angled, indicative of a cautious optimism, while his left eye angles down. This signifies compassion attained through personal suffering.

Finally, Marshall's **Priority Areas** evolve. Which of the three face lengths is longest? On Photo A, it's Area I, hairline to eyebrows, which marks a personality best designed to be effective with intellectuals. On Photo B, all three areas equalize.

Five Famous Faces **73**
Remember, technical terms in this chapter can be found in Index II.
Explanations follow later in this book.

Marshall's personality has gained greater appeal to all three types of people: intellectuals, ambitious strivers and the salt of the earth, practical folks.

The wrinkles

Marshall has not wrinkled. It's that simple. The **suffering lines** that show in Photo A actually shrink over the 13 years until Photo B.

Looking casually, you might think that Marshall has developed anger flags, but if you look more carefully you'll see that these are shadows. What has happened, really, is that his **eyebrow bulges** have grown more pronounced, casting those shadows. The bulges signify greater intellectual forcefulness.

Although the justice's face has not developed wrinkles, you may feel that he has come to look physically tired, an impression caused by a more detached eye gaze, the increased cheek padding and the heft of his eyelids. None of these factors necessarily gives that impression, however. Consider:

- Warren Harding's **detached eye gaze** caused him to look sinister, not fatigued.
- **Increased cheek padding,** being a symbol of social support, added to the clout of Nixon and Kennedy.
- And **huge eyelid thickness** didn't make George Washington look tired, as you can see by consulting his image on the nearest $1 bill.

But if you still can't shake off that impression of exhaustion in Marshall's image, it could be that you're picking it up from his aura. By reading his energy field, I'm struck by the dramatic contrast between his aura in the two photos shown here.

The younger man's **root chakra** (the layer of his aura corresponding to pure physical vitality) is dazzling. He has the kind of charisma where you'd feel him enter a room even if your back was turned. In the older man, the root chakra has lost dazzle but gained solidity; there has been a staggering loss of physical vitality in exchange for a deepened ability to endure.

Marshall was one of America's great warriors. Instead of a military uniform, he dressed in judicial robes, wearing a face whose intellectual power grew greater, more principled and compassionate, through the years.

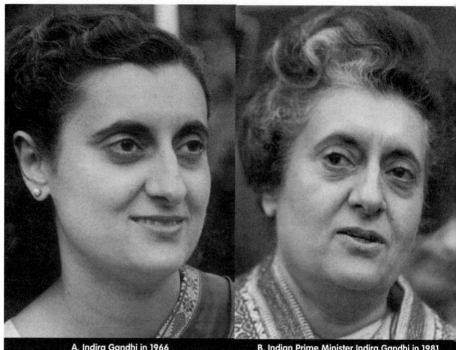

A. Indira Gandhi in 1966

B. Indian Prime Minister Indira Gandhi in 1981

Indira Gandhi
Great promise, mixed results

- The first woman elected to lead India, the largest democracy on earth.
- Was the daughter of Jawaharlal Nehru, the first Prime Minister after India won independence from the British Empire (Gandhi was her husband's last name).
- Helped her country to improve food production and develop industry. Her slogan: "Remove Poverty."
- After convicted of breaking election laws, she refused to resign. Instead, she imprisoned her enemies and imposed censorship on the press.
- To crush secessionists, attacked the Sikh religion's holiest shrine. Over 600 Sikhs were slaughtered.
- Was Prime Minister of India 1966-77. Was re-elected in 1980, then assassinated in 1984.

Remember, technical terms in this chapter can be found in Index II.
Explanations follow later in this book.

Great promise, with mixed results, shows in the evolution of Indira Gandhi's face. In a country where women have endured subservient status and few legal rights for thousands of years, Nehru's daughter is born with the unlikely destiny of prominent political leadership. Soul signature traits will help her to carry out this life contract.

The early face

To explore Gandhi's gifts for leadership, let's start with her face data for communication.

- IG has the **up-angled mouth** often found on favored children of political leaders, conveying a lifelong expectation of praise from others.
- A **mouth higher on the right side** indicates the habit of saying expedient things in public, things not necessarily believed in private.
- Problematic when interpreted in conjunction with her other mouth data, Gandhi's **smile depth** is remarkably small. To appreciate the inner significance, try this experiment. Take out your mirror and mimic the minimalist parting of her lips, then notice how you feel. To intensify the feeling, hold that faint smile while saying, "I'm so open to sharing my genuine inner self with you." As if!
- Other interesting asymmetries on the young Gandhi relate to her social outlook. First: **lower eyelid curve** is greater on the right than the left, signifying that she seems more open to people than she really is.
- Second: if you look closely, you'll notice that IG has a **deep-set left eye**, in contrast to a right eye with average depth of set. This suggests a gift, in her personal life, for hiding her true reactions to people, whereas in public she can more easily appear forthright.

To appreciate the potential charm in these two asymmetries (both depth of set and lower eyelid curve) consider that two of Hollywood's hottest actresses have exactly the same combination (with asymmetries in the same directions as Gandhi's). Who would have thought that both Julia Roberts and Sandra Bullock would look so much like the Indian leader? Also, like Gandhi, their **noses angle toward the right**—a fame trait that you'll read more about in Chapter Eight.

Besides face data related to worldly success, the young ruler also shows notable sensitivity traits. **Large eyelid thickness** suggests closeness to people she works with, as well as friends and family. **Curved eyebrows** indicate thinking driven by emotion.

And ear proportions are dominated by **huge inner ear circles**, meaning that IG is unconsciously driven by her personal belief system and, therefore, has little inclination to view life objectively. You'd love the ruler of your country to have these sensitivity traits, on the condition—and it's a big condition—that you agree with her politics.

Other soul signature traits include **high ears**, suggesting a quick speed of intelligence (with the potential for impulsive decisions); a **long, broad chin,** indicating exceptional ability to recover from adversity (and potential challenge with ethical choices); plus a **narrow nose bridge,** relating to the desire to be accountable only to herself when working (or, in her case, ruling).

Were Gandhi to come for a face reading when first elected to high office, I would congratulate her on the combination of astute political instincts with a deep inner life. For this very reason, however, I would warn her against going politically overboard based on personal attachments.

This challenge helps to explain, if not excuse, the great mistakes of her rule. But though she'll later try to bend the rules of democracy, I wouldn't be too quick to judge. How easy would *you* find it to rule her fledgling nation, beset by ancient traditions of prejudice, oppression, ignorance and poverty?

What changes?

Good comes of Gandhi's rule, despite the political corruption. And some of her face changes suggest that she grows as a leader. For instance, Photo B shows that she develops a **nose bonus,** that extra bit below the nose tip, between her nostrils. This symbolizes service as a major motivation for work.

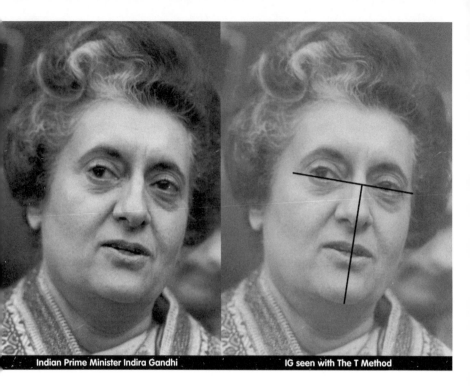

Indian Prime Minister Indira Gandhi | IG seen with The T Method

The **T** Method

Eye height asymmetry can be hard to spot in photos. Sometimes they're designed to make the eyes appear level, as is the case with the photo before you. Use the T Method to outwit photographers.

Imagine the down stroke of a **T** from the bridge of the nose to the chin. Then imagine the crossbar of the **T;** use one of the eyes, at the tear duct, as your reference point. Extend your imaginary crossing line from the bridge of the nose, past that tear duct, to the other side of the face.

Now, do the eyes line up above or below that horizontal line? Photos like these trick casual viewers, who glance at the eyes and never notice how far the rest of the face has been skewed to create the illusion of evenness.

Her **ear position** changes, too, from average to low. This physical change registers a shift in decision-making style, with increased willingness to deliberate.

Responsible to India's starving millions, how could this sensitive ruler *not* worry about money? Identifying with her people's financial worries, IG's **flared nostrils** turn triangular. This suggests a shift in spending style from cautiously experimental to deeply fearful of financial waste. This face change proves that Gandhi's most famous slogan, "Remove Poverty" is no mere rhetoric. She really cares about this.

Witnessing ample pain (including her own at eventually being ousted from power), the angle of Gandhi's left eye drops. This **down-angled eye** relates to personal suffering, normally leading to greater compassion for others.

As her political troubles intensify, however, IG grows increasingly power hungry rather than more compassionate. Her **wide jaws** thicken, indicating a stubborn commitment to staying in power. Enhancing the asymmetry to her **depth of eye set**, her left eye moves farther inward while she develops a **protruding right eye**. This suggests divergent social behaviors: secrecy in private, high involvement in her public role—and a loathing of being disrespected.

Another shift, subtle but noticeable, intensifies the dominance of IG's **right eye height.** (To see it, use the **T Method,** shown on the previous page.) The meaning for Gandhi is simple. Increasingly she values her public self over her private self. Frankly, these eye changes are ominous.

In addition, a fascinating shift to lip proportions has her go from blarney lips to **outspoken lips,** where the upper lip has grown fuller than the lower lip. Feeling increased license to speak her mind, IG surrounds herself with sycophants, resulting in a vicious cycle of believing that she can get away with whatever she chooses to say or do. However, assassins cut that cycle short.

The wrinkles

In contrast to her many other face changes, IG develops relatively few wrinkles. A faint **anger flag** on the left suggests that she finds it harder to control her personal life than her public domain.

Five Famous Faces **79**
Remember, technical terms in this chapter can be found in Index II.
Explanations follow later in this book.

Eye deepeners develop, but not eye extenders; those circles beneath her eyes reveal that in times of trouble she looks inward more than her detractors may suspect. Flaws aside, Gandhi's face does suggest that she is a deeply sensitive woman who feels personal responsibility for her choices as Prime Minister.

Most touching of all the face changes are her **nose grooves**—vertical lines that develop on either side of IG's nose tip. Evidently she feels cut off from financial support.

As I read it, that change demonstrates how deeply India's first female Prime Minister has identified with her nation's notorious poverty. In this period of post-World War II history, both China and India faced nearly insurmountable obstacles. But unlike China, India made a commitment to freedom. In struggling to hold her young democracy together the best she could, Indira Gandhi paid with her life.

Abraham Lincoln
Conservative values, radical change

- Elected as the first Republican president.
- Extraordinarily difficult personal life included political and financial losses, early deaths of significant others and marriage to an emotionally unstable wife.
- One month after his inauguration, the Civil War began.
- Freed all slaves in Confederate territories with his Emancipation Proclamation.
- Supported creation of a national banking system and the first federal income tax.
- Assassinated one week after the end of the Civil War.
- President from 1861-1865

Lincoln's youthful portrait is a far cry from the ravaged countenance we usually associate with him. In his unconventional way, isn't he a startlingly attractive man? Maybe the biggest shock, from a face reading perspective, is his movie-star caliber **philtrum definition.** Those well sculpted grooves from nose to mouth attest

A. Abe Lincoln in 1848　　　**B. President Abe Lincoln in 1863**

to strong sex appeal. Who knew? History informs us that the man was physically awkward, lacked social graces and had no fashion sense whatsoever.

But sex appeal isn't the same as conventional good looks. Even in glam-obsessed, post-modern America, senators don't look like runway models. Sexiness can take the form of charisma and, thus, have impact that goes far beyond the boudoir. Someone with Lincoln's juicy kind of presence makes you feel more alive. Outright seduction may be unlikely, but at least you'll perk up and listen to what the man has to say.

Whether you call it charisma, chemistry, or It, Lincoln is well endowed. No doubt he needs that It, has It packed into his suitcase of soul signature traits to help him fulfill his destiny. Otherwise, given the lack of marital happiness in Lincoln's personal story, wouldn't that chiseled philtrum later sink into his face? (That's exactly what happened to Mr. and Mrs. FDR, as you'll read in Chapter Eight.)

Lincoln is, in fact, supplied with a generous share of face data that doesn't change. Spiritual talent scouts will find this especially fascinating because so much of his face data is extreme and unconventional—for a president, for anyone.

Five Famous Faces 81
Remember, technical terms in this chapter can be found in Index II.
Explanations follow later in this book.

The early face

Cheeks are astonishing for Lincoln, considering that he is destined to be president. Pay close attention to those cheeks in Photo A: *very* prominent, the widest part of his face by far, and relatively unpadded. No other American president has had such a high-profile leadership style.

Also rare for someone who will later become president, his dominant **Priority Area** is hairline-to-eyebrow, indicative of a personality that emphasizes learning. The challenge is criticism from those who are annoyed by abstractions or lofty ideas.

Lincoln's extreme **lower eyelid curve** is likewise unusual for a politician, especially when paired with his enormous **eyelid thickness.** Together, these traits reveal uncommon sensitivity. Besides being open to people, he cares about having genuine closeness in relationships.

Yet his **ear angles** are outies, conveying that he's used to playing by his own rules—helpful for a man who later will have to improvise a way to hold a warring nation together.

Unusually **large inner ear circles** balance his outer ear circles, which suggests a natural balance between sensitivity and realism.

And the extreme **ear size** in proportion to his other features tells us that Lincoln is a remarkable listener.

Another unchanging *very* for Lincoln is his **lip proportions**, with the lower lip about four times fuller than the upper lip. Most high-level politicians share this trait, though to a lesser degree. Honest Abe's integrity, however, is unusual for a politician; my aura reading of him suggests that few presidents have been more scrupulous about telling the truth. (See his Integrity Rating in the Online Supplement.)

How would we caution the young Abe Lincoln if he came for a face reading? "Isolation is your biggest life lesson."

In private life, it might be hard for him to find a partner with a compatible combination of sensitivity and enormous personal power.

The pull of interpersonal closeness is strong, as evidenced by the eyelid thickness, under-eye curve and deep inner ear circles. Yet other traits show an equal and opposite push: those *very* out-angled ears and his unpadded cheeks symbolize independence.

And Lincoln's **near-invisible upper lip** suggests potential difficulty with speaking up for himself; the challenge is compounded by what shows in the relative sizes of his ears, eyes and mouth—proportions that indicate he's far more likely to learn about others than to speak up for himself.

A face reader might also draw Lincoln's attention to the **power scar** on the right side of his face. Being a deep vertical, positioned between cheek and mouth, this scar reveals life lessons related to dealing with power in his career, plus challenge requiring self-defense through speech.

What changes

Lincoln masks his power scar by growing a beard. But he cannot hide the **war mound** that develops on his right cheek; it's similar to marks evolved by two other wartime leaders, Grant and FDR. The war mound relates to a long-term battle and shows a soul's close identification with the fate of his side during the conflict.

The Civil War president also develops **deep-set eyes**—a highly unusual kind of face change—indicating that, through bitter experience, he has learned to keep his own counsel.

He also develops a third white showing beneath his eyes. Usually this **sanpaku** trait suggests a feeling of personal inferiority or even giving away personal power; with Lincoln, I wonder if it isn't more a reaching out for someone he can look up to, a search that is never satisfied.

Growing a **beard** is a good choice for Lincoln. Accentuating his chiseled jaws, the beard symbolizes determination.

The wrinkles

Suffering lines are a soul signature trait, evident early in Lincoln's life. But he develops other wrinkles as he grows in spiritual stature.

Remember, technical terms in this chapter can be found in Index II.
Explanations follow later in this book.

Lincoln acquires **horizontal forehead furrows**, mostly on the left. Since this corresponds to drawing on intuitive, inner strength, it's especially impressive to find it on someone with such high status in public life.

Eye deepeners grow, particularly on the left. These horizontal wrinkles signify looking deeper for truth, particularly in his personal life.

Nose grooves develop, cutting off the small flanges to the side of Lincoln's nostrils. These lines show that he has ceased to expect financial support from others. Given the degree to which he identifies with his people (related to his eyelid thickness), these nose lines suggest that he's taking on suffering connected to the material hardships of the American people on both sides of the Civil War.

At the top of Lincoln's nose, a **burnout line** is etched, indicating that work responsibilities deplete him.

In the last two years of his life, Lincoln will evolve even more dramatically than in our Photo B, taken in 1863. Lincoln's face shows about 10 years of facial wear-and-tear for each of his years in office. By the time of his assassination, Lincoln has the look of the frail elderly—although he's just 56 years old.

To a face reader, Lincoln's face was remarkable from his earliest days. His countenance evolved magnificently, inscribed with his heroic struggle to preserve the United States.

Eleanor Roosevelt
Extraordinary evolution

- Textbook example of the childhood from hell: alcoholic father, cold and neglectful mother.
- America's most active First Lady, her causes included the rights of women and minorities, the pursuit of world peace.
- Nursed husband, Franklin Delano Roosevelt, around the clock when he developed polio in 1921.
- For 24 years, helped FDR hide the secret of his disability.
- First Lady from 1933-1945.

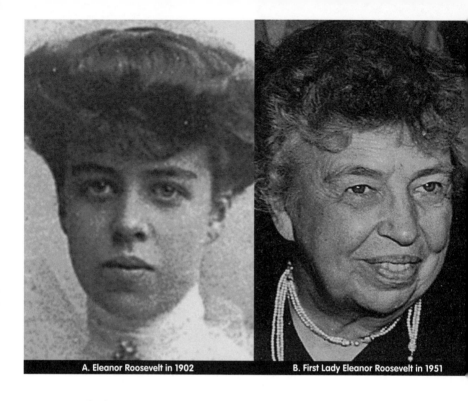

OK, I'll admit it. Seeing these paired photos of Roosevelt, my first reaction is that she goes from a sweet young thing to a grandmother. Yet a face reading transcends the bland social stereotypes. That's especially important to do in ER's case since she changes more dramatically than any other politician in American history (including Lincoln). How appropriate, given her role as America's most influential first lady!

The early face

Look carefully at Photos A and B. As with the other Transformation Readings in this chapter, I consider only traits that show from the front. (Profile shots, though very informative, are hard to locate consistently for all subjects.) Even with this limitation, I find 20 significant changes, *plus* some wrinkles, for Eleanor Roosevelt. Only four bits of data don't change. See these soul signature traits in both photos:

- Her *very* **full, ender eyebrows** signify a brilliant mind, with exceptional follow through.

Remember, technical terms in this chapter can be found in Index II.
Explanations follow later in this book.

- Her **ear structure** reveals huge earlobes, unusually large inner circles and almost no outer ear circles. This pegs her as street smart and observant, yet most interested in abstract causes.
- Unusual for a politician, ER has a **short mouth**, signifying a gift for truthful speech—most effective when delivered one-on-one. This face data goes with a challenge about fear of public speaking; Roosevelt's biography shows that she worked long and hard to overcome this.
- Most distinctively, notice her *very* **outspoken lips**, with her upper lip proportionately fuller than the lower. This symbolizes Roosevelt's penchant for telling the truth that is hidden (even embarrassing).

What advice would a face reader give the young ER? I'd encourage her to have more confidence in herself. The four bits of unchanging face data that I've described all contribute to her vulnerability. She has a knack for unsettling others, yet does it as a highly sensitive person rather than someone who enjoys confrontation.

What changes

From top to bottom, Eleanor Roosevelt's face changes in ways that you may not have thought humanly possible.

Eyebrow angle on the right goes from even-angled to down-angled. This parallels an intellectual shift. In public, when young, she's most effective in the here-and-now; later she's more apt to view the present in a historical context.

That's not due to aging, either. It's not unusual for seniors to have fond *thoughts* about the past (e.g., preferring the Beatles to Eminem). By contrast, eyebrow angle shows deep *understanding* of the past, related to a personal style about intellectual functioning. ER's down-angled right brow sheds perspective on her thoughtful comments, placing everyday life in historical context, that enlivened the syndicated newspaper column she wrote from 1935 to 1962.

Usually eyebrow angle is a soul signature trait; I'd estimate that a shift like hers happens no more often than once in 5,000 faces.

Her eyebrow shape changes, too. In Photo A, her right eyebrow **angles**, suggesting managerial skills in her public life; her left brow is **straight**, corresponding to a fascination with ideas. By Photo B, both eyebrows **curve**, revealing compassion for others as a basis for thinking.

The very fact that ER lives for extended periods with all three of the basic eyebrow shapes is highly unusual. It tells us that she gains a deep familiarity with variations on the human thinking process, learning to appreciate all three styles with the most powerful teaching tool of human life, personal experience.

Over four decades of life in politics, changes to ER's face includes five different eye characteristics.

- Her **sanpaku** eyes, in Photo A, reflect a tendency to look to others for reassurance; this changes to two-whites, indicative of greater self-confidence (and, presumably, her emotional recovery from an extremely difficult childhood). Rather than bemoaning the damage to her Inner Child, she becomes an advocate for others in need of help.

- Her **right eye angle** shifts from up-angled to down-angled as ER's public self evolves from an idealist to a problem solver.

- The bottom half of her eyes changes shape, particularly on the right. Her **Wariness Index** goes from maximum curve (10 on a 1-10 scale) to an asymmetrical 3 on the right, 8 on the left. Most high-level politicians become extremely wary; she confines wariness to her public life, staying relatively open in her personal relationships.

- **Eyelid thickness** starts small for ER. By her senior years, she has none. This symbolizes a changing style of intimacy in relationships. Increasingly she comes to prize emotional independence.

- ER's most startling eye change makes perfect sense to face readers. Look at her remarkable reversal of **eye height asymmetry**.

In Photo A, her right eye is higher than the left, corresponding to respecting men more than women. In fact, ER grew up with a father who was a much stronger influence than her mother. Roosevelt's eye height asymmetry reflects this.

Remember, technical terms in this chapter can be found in Index II.
Explanations follow later in this book.

Later, however, ER forges strong relationships with female friends and colleagues. And, by Photo B, her eye height asymmetry reverses, with her left eye held markedly higher. This symbolizes her coming to hold women in higher regard than men.

Roosevelt's **ear angles** also show reversing asymmetries. In Photo A, her right ear angles in while her left flares out. This relates to maintaining decorum in public while, in private life, ignoring other people's rules.

By Photo B, however, she has evolved a remarkably out-angled right ear while the left one in-angles. This symbolizes developing an outsider's perspective in public life, with the potential for being controversial. In personal life, she becomes less outrageous than in her public role.

Nose data also changes for ER, with **nose length** going from medium to long. This reveals an increased interest in strategic planning.

ER's **money-related nose data** evolves even more drastically. While Photo A shows large, round nostrils paired with a moderately-sized nose tip, by Photo B she has tiny nostrils with a flared shape, plus a larger nose tip. The meaning? Increased respect for financial security is backed by a frugal spending style.

At the risk of going out on a limb (or a nose), I believe that this change involves a transition from thinking of herself as a wealthy young woman with no financial problems to someone who comes to identify with the people she's tried hardest to help, the poor and oppressed.

Noses being the most emotionally charged part of the face, some of you readers may be wrinkling *yours* at the previous paragraphs. Go ahead. Supply a better explanation for ER's nose changes. But traditional views of heredity won't help you to explain why, over time, Eleanor Roosevelt's nose tip doesn't resemble her biological parents so much as Mahatma Gandhi and Mother Teresa, who also made it their life work to help the poor.

Much as I enjoy contemplating Roosevelt's natural nose job and its spiritual implications, my favorite ER face change involves her **cheek prominence.** Photo A shows no visible cheeks, which corresponds to the polite power style. Basically she makes her debut into society as a good little woman getting things done behind the scenes, with no show of power.

Oops! By Photo B her cheeks have evolved into some of the most prominent and powerful in American political history.

See how those cheeks come to dominate her face? They also develop a fascinating asymmetry of **cheek emphasis**: high on the right, low-slung on the left.

After her youth, when she shows no visible cheek emphasis, Roosevelt develops distinctly different styles for handling power: one for public life, another for private life.

- Publicly, she becomes the conscience of America, as when she resigns from the Daughters of the American Revolution to protest their barring Marian Anderson from giving a concert. (This sets in motion a bigger, and better publicized, venue for the African-American singer.)
- Privately, Roosevelt develops—and, probably, needs—exceptional tolerance for allowing her loved ones to make their own choices and mistakes (helpful for handling her husband's long-term extra-marital affair).

ER's **cheek padding** changes belie the stereotype that cheeks become gaunt with age. Just the opposite! Her cheeks grow plumper. The padding increases to such a degree that it extends over her jaws. This highly unusual facial display symbolizes dramatically increased support from others inspired by reliance on her own personal conviction.

Many people expect jowls in more mature people. Forget it! ER's **muscle tone for cheeks** is superb, becoming firmer and more supple as she ages.

Roosevelt's moderately sculpted **philtrum** does lose its definition, however. This signifies that sex appeal, never her strongest selling point, has become even less important in later life.

Perhaps this dimension of self-presentation makes it easier for ER to become increasingly powerful as she ages; the Chers and Madonnas of the world, who vest their identity in youthful glamour and sexiness, retain their highly defined overlips. But who knows how hard a time they have inwardly, keeping up appearances as aging sex kittens?

Roosevelt's lips do thin, especially her **upper lip.** Although she continues to fit into the category I call "outspoken perceptiveness," her shock value diminishes over time.

This could be considered part of her response to decades of intense public scrutiny. Another part of this response shows in her changed **lip texture**. ER's

Remember, technical terms in this chapter can be found in Index II.
Explanations follow later in this book.

lips go from smooth to significantly worn, almost calloused. Another prominent figure in American life has undergone similar wrinkling of her lips, more than any other part of her face. For Oprah Winfrey, as for Eleanor Roosevelt, the significance is courageous action through controversial speech. This takes an inner toll, especially when the speaker is a long-term mega-celebrity.

Still speaking of mouths, **smile depth** evolves for Roosevelt. Photo A shows a lips-only smile, symbolizing that she does not readily open up to people. By Photo B, however, she has learned to do a classic tooth framer, which symbolizes giving to others yet respecting one's personal boundaries.

Next comes the change to her **chin length**. Initially large in proportion to the rest of her face, ER's chin diminishes, suggesting greater refinement of her conscience, along with increased vulnerability to criticism.

Chin thrust alters too, from even to *very* in-angled. Sometimes called a "weak" chin, this data really means that a person is socially minded. When conflict arises, someone with this kind of chin thrust cares more about creating community than browbeating opponents. Cooperation trumps aggression.

Finally, ER's **Priority Areas** shift. Initially, the nose-to-chin area is longest, suggesting a down-to-earth personality. Later, her eyebrow-to-nose tip area matches its length, meaning that accomplishing things in life has become just as important to her as fitting in socially. Although ER has been raised with upper-class Victorian values, expected to disdain work outside her own household, her soul has called her to a life of principled activism, as shown in her many face changes.

The wrinkles

As a senior, ER develops fewer wrinkles than many people half her age. She acquires some **eye extenders** and **eye deepeners**; their balance suggests that, under stress, she's as likely to look within as to seek perspective from others.

On the right side only, notice an unusual configuration of eye extenders moving upward into a small array of **forehead horizontals**. This indicates a pattern in her public life, where ER takes what she learns from others and wrestles with it intellectually.

Her short **suffering lines,** from nose to mouth, evolve to frame Roosevelt's smile. Undoubtedly, she's aware of suffering in others. Yet a lifetime of service is the best antidote to pain, as demonstrated by her life... and her face.

Any face reader will wonder why Eleanor Roosevelt developed so few wrinkles, kept so few of her original face traits and changed so much. The answer, I believe, is that she consistently chose to grow.

All of us can use free will, a more powerful force than biography, life contracts or any other limiting circumstances. Overcoming our personal challenges, we are rewarded with ever greater opportunities to serve and evolve. The extraordinary number of changes to Eleanor Roosevelt's face parallels her exceptional commitment to fully express her soul.

6. God's 30-Day Makeovers

Like the makeover articles in women's beauty magazines, but deeper, God's makeup is at work in all of us. During your lifetime, you're likely to receive four different kinds of makeover.

- Nearly everyone qualifies for **God's Lifecycle Makeovers.** For this one, all you need do is survive for seven years straight. During that cycle, every cell in your body will be replaced, down to your blood, organs and bones.
- **God's Long-Term Makeovers** will fine-tune your body even more. Over the decades, your physical face will keep pace with the nuances of your inner evolution.
- If you're in a spiritual growth spurt, you can receive a faster, all-natural makeover. At times of accelerated outer pressure or inner growth, your face will change significantly in a month or less. That's what I call **God's 30-Day Makeovers,** the subject of this chapter.
- **Zit Makeovers?** Sure we don't wish them on ourselves, but they can be part of a 30-Day Makeover. They do give a person an instant new look! One of the consolations of face reading is that you can find meaning (if not joy) in blemishes. Can't wait to find out? Turn ahead to page 115.

Social security

In my system of Face Reading Secrets, **cheek padding** reveals patterns of coop-eration—in all social situations except the workplace. (For insight into your teamwork style at work, read noses.)

The Data

Physically, **cheek padding** is the stuff that a grandma could pinch, located towards the sides of the face, anywhere from nose tip to jaws. The category has two main options: **padded**, meaning there's a lot to pinch, and **unpadded**, which means there isn't.

Among U.S. presidents since World War II, Clinton has had the largest amount of cheek padding. Kennedy, the runner up, had a considerable amount, distributed throughout the full range of his cheeks and accentuated by superb muscle tone.

Eisenhower and Truman had relatively unpadded cheeks.

The Meaning

Padded cheeks signify a flair for teamwork. Basically, you attract support from others. If you have cheeks like these, please reread this last sentence because you're likely to give everyone credit for this but yourself.

Maybe you'll recognize the following challenge more readily. How frequently do you inconvenience yourself to please others? Often, probably. "I'm easy," you'll say. Seldom does one hear people with unpadded cheeks say that... convincingly, at least.

Unpadded cheeks reveal the strength to do things on your own. Secretly, you may believe that nobody else could do as good a job. Not surprisingly, your challenge involves delegating power.

Where's the talent in that? You've just described me and my cheeks perfectly, but it doesn't sound good at all.

Sometimes a soul has been shaped this way to prepare for circumstances where, like Lincoln, you will have to show courage regardless of criticism. With unpadded cheeks, you get practice in persisting despite the lack of support from others.

Pity the aspiring politician with hollow cheeks. Of course, you won't find many.

Hold on. Everyone knows that what you euphemistically call "cheek padding" really means whether you're fat or thin. Admit it. Don't fat people have fat cheeks and thin people have thin cheeks?

President John F. Kennedy

First Lady Jacqueline Kennedy

President John Adams

Ah, the **Adipose Assumption!** People assume that padding *above* the chin corresponds to weight *below* the chin, or that big upper cheeks correspond to big cheeks lower on the body.

Question this assumption. I've read faces of anorexic people with chubby cheeks as well as very large people with tiny endowments of cheek padding.

History gives us many examples that contradict the weightist assumption. Kennedy wasn't fat, nor was Dr. Martin Luther King. And John Adams, though leaner than many presidents before modern times, had enormous cheeks. He also may have been the most sociable president we've ever had.

Andrew Johnson, the successor to Abraham Lincoln, had *very* unpadded cheeks along with an otherwise portly body. Politically, his power base was so unstable, he was nearly impeached.

If you're more familiar with actresses than presidents, consider Renee Zellweger, your typical turn-of-the-millennium rail-thin actress, except for her ample cheeks. Then contemplate the unpadded cheeks of gorgeously plus-sized actress Camryn Mannheim. The ultimate glamourous example of plump cheeks on a slender body has to be Jackie Kennedy, whose immensely prominent, far-set cheeks are half hidden under all that cheek padding.

Sometimes a novice to face reading will confuse cheek padding with other face data: cheek prominence, jaw width or cheek proportions. That's why I recommend that you practice reading this category by looking at people you know and, with permission, gently pinching their cheeks. (The upper ones, of course.)

Doesn't age always change cheek padding?

According to stereotypes it does. But take a closer look. Our photo of Dr. Martin Luther King in Chapter Three shows enormous cheek padding. That picture was taken in 1964, but photos from just a few years later show significant loss of that padding before his life was cut short. How would age explain this? He was just 39.

As bad as the Adipose Assumption, there's an equally unhelpful (and often inaccurate) stereotype promulgated by cosmetic surgeons. Some of their ads suggest that middle-aged people invariably suffer **"gaunting"** in their cheeks? This ominous medical-sounding term simply means a decrease in cheek padding.

Daunting though gaunting may sound, it's not that big a deal from a face reading perspective. All it means is that the individual has gained a greater sense of social independence. See how stereotypes get people coming or going? Less cheek padding, you're old; more of it, you're fat. Please! Investigate your fellow cheek wearers and you'll demolish these pathetic stereotypes. Then you can go on to find *meaning* in the faces of your fellow free-willed human beings.

Do you have any idea what a painful subject cheeks can be? For the last 30 years, people have teased me about my chipmunk cheeks.

Laugh back at those sillies. Even better, send those animal namers to me. I'll badger them back. After that, I'll pester them and horse around at their expense until all they're good for is playing Scrabble for Poodles! (For more of my vengeance, turn to this book's Online Supplement, "Glossary of Nasty Names for Face Parts.")

Seriously, what if you hate your cheeks?

Seriously, stop worrying about insults from ignorant people. Big cheek padding means a leadership style where friends, neighbors and family members are as helpful to you as they could be. Isn't that true for you, except for the occasional wisecrack about your cheeks?

Well, yes.

Then I rest my case, right on your cheeks.

Change

Sure, weight and cheek padding are sometimes gained together, but one factor or the other can change independently. Face readers interpret what shows on the face alone. So read nothing below that first chin!

For best results, avoid weightism as much as racism or ageism. Interpret the face data on one person at a time. When you can, follow up by asking for feedback.

Let's face it. Even if it were possible to have in-depth conversations with stereotypes, feedback from real live people would be far more interesting.

Gifts of gab

To learn how a person communicates best, a face reader reads **lip proportions,** a category that can easily change in a month or less. To read this, you compare the relative fullness of top and bottom lips. The trick lies in comparing the fullness of the two lips relative to each other, i.e., not comparing either lip to what's on someone else's face.

The Data

Most intriguing visually is the configuration called **blarney lips.** That's the name physiognomist Lailan Young has given to lip proportions that include an extra full lower lip. It could be anywhere from two to five times fuller than the upper lip. Although more than half of U.S. presidents share this face data, usually it's found on just 1 in 50 people.

Outspoken lips is my term for an upper lip that is at least as full as the lower lip. Though it's uncommon for presidents, you'll find it on Jimmy Carter and Andrew Johnson.

Most people have **everyday persuasiveness,** a slightly fuller lower lip that's fuller than the upper lip, but not by a lot. Witness the mouths of such averagely scintillating speakers as James Polk and Chester Arthur.

The Meaning

Blarney lips spell persuasiveness. If you have them and your lips are also **long** (as on the "read my lips" president, George H. Bush), you could easily sell ice to Eskimos. And regardless of lip length, your blarneys correspond to a knack for convincing others with relative ease. What's the catch? It's being tempted to push your gift too far, because you're such a good convincer.

By contrast, **outspoken lips** symbolize talent in a different direction, perceptiveness. With lips like these, you can figure out what's really going on with people under the surface. And do you ever want to tell! (That's the challenge. Ever notice?)

The majority of people have **everyday persuasiveness.** This denotes the ability to convince people when you try really hard, but you have to work for it. On

President James Polk

President Jimmy Carter

President Ulysses S. Grant

President Chester Arthur

the other hand—or lip—you're less likely to be tempted ethically than the folks who are natural persuaders.

For presidents who have blarney lips, how does that data correlate with being known as an orator?

You'll find plenty of correlation. In the electronic age, persuasiveness and personality have taken on more importance than character. Is it a coincidence that every president since Johnson (except for Carter) has had blarney lips?

Johnson's predecessor, Kennedy, didn't, yet some would consider him the greatest orator of modern times. How do you explain that?

Kennedy's mouth showed two important soul signature traits. **Trendsetter lips** are the diamond-like structures on the upper lip that are more commonly known as "cupid's bows." This rare gift enables a person to effectively speak on behalf of a group he identifies with. Kennedy spoke for liberals just as, later, trendsetter-lipped Shirley MacLaine spoke up on behalf of New Agers and Donald Trump represented yuppies of the 1990s. Lincoln *developed* his set (see Photo B on page 80), which is even more rare than having trendsetter lips as a soul signature trait.

Kennedy's second unusual mouth gift was extreme **lip definition,** which means he had naturally chiseled ridges around the edges of his mouth. The associated gift is high standards for communication... to the point of fussiness. An additional challenge can be impatience with others since, judging by those same high standards, most people come across as undisciplined blabbers.

Change

Whatever your lip proportions are today, they could change tomorrow. One month from now, your lip proportions could reveal a different emphasis in your speech. One of my clients went from extreme blarneys to everyday persuasiveness; decades later she developed an extreme version of outspoken lip proportions. Sound strange? One way or another, your face could change that much, too.

Don't lip proportions change when you smile?

Sure can! You know from Chapter Three about the meaning of smiles: Your mouth in repose shows your deeper self, whereas smile style reveals how you adapt your personality when reaching out to others. Grab your mirror right now to research instant changes to your communication style.

Handling conflict

Want to predict a person's instinctive reaction to conflict? Check out the width of the jaw compared with the rest of the face. Choices in the **jaw width** department are wide, narrow and medium.

The Data

To see them, take a quick look at the hinge part on the lower third of the face.

Wide jaws make their presence known by a significant spread, as in the case of General (later President) Ulysses S. Grant. **Narrow jaws** take a little more care and attention to see. Given the width of the face at cheek and forehead, are the jaws relatively skimpy? For an example, see last chapter's Photo A of Eleanor Roosevelt. Compare that with the **medium jaws** in her Photo B.

The Meaning

Endurance goes with the trait of wide jaws. Athletic competitions aren't the only situations where this stamina comes in handy. If you have **wide jaws,** you're well equipped to tough your way through any form of conflict.

A related talent involves handling commitment. With these jaws, when you decide on a cause, a company or a spouse, that's a big deal. You're committed for the duration. (People with narrower jaw widths stay committed only so long as things remain pleasant; that's their challenge, at least.)

You mean that wide jaws involve being stubborn?

Others may call it that. However, I've noticed that people who have wide jaws either avoid that term or take it as a compliment. To them, "stubborn" evokes an admirable tenacity. And they just might be right. If it weren't for Winston Churchill's grit, as outpictured in his *very* wide jaws, all of us might be living in some Nazi suburb.

Narrow jaws go with a wonderful gift, too. It's an Early Warning Detection System for conflict.

If you have these jaws, give yourself credit. Aren't you usually the first to recognize an interpersonal problem? Besides being extra sensitive to conflict, you're equipped to initiate conversation about what others hold in denial. Sure, it takes emotional and spiritual courage to tackle forbidden subjects, but that's standard issue if you have that Early Warning Detection System. You're wise to resolve conflicts early, before hurtful behavior becomes habitual.

The downside of your gift is that it's needed. If you have narrow jaws, long-term conflict is poison for you—both emotionally, spiritually and physically. So it's imperative to take advantage of your Early Warning Detection System. When that inner siren starts blaring, either resolve the problem fast or get out.

Medium jaw width signifies an average amount of conflict endurance. This gift is so useful, it could be considered Conflict Endurance Insurance. Stamina is available if needed, but so is emotional courage. Your only challenge is a lack of tolerance for the rest of humanity, in yet one more guise.

Change

One month's heavy lifting—of stress—can cause your jaws to widen.

To change your face on the outside, and then create the inner correlate, try chewing gum vigorously for several hours a day for 30 days. Before embarking on a Jaw Makeover program, however, consider how the change would fit with the rest of your face (plus whether you really like gum that much). If you really, really like gum, you can do even more extreme jaw widening by chewing it vigorously over a period of several years. Usually, though, jaw width changes come from within.

Teddy Roosevelt took years to build himself up, physically and inwardly. On a more sinister note, Muammar Al Quadhafi has tripled his jaw width since he's been in power, bringing joy to his Libyan stalwarts but not necessarily to you or me.

Can't jaws diminish, too?

Sure. Examples include Lyndon Johnson and Golda Meir.

But couldn't jaws narrow for health reasons, rather than an inner lack of endurance?

Inner and outer causes mesh, just as jaws do. The physical hinges can turn narrow as a result of illness or dental work. For instance, when all the teeth have been extracted, should dentures not be worn regularly, the lower face will cave in.

Tooth extractions and gum chewing are good examples of physical circumstances that have inner correlates. Why shouldn't many levels of life create a meaningful synchronicity?

If you're metaphysically minded, it makes perfect sense that the extra groundedness cultivated by massive, persistent gum chewing would bring about inner consequences. And regarding removal of teeth, that's highly significant in physiognomy because **teeth** carry data about life lessons. Removing them all would symbolize that a person no longer faces inner struggles the way she used to.

Wearing dentures signifies taking on generic lessons, not ones closely associated with the soul. When someone can't afford false teeth, or can only buy ones so ill-fitting that they're painful, failure to wear the teeth corresponds to living on one's own terms in a state of enforced humility. This sets in motion a drastic reorganization of personality. The appetite for life can be severely diminished after full-scale dental extraction.

Interpreting teeth? Trying to find meaning there seems far fetched. To paraphrase Freud, sometimes a tooth is just a tooth.

Teeth are meaningful in face reading, to paraphrase me! See more about teeth in *The Power of Face Reading,* pages 268–272.

With so many kids going to orthodontists, loads of people have changed their jaws and teeth. Doesn't science explain away any supposed inner meaning?

These changes can be explained on a physical level, but why assume that categorically excludes all other explanations? I've had **scientific reductionists** tell me that asymmetries to their ear angles are due to how they sleep on a pillow, and so forth. In the unlikely event that such a person notices a change to her jaws, she'll dismiss it out of hand—or maybe I should say, out of face.

Personal confession here: My own jaws, being narrow, may help explain my strong distaste for arguing with **skeptics**. Although the term skeptic means keeping an open mind while considering the evidence, most people who call themselves skeptics are really **cynics**, people whose minds are adamantly closed. Rather than argue with them, I prefer to walk away. In my opinion, the cynics lose out, and not only because a mind is a terrible thing to waste. When I refuse to argue with them, cynics miss the "entertainment" of an argument. They also disqualify themselves from enjoying the fun and informativeness of face reading.

Expecting the worst

Mouth angles show how you expect others to talk about you, especially behind your back. To read this, study lips when they're in repose: not smiling, talking, or kissing you passionately. Read one side of the mouth at a time, because asymmetries are definitely possible.

Then use the **Dot Method.** Imagine a dot in the center of the lips, plus one dot at the mouth corner. Connect those dots with an imaginary line. Is the direction up, down or even?

The Dot Method

To see angles on faces, use a grownup's version of Connect the Dots. I call it The Dot Method. Use it to see mouth angles, eye angles and eyebrow angles. In profile, you can use it for nose tip angle and ear tilt, too.

In each case, you imagine a dot at the outer edge or corner. Imagine a second dot at the opposite side. Then connect the dots with an imaginary line. For mouth angles, you'll need a third dot. That's because the left and right sides of the mouth must be read separately.

For either side of the mouth, your reference point is the dot in the center of the mouth. (If lips are parted, use only the top lip.)

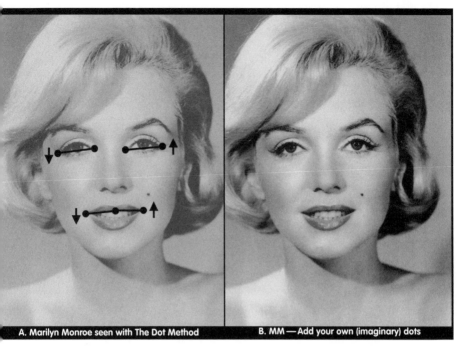

Let's demonstrate The Dot Method on Marilyn Monroe. As with other famous faces, its familiar look will change when you use face reading. Photo A shows how to use The Dot Method. Photo B gives you a regular head shot. This time, use your imagination to connect the dots.

Following the dots, you'll find two different eye angles. (Right down, left up.) For extra practice, try it on her mouth angles (Also right down, left up.)

What's the meaning of these asymmetries? In public, Monroe expressed her vulnerability; in private, she was guardedly optimistic. Eyes show her outlook while mouth reveals her reaction to other people, especially when handling criticism. Monroe expressed vulnerability through her body language and aura, as well as her face. This congruence contributed to her extraordinary impact as a performer.

The Data

Mouth angles on most adults go down to varying degrees, except when they're smiling. Finding photo examples with natural mouth angles can be difficult since portrait-style pictures generally show people smiling. For an exception, turn to pictures of presidents before Nixon. Remember, those old-time authority figures didn't grin for their official portraits, so you'll see plenty of **down-angled** mouths.

For an **up-angled** mouth look at old and new presidents whose fathers were also presidents: John Quincy Adams and George W. Bush. But you may have the same mouth angle even if you've never run for public office.

Examples of **even-angled** mouths are found on James Polk and George Washington.

The Meaning

People with **down-angled mouths,** like many we've already seen in this chapter (Grant, Arthur and Johnson), tend to be verbally considerate. If you're in this group, you've earned your chops the hard way, having suffered from criticism in the past. Your challenge is over-sensitivity when being talked about by others. Do you expect people to praise you or does your mouth flinch in anticipation of insults?

Hold on. Are you saying that people with down-angled mouths are guaranteed to be tactful?

Only one aspect of tact is guaranteed here, actually. It's the lack of direct verbal put-downs. For other aspects of tact, see eyebrow shape, eyelid fold, ear angles, cheek proportions, dimples, lipfulness, chin thrust and Priority Areas.

Face reading is so complex, how can I pull all the pieces together?

It's easy. Use the indexes. If you're looking for information about a particular aspect of behavior, like tact, Index III will refer you to the related face data. So don't worry, you'll be able to read faces one piece of data at a time. And speaking of not worrying....

People with **up-angled mouths** are a different breed, when it comes to how they expect others to talk about them. Praise is expected. If you have this trait, congratulate yourself on having mastered a vital component of high self-esteem. Your potential challenge is verbal insensitivity: hurting people's feelings, then being oblivious to it. Since you bounce back from teasing so easily, you may wrongly assume that others do, too.

Those fortunate mortals with **even-angled** mouths display a rare form of equanimity, neither expecting to be disrespected verbally, nor likely to diss without provocation. Your only challenge if you have this trait is that pesky lack of tolerance for the rest of humanity. What's with all those bashers and sulkers?

Change

Whenever I see a new person, I start with the mouth. A down-angled mouth shows bitterness. Don't you think these people should get over it?

Note: Friendly reader, you might expect that the woman asking me this question has an up-angled mouth. But in repose (and apparently unbeknownst to her) she's in the down-angled club herself. Questions like this are fairly common. One more reason to avoid judgmental habits of seeing others!

Because I view face data as God's makeup, I'm not so quick to condemn people based on what the face shows. Especially in the case of mouth angles! I can remember when mine began to turn down.

Spiritual talent scouts appreciate that facial scars aren't restricted to marks on the skin. Many changes to face data could be interpreted as "scars."

Like most children, I began life with a perfectly even set of lip angles. Mine changed after I started attending a small private school where I was mercilessly teased by the ruling clique of girls. Every day, I'd leave the school in tears.

Since then, I've worked hard to release the emotional pain. Yet it's part of my story and, not surprisingly, has become part of my face.

People who have been deeply wounded by criticism usually develop down-angled mouths. Can it happen in a month? I'm living proof. More commonly, it takes years for a mouth to turn down. Accumulated suffering, not bitterness, is the more compassionate explanation.

And if you do lift yourself up emotionally, will your mouth angle change?

Even though a person works hard to forgive, the body doesn't forget. Until you completely release the old pain, your mouth will keep that downward slope.

To supplement emotional healing, you might also consider adopting a new habit. Are you willing to hold your mouth in a relaxed smile with lips closed? Can you remember to do this while you're alone, just you and your face?

Over time you can nudge your mouth angle upwards. As a consequence, you'll feel more socially confident. Just take care not to force the smile. To clench your closed lips into a smile will make you look like you're mugging, plus it could give you lip puckers. Only a relaxed smile brings the desired results.

When you sleep, and your face relaxes completely, your default down-angles may return. (But that can be your little secret.)

Marking sexual territory

Mustaches display masculinity, good reason why most women aren't thrilled if they develop facial hair. Out of kindness, we'll feature male examples only.

The first mustache category we'll consider is horizontal, **length of mustache,** which relates to the range of a man's sexual forcefulness. Not only is this category relatively easy to see but, assuming that the facial hair belongs to a man, chances are he'll be flattered when you stare openly at his data.

The Data

To gauge mustache length, compare it to mouth length. Is the mustache relatively **short** (i.e., narrower than the mouth)? Fortunately for America, we've never had a president with this variety, but you've seen it on Adolph Hitler and Charlie Chaplin. Is a mustache **long** (wider than mouth length), as worn by Grover Cleveland? Or is it **mouth-length** (approximately even with the ends of the mouth), as grown by Chester Arthur?

The Meaning

If you've grown a **short mustache,** be honest. Don't you have enormous pride in your masculinity? For you, there's a "guy" way to drive; there's also a guy way to open and close the car door, to sit in the driver's seat, even to sit (if you must) in the non-driver's seat.

Hitler demonstrated the extreme need for sexual recognition that can go with a very short, full mustache.

Charlie Chaplin made millions laugh as the Little Tramp movie character when he pretended to be an insecure man pretending to be confident.

Behaviorally, a man with a short mustache can pretend to be anything he likes but, deep down, he demands that his masculinity be taken seriously.

Wearers of a **long** mustache may be flirtatious. You're probably trying to expand the number of your romantic conquests. Certainly it's important to you that as many people as possible admire your studliness.

The **handlebar,** as worn by William Taft, is a *very* version, being not only super-long but turned up at the ends. This is the most elegant, self-conscious statement a man can make about his masculinity.

Handlebar mustaches show the desire to be considered an artist, a gentleman or both. Other longer-than-mouth-length mustachio can blend into beards, which will be discussed later in this chapter.

By far the most moderate form of stand-alone facial hair is the **mouth-length** mustache.

This shows a balanced self-confidence, declaring that you're forceful in all communications, sexual and otherwise. Do charm and wit back you up, or are you more likely to use physical force? The next mustache trait gives a clue.

President Grover Cleveland   President William Taft

Masculine or macho?

Mustache depth reveals how a man defines his masculinity. Options in this category are lip-accentuating, lip-hiding and lip-framing.

The Data

A **lip-hiding** mustache looks untrimmed. How untrimmed? Hair covers at least part of the upper lip. *Very* versions conceal the upper lip entirely and maybe even the lower lip, too. So far, America's presidential record for lip-hiding belongs to Rutherford Hayes. Maybe he should have campaigned on the slogan "Read what lips?"

The opposite is a **lip-accentuating** mustache—trimmed to expose the upper lip and part of the philtrum. No American head of state has dared to wear this, but it decorated the British monarch, Henry VIII.

The compromise depth, **lip-framing,** demands scrupulous maintenance, with the mustache trimmed to show the full shape of the upper lip without covering it up. Ulysses S. Grant managed to perform this neat trick.

The Meaning

A **lip-hiding** mustache tells the world that you consider yourself the strong, silent type. Should someone push you around, whether literally or figuratively, you'll shove right back. Without necessarily uttering a word!

But face readers can expect just the opposite type of behavior from the opposite type of mustache. Do you wear a **lip-accentuating** mustache? Then I'll bet you consider speech to be one of your greatest sexual assets. Your prospective dates expect charm, hope for wit and pray that they'll stay on your good side. Owners of such a mustache know very well what happens when you're angered—your ripostes can cut like a knife.

Lip-framing mustaches belong to men who feel relatively comfortable about expressing their masculinity. You'll speak or be silent as the situation demands, and it's relatively effortless for you to project a confident, manly image. Lucky guy, you've got it made… except for that little potential problem, a lack of tolerance for the rest of humanity.

So you're saying that men can give themselves any communication style they choose, depending on how they shape their mustaches. But women can't. How is that fair?

Fairer than you might think! Depending on what a man would like to emphasize about his sexual style, his choice of facial hair does more than project an image. The face data he shapes on the outside will also affect who he is on the inside.

A man who's not using his abilities fully in life may make a poor choice, then have to live with the consequences. Hitler, for instance, wasn't in touch with his vulnerability (to put it mildly). His *very* short mustache didn't cause this problem but may have exacerbated it, especially since that mustache became his facial trademark.

Women who lack the opportunity to shape mustaches finesse the opportunity to make a bad choice. Women also avoid frustration: Not all mustaches can be coaxed to grow to the desired length or depth. And scissors or razors can change a man's facial hair in one direction only.

Change

Mustaches are an instance where free will takes us as far as it can, but ultimately we bump into limitations. Given our personal contracts about who we are as soul in this life, men can take personal choice only so far. In that sense, they're absolutely equal to women.

What's the consequence of growing a mustache and beard combo so huge, it's as though the guy has no mouth at all?

Ah, the Rutherford Hayes look! It's a great choice—but only if you'd like to say as little as possible, then have it be quickly forgotten. When I read this president's aura from his photo, the part that relates to communication reveals a fascinating blend of timidity and stubbornness. Even Reagan wouldn't have seemed like a great communicator with that mustache and beard combo.

What was in it for Hayes, wearing that much facial hair? He upped his machismo. Ultimately, only the beard wearer can decide how much is too much.

I'm the kind of guy who hates touchy feely stuff. What's the big deal if I prefer a mustache that shows off my upper lip?

Sending a mixed message, that's the only catch. When you grow facial hair that sends a message in conflict with your personality, your love life will suffer. Try growing your mustache a bit longer. It could help you attract women who are more appropriate for you. Such an experiment would take what, half an inch of hair? And how long, 30 days?

Bossiness and compassion

Beards are another guys-only way to swap old face data for new. When the growth extends past the stubble stage, it can change the shape of **chin bottoms**. So beards do count as face data.

What, women lose out again?

Beardless or bearded, female or male, everyone's face has a bottom line. The only advantage men have is being able to alter it, and plenty of men do themselves no favor by growing facial hair that sends the wrong message.

Like chin bottoms, beard bottoms reveal a person's basis for making decisions, including (to put it bluntly) how much that person needs to boss others around.

Chin bottoms come in three persuasions: curved, straight and angled.

The Data

Curved chin bottoms are most common, whether on chins or as beards. You'll find them on most presidents. One particularly extreme example belonged to Lyndon Johnson; for a bearded instance, see our portrait of Rutherford Hayes in Chapter Three.

Straightness of chin or beard bottoms shows in Founding Father George Washington and the hirsute Benjamin Harrison, respectively.

When you see a letter V at the bottom of a chin or beard, either you're seeing an **angled** shape or else someone has been doodling strangely with a felt-tip pen. Unimaginable that Dwight Eisenhower would do something so frivolous? You bet. His angled chin wasn't drawn in, any more than James Garfield's beard.

The Meaning

Here's the scoop on **curved bottoms,** whether on chins and beards. They correspond to making decisions based on respect for people's feelings. If you're one of these humanitarians, you run the risk of being called too caring. Ooh, now that's a scary thought!

Straight bottoms on chins or beards relate to a different driving passion: fairness. Do you base your decisions on "the principle of the thing?" Then your bottom line shape is most likely straight. Under Washington's leadership, America became defined by the search for each individual's quality of life, liberty and the pursuit of happiness. With a less defined chin, who knows? Maybe our national motto would have been "Whatever."

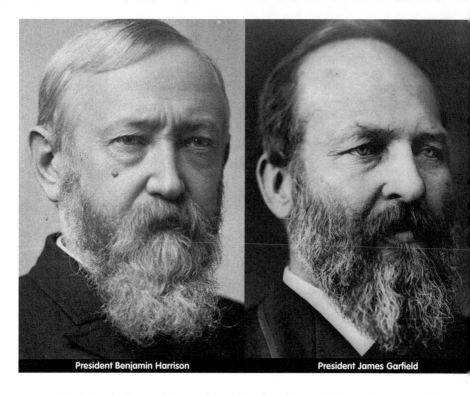

President Benjamin Harrison

President James Garfield

What's the challenge with a straight chin or beard bottom? Your values may tend toward black and white, causing you to miss life's wonderful shades of gray.

Angled chin or beard bottoms signify that your decisions will be based on the need to stay in control. Nobody, and I mean nobody, is going to tell you what to do. Benefits of this personal style include inner strength, executive ability and (in some cases) having your will of steel balance an otherwise sensitive nature. Sometimes, however, the bossiness that goes with an angled chin bottom can be downright scary.

Many people instinctively shudder when they see a *very* pointy beard. If you're the one with chin or beard angling, enjoy the benefits of having a strong will. The trick is to avoid giving people the impression that you're a control freak.

Change

Beards can be trimmed in minutes. But a beard's rate of growth, and consequent clout enhancement, are more iffy. After all, Nixon's five o'clock shadow didn't help him on camera with Kennedy during the nation's first televised presidential debate.

Face reading tells us that what matters with facial hair isn't your personal whisker endowment but your chosen style of wearing it. That makeup kit you've been issued by God, supplemented by your chosen collection of razor and aftershave, may contain just what you need to express your soul.

Temporary Rage

At last, everybody's favorite topic! What, you don't adore **zits?** Hey, at least it helps to know what they mean. Stay tuned

The Data

How many ways can a face have **zits**? Thousands. Ask any teenager. Which is why, for this age group, this aspect of face reading should be *required* reading. Physiognomists of any age won't be freaked out by zits, however. We'll notice the location, then the type of blemish.

The Meaning

Zits and the like represent problems. This is news to you?

But cheer up. Most zits are temporary. And even the recurrent ones have meaning, which should come as some consolation. For the meaning of pimple locations, turn the page and read "If Zits Could Talk."

As a spiritual talent scout, you can raise your consciousness about all the forms of vulnerability that show in a face. Because zits, birthmarks, moles, and wrinkles are just the more obvious forms of what I call **visible vulnerability.** And I call it a blessing.

Lack of apparent perfection shows in non-facial ways, too, such as physical disability, obvious emotional or social difficulties, poverty and more hidden forms of medical and psychological problems.

Of course they're embarrassing. But let's not react like one man I know who told me he was traumatized at age 14 when his first cavity was found by a dentist. Frank went into a deep depression because it was the first time he'd ever considered the possibility that he wasn't perfect in every way.

There's no way I would ever consider zits a good thing. Or meaningful. Zits tell me one thing and one thing only. Embarrassment.

It's human to wish to look perfect. Hollywood stars will pay over $20,000 on personal grooming before a single public appearance. Even the "little people" wish to hide blemishes, yet one way or another our human struggles will show through.

Why do we think we want perfection? Apparent perfection enables us to relate to people in superficial ways. We can slide through our dealings with them like skaters at an ice rink that has just been smoothed over. Flawless appearances seem ideal. However, that's not where the growth is. First and foremost, earth is a learning planet. We start a new phase of life, master it, then go on to our next assignment.

The mark of success in your personal evolution
is bliss followed immediately by a new set of lessons.

This pattern repeats in all its relentless variations. Along the way, some of us manage better than others to hide our struggles. Over time, though, everyone's song is the same: Something's gotta give. When others can see what we're going through, that's visible vulnerability.

How our human pride hates it. Zits are an "in your face" lesson that's hard to ignore. But you, remember, are becoming a spiritual talent scout. So, for you, faces with visible vulnerability represent an invitation to have greater compassion.

Change

Zits can heal in days. To accelerate the process, you might wish to study our chart on the facing page. If the inner message, as given, resonates for you, do what you can to change on the inner. That just might help you to avoid repeat breakouts in the same spots. (Of course, it's still wise to call on a holistic physician to address underlying medical problems.)

If Zits Could Talk

Face Location	General Significance	Zits Speak Out
Chin	Ethics, Need for physical courage	*Did I make the right choice?*
Jaws	Commitment	*Following through on my choice is taking too much out of me.*
Lower lip*	Persuasive speech	*I have to work too hard to get people to believe me.*
Upper lip*	Perceptive speech	*I told the truth and this is all the thanks I get? Geez!*
Overlip	Sex appeal	*You call this a sex life?*
Cheeks	Social pressure	*I wish other people would get off my case.*
Nose tip	Handling money	*My financial situation is driving me nuts.*
Nose middle	Work or school	*Doing my job is a real hassle right now.*
Nose bridge	Starting a new project at work	*This latest project is going to be (or already is) a real pain.*
Earlobes	Unconscious response to life at a physical level	*Someone or something in my immediate environment is incredibly annoying.*
Right eyebrow	Ideas for work or school	*Someone I work with doesn't appreciate my ideas.*
Left eyebrow	Ideas about my social life	*Someone I care about doesn't appreciate my ideas.*
Forehead, lower third	Short-term memory	*Something that I keep thinking about (or trying to deny) upsets me.*
Forehead, middle third	Spiritual life	*I've had to sacrifice too much for my spiritual life. Why me?*
Upper forehead	Concentration	*All this worry is getting to me.*

*In this location, the mark would more likely take the form of a cold sore than a pimple, but the meaning is the same.

It bothers me that zits are bypassed by the wealthy and healthy. Maybe face readers like me could take vengeance by making them read your scary chart about zits talking. What do you think?

Take consolation in the fact that zits can be avoided but wrinkles come to everyone. No vanity surgeon has the means to hide them forever, just as wealth can't protect us from the long-term consequences of our actions. Live long enough and your vulnerability *will* become visible for all to see. From a spiritual perspective, that's all to the good.

More markings from God's makeup kit

Zits are just the beginning, it turns out. The face has a variety of skin-level markings. And each type of God's face paint holds a special significance, as described below:

- **Zits,** as we've seen, are about anger.
- With **boils,** the anger is seething.
- **Warts** show shame.
- **Freckles** are more about spunkiness and rebellion than anger.
- **Age spots,** a.k.a. "liver spots," reveal accumulated (tough) learning.
- **Scars** record that life contract debts have been paid—either major struggles in this lifetime or important memories from a past life to be applied to this incarnation.
- **Keloid skin** reveals sensitivity towards trauma. Events from the past tend to leave a lasting impression.
- **Moles, beauty marks** and **birthmarks** tell the spiritual talent scout, "Pay special attention to this part of the face." Note size, since a relatively large mark counts as a *very*. Then notice the color.
- **Brown or black marks** (or light **discolorations** on dark complexions) reveal a talent or issue with life-long significance. The latter can relate directly to patterns set in motion during a past life, something a skilled regression therapist can help you to release.
- **Red marks**, in general, show anger.

I'd be less skeptical of your theory if you could give an example. Can you?

Sure, **war mounds**. I've noticed these raised blemishes on presidents who serve during wartime and are deeply affected by their responsibility. War mounds appear on the right cheek; in terms of pure physiognomy, they relate to power in the context of work. Take a look at Abe Lincoln, Benjamin Harrison and Franklin Roosevelt. All three developed war mounds. This book's photo of Grant as president doesn't show the mark, but he had it when responsible for the Union army during the Civil War (see the Online Supplement); afterwards the mark disappeared!

How about accidents that change the physical face? Would you consider them meaningful, too?

With faces, there are no "accidents." Dramatic changes, like noses that break and change shape, have meaning. Circumstances show us the surface level. To gain a deeper understanding, interpret the face traits that change.

When clients request it, I'll interpret **scars** as part of a reading. Feedback verifies the accuracy of these interpretations. As with pimples, the meaning relates to the scar's location. Unlike pimples, scars are usually preceded by a long-term buildup of frustration; then an "accident" creates the physical mark.

Are scars or injuries reasons to jump for joy? Of course not. But, unquestionably, they are part of God's makeup.

What's the meaning of a lot of acne, or acne scars?

The person has gone through challenges about relating to society, such as feeling like an outsider. Because severe cases of acne usually appear during the teenage years, they can also be understood a part of a life contract. (See Chapter Ten for further discussion of this.)

And what if someone is physically deformed? Grotesquely ugly?

Face readers don't make light of this. Without discounting the suffering involved, we consider the possibility that a soul has chosen the face as part of a life contract. Granted, the specific reason for the choice isn't always clear. Still, your view of deformity need not be our society's prevalent and ultimately trivializing response: calling people "victims." And ugliness, as you'll see later, is linked to talent.

Anyone with a disability is on an accelerated learning program, with intense and powerful information available about spiritual truth.
Auras of people with disabilities are often magnificent.

A three-year makeover plan

God's makeovers can take 30 days, 30 years, or any amount of time in between. For perspective, let's examine what happened to one man whose contract with God brought him intensive change over a three-year period.

Photo A shows Colin Powell during Campaign 2000, where he emerged as one of the most popular leaders of the Republican party, although he declined nomination for high office. Photo B, from February 2001, shows him as the newly appointed Secretary of State. By Photo C, in June 2002, Powell was contending with the War on Terrorism, conflict with the Middle East and the threat of nuclear war between India and Pakistan.

Before he moved onto the national stage, General Powell's life was scarcely uneventful. But the pressures of military life were slight compared to new responsibilities that he clearly took to heart. To a face reader, it's significant that his face evolved more, from 2000 to 2002, than the faces of either President Bush or Vice President Cheney. For that matter, facially Powell evolved more in one year than President Reagan did in 40.

Cheek padding for Powell was taut and muscular in Photo A; that padding increased by Photo B; then increased further by Photo C. Note that it also became *looser*, forming jowls. These changes symbolize a shift in personal power, from confident mastery to moving beyond his comfort zone.

The **jowls** suggests decreased support from others and, perhaps, frustration over lessened control. Lessons about power were being learned on a personal level. Clearly Powell took on enormous responsibilities—power struggles with no easy solution, impossible for any one man or nation to resolve.

Lip proportions changed, too. Photo A shows blarney lips, an extra-full lower lip, symbolizing a gift for easy persuasiveness. By Photo C, Powell developed **everyday persuasiveness** lip proportions, with his lower lip just slightly fuller

A. Colin Powell in 2000

B. Colin Powell in 2001

C. Colin Powell in 2002

than the upper. Meaning? His communication may have gained nuance but it lost impact.

Other meaningful mouth changes happened, too. Photos A and B show strong **lower lip definition**, a chiseled ridge that lost its edge by Photo C. A meticulous communicator before becoming Secretary of State, CP learned to speak in the role of the president's representative. Speech became a matter of compromise, rather than personal communication, precisely shaped.

Comparing **mouth angles**, we must take into consideration that Powell displays a slight smile in Photo A but not in the other pictures. (That smile is extraordinary for a high-level politician, incidentally. Notice how his eyes crinkle, looking more expressive than his mouth? It's exactly the opposite of political business as usual, suggesting a genuine inner warmth and concern.)

In his two non-smiling photos, the left side of Powell's mouth goes from up-angled to down-angled. The left side also takes on a sizeable length of **line without lip.** These asymmetrical changes indicate growing secrecy about what he will communicate publicly. Diplomacy is the related talent. The challenge? Reticence is a symptom of fear and/or pain.

Eye changes are particularly fascinating in Powell, since they developed over such a short time period. For starters, notice how level his eyes are in Photo A?

To compare how his eye height changed in the other two photos, you must compensate for the tilted camera angles. Practice using the T Method discussed in the last chapter. It may also help to use Powell's ears as reference points for asymmetry. If you look closely at Photo B, you'll see that his right eye has become higher than his left. In Photo C, the right eye is higher still.

A **higher right eye** indicates valuing public image over private life. As you'll see in the next chapter, it's often associated with a career in politics. To counterbalance this shift, however, Powell has developed **nose angling toward the left.** This symbolizes a desire to work according to private values, more than playing a public role.

Hold on. First you said that Powell values his public role. Now you're saying his job satisfaction comes from within, not his public role. How could both these interpretations be true?

Welcome to the world of human complexity! You've just seen what happens when a person struggles with deep inner conflict. Remember, CP had a good chance of being nominated for U.S. president, yet he declined for personal reasons. Later, though, he accepted the opportunity to become secretary of state.

Did Powell want to be involved in national politics or not? Even on the level of action, these choices imply inner conflict. Now you're seeing how his face came to out-picture his inner ambivalence.

And there are more examples. For instance, look closely and you'll see progressive changes to Powell's **eye angle.** His right eye shifted from slightly up-angled in Photo A to down-angled by Photo C.

This suggests that, in his career, Powell went from an optimistic orientation to one of pessimism. Few face changes come with deeper emotional and spiritual pain; this is as rough as developing an earlobe crease.

Speaking of which, guess what? He got that one, too. (Earlobe changes for Powell can be read on his right ear only, given the camera angles in our sample photos. Even one ear reveals a lot, however, and this is the ear related to public life.)

On the topic of earlobes, first notice CP's **puffy earlobe texture** in Photo A. That's rare for most people (though common with high ranking military officers) and it relates to exceptional street smarts. This gift faded by Photo C, when General Powell adapted to serve in a government position that required more abstract management than his former job.

A **diagonal earlobe crease** tracks the impact of deep stress, a wrinkle often having the emotional undertone of disillusionment, as will be discussed in Chapter Nine. His earlobe crease is the only wrinkle in Powell's collection at the time of Photo C.

Time for change

We've seen how Colin Powell's face evolved over a three-year period. Why did he change so much, so fast?

If he'd been under less pressure, the same changes might have taken three decades. Constant media attention and high-level responsibility can be factors in facial evolution. Ultimately, however, inner growth is what makes for an altered visage. Powell's rapidly evolving face is a tribute to his internal sense of responsibility, more than a consequence of his politically important position.

As Secretary of State, Powell *evolved* facially far more than either President Bush or Vice President Cheney. The reason, I suspect, was that he felt more *involved* on a personal level. For Powell, these three years may have seemed to take longer than the three previous decades.

You don't need to be an Einstein to notice that time is relative. Waiting in line at the supermarket for 10 minutes can feel like a brief, relaxing interlude or a lockdown in purgatory.

As a spiritual talent scout, you should be grateful if you've learned how much leeway there is in whether time flies or it doesn't. Even if learned the hard way, this knowledge is worthwhile. It helps you to overcome one of earth's major illusions. Not one single clock on the planet is calibrated to show the increments of spiritual growth.

Realizing this will motivate a spiritual talent scout to examine face data closely. Comparing before-and-after pictures, you can look for changes as they really are. That contrasts with the more common approach where people assume a certain amount of change, or lack of it, due to chronology.

Sheer quantity of life drama doesn't predict the amount a face will evolve. An exquisite accounting is made by each soul. The calculation includes external stress, internalized stress, conscience, character, spiritual awareness and the soul's chosen pace of evolution.

Not all changes involve the facial wear-and-tear associated with aging. After a healing conversation, a face may visibly lighten up—grow more symmetrical, for instance. If you're lucky, you've seen that happen to yourself at least once.

In general, God's facial makeovers can be subtle. Non-face readers may not notice any physical changes at all. To read the story, you'll need an attentive eye and appreciative heart. Makeovers like Colin Powell's—or yours, or mine—are not the kind touted in magazines. They're recorded in God's great Book of Life.

7. Long-Term Changes

Hold onto your hat… and as many face parts as you can grab, should you think they're in any danger of falling off! Our mission here is to explore the long-term ways your face has evolved. How many ways? Enough to fill two chapters. This one's dedicated to the upper half of the face: eyes, eyebrows and ears.

Family values

Did you know that, over time, many of us hold one eye higher than the other? **Eye height asymmetry** reveals deep values about your place in the family of humanity.

The Data

To see this category, be sure to look at a face from an even angle.

- Hold your mirror directly across from your face.
- If you're reading a photo, don't leave it on a table. Pick it up and lift it until the eyes in the photo are straight across from your own.

A higher right eye or **higher left eye** will become obvious, assuming that the asymmetry is strong enough to matter. Don't squint to see it. Only the *verys* are worth reading, like Ronald Reagan's higher right eye and the higher left eye on John Quincy Adams.

The Meaning

If you value your public image over your personal self, over time, you'll develop a **higher right eye.**

Are you saying someone like me is a phony?

Not necessarily. You could be deeply committed to actions that make a difference in the world. And wonderful though your personal life might be, your career's your priority.

Over a 10-year period, inner priorities brought dramatic change to James Monroe's eye height asymmetry. To see the shift, compare his portraits. In 1817, at the start of his first term as president, his right eye was significantly higher than the left. But after his second term, in 1828, the direction of his eye height asymmetry reversed, making his left eye higher. Sound strange? The very same thing happened to Thomas Jefferson. Compare the portrait in Chapter Three to his image on a $2 bill.

If your private life and relationships matter more to you than work, don't be surprised if you, too, find your left eye edging upwards. Does that mean you can't be responsible or financially successful? Spy Robert Hanssen did fine (according to his dim lights) until he was caught.

For an ethical person, a **higher left eye** can signify a far-reaching personal mission that winds up augmenting your worldly success. For instance, what if you decide to make service to others a life priority? You'll put this personal value first in every aspect of your life, which could improve all your relationships, making your work extra influential.

Guess what? That's Oprah Winfrey's story. Over the years, her face has changed in many ways, but not her eye height asymmetry, which has consistently been higher on the left. According to an interview in *Redbook*, every day of her adult life, she has prayed to be of service to others.

Change

Golly, I don't think I'll ever enjoy putting on makeup again, now that I know my left eye is higher. Do you realize you've spoiled my face?

Fruit may spoil, faces ripen. Consider the possibility that what's been destroyed, really, is your old belief in faces as simple, decorative objects. Raising your consciousness about this will bring you greater wisdom and, ultimately, happiness.

A. President James Monroe in 1817

B. President James Monroe in 1828

Oprah Winfrey

The honest truth is, I'd rather be beautiful than wise.

Even "beautiful people," like movie stars and supermodels, show eye height asymmetry. For right eye higher, it's Gwyneth Paltrow, Cameron Diaz and Tyra Banks. For left eye higher, there's Cindy Crawford, Keri Russell and Charlize Theron.

What's really weird is that my whole right eye is bigger. Not just higher, bigger. If it keeps on getting bigger over the years, it might devour Texas. What does that mean?

Eye size asymmetry is the term I use when one eye is larger than the other. It's a soul signature trait.

A **larger right eye** means that you're destined to be socially adept in your career, as in the case of Indira Gandhi.

A **larger left eye** suggests a contract where you're especially skilled at making social connections in your personal life. John Adams is an example.

Philosophical bent

Eye angle shows outlook. Eyes can be up-angled, down-angled or even-angled. Although this category takes some practice to see, you'll be glad when you manage it, because this is one of the most meaningful ways a face can change over time.

The Data

Popular clichés about eye structure don't help face readers one bit. Most of us are familiar with expressions like "almond eyes," "doe eyes" and, even, "sloe eyes." Yet we'd be hard pressed to describe them. (Or their opposites, for that matter. Might I suggest "walnut eyes," "turtle eyes" and "faste eyes"?)

To see **eye angle** properly, read each eye separately. Then, as with any angle on the face, use your trusty technique, The Dot Method from the last chapter.

Holding your mirror on the level, imagine a dot at the inner corner of one eye, positioned just at the tear duct. Imagine a second dot at the opposite corner, which marks the three-way intersection of upper eyelid, lower eyelid and the white of the eye. Then, using your imagination only (no blunt instruments, please), connect the dots by drawing a line. Does the eye angle up, down or straight?

President Harry Truman

President Teddy Roosevelt

President Gerald Ford

Most presidents, like most human beings, have **up-angled eyes**. Extreme versions show on Carter, Truman and Coolidge (just their right eyes, corresponding to their idealistic selves at work).

Examples of **down-angled eyes**, also on the right, are Teddy Roosevelt, Kennedy and Grant.

Folks with **even-angled** eyes are rare (only an estimated 1 in 2,000 people has even *one* eye in this category). Count Ford, Clinton and the elder Bush in this elite group (their public-persona right eyes, anyway). Or, for a loathsome example, consider the right eye of Osama Bin Laden.

The Meaning

Up-angled eyes signify optimism, idealism and high expectations. The more *very* the angle, the higher those expectations tend to be.

Advantages of up-angled eyes are obvious. Should your eyes be down-angled, however, I'll bet you've already figured out the catch. Since we live on The Learning Planet, up-angled high expectations guarantee frequent disappointment.

By contrast, **down-angled** eyes correspond to a gift for finding—and solving—problems. Remember the puzzles for kids, "What is wrong with this picture?" Down-anglers find this kind of puzzle everywhere they look.

Compassion is the strength related to this tendency. Your challenge is holding onto problems the way a toddler clutches a security blanket.

As for **even-angled** eyes, congratulations. You're one of the world's rare realists, seeing things pretty much as they are. Your only problem with this, as you'd expect by now, is a lack of tolerance for the rest of the humanity. Why are some folks such dreamers? Why do others grouse and grump?

I've got something genuine to grouse about. Why are Americans of Chinese ancestry, like me, singled out as having "slanted eyes"?

All human beings have slanted eyes (also slanted eyebrows, ears and mouths). With eyes, confusion probably comes from unfamiliarity with the part of eye structure called the **single eyelid fold**, described in Chapter Three. George Washington's right eye angles up more than Ang Lee's (see page 25).

Maybe it's my down-angled eye talking here, but I find it scary that one of my eyes goes up and the other goes down.

Cubism in everyday life—it *is* kind of scary. However, if you've ever studied drawing you know that literal reality is far stranger than the blur that meets the casual eye. So go ahead and be an artist. Or a face reader. Or both. Your life will be enriched by the strangeness of reality rather than the slickness of stereotypes.

Okay, I'll be an artist. But I don't want to feel as loony as Van Gogh after he cut off his ear. So what comforting things can you tell those of us who just discovered we're cockeyed?

By the age of 40, most people develop some degree of difference between the angles of their eyes. Asymmetries can show up earlier, too. Remember, the angle of your left eye reveals your outlook about personal relationships, whereas your right eye reveals career concerns. Why shouldn't they differ?

So what does it mean that my right eye goes up while my left one goes down?

It means that you're in good company, including Abe Lincoln. At work you're optimistic, the kind of person who holds onto a vision of what's possible. But, thanks to that problem-oriented left eye, you have the courage to recognize the truth, pretty or not.

How about me, with my down-angled right eye and up-angled left?

You've got something in common with Jack Kennedy. The eye angles you've developed suggest that, in personal life, you're an idealist. But when you move out to the workplace, you aim to find, and fix, what's broken.

Change

Changes to eye angles can sneak up on you, most commonly after a difficult period in your life. You'll glance at the mirror and bam! Suddenly you notice that one eye dips downward. Less commonly, change goes in the other direction as well. Youthful photos of novelist Norman Mailer show his eyes to be very down-angled.

But life has been good to him, resulting in a set of conspicuously up-angled eyes. To see another example, turn to the photos of your trusty author at the end of this book. Check out the change to my left eye.

The whole right side of my face was affected by Bell's Palsy. Can't eyes change their angle for strictly medical reasons?

Illness can be understood on so many levels. Face reading brings the comfort of inner meaning. In your case, I'd invite you to consider why your right eye was stricken rather than the left. Could you have felt challenged in your career, rather than your personal life? Having gone through your bout of illness, which included that change to your right eye angle, do you now bring more compassion to your work life?

Although illness is widely considered the sole cause of face changes, physiognomy can help you to remember life's inner component. The soul has learned a new outlook about relationships or the workplace. To a spiritual talent scout, your hard-won asymmetry shines like a medal earned on the battlefield of life.

You are all sanpaku? Hope not!

Did you ever read *You Are All Sanpaku*? A bestseller during the 1970s, it's still the definitive book about macrobiotic facial diagnosis. Not exactly cheery, George Oshawa's book warns readers against the dire consequences, as shown in the physical face, of macrobiotically undesirable behaviors, such as eating dairy products.

The Data

With **sanpaku eyes**, a third white develops *below* the two white areas that usually show in an eye (one white on either side of the iris). Examples include JFK and the young ER.

The Meaning

Oshawa's biggest claim to fame was alerting Westerners to the alleged dangers of sanpaku eyes. The prognosis was fatal: early death.

Personally, I haven't found a direct correlation between any face trait and death. But it's true that, over time, some people do develop sanpaku eyes. Eleanor Roosevelt's not a great example of early death, having lived to age 78. Kennedy is a fair example, except that he doesn't appear to have suffered from one of the major symptoms alleged by Oshawa, low sexual vitality.

In my system, sanpaku eyes convey a different meaning. I agree with Oshawa only to the extent that I, too, find this particular face data to be primarily about challenge, rather than talent.

Eyes with **a third white under** suggest a challenge with pedestal-itis— as in putting people on them. Obviously, plenty of people with an inferiority complex don't develop sanpaku eyes, only those for whom the psychological problem is extreme and chronic. In life, as in face reading, it's always recommended to see people on the level, rather than looking up or down.

Change

What fascinates me about sanpaku eyes is how often they change, whether through the dietary improvements favored by Oshawa, by means of living in the White House for a decade or via other lifestyle possibilities. *How* this is achieved doesn't show in the eyes, unless it's written so small that I ought to be reading faces with a special macrobiotic magnifying glass. What does show is that eyes can lose that third white, as happened with Eleanor Roosevelt.

How about having a fourth white show, one under plus another one over?

It's rare. When I say rare, I mean that since I began reading faces in 1975, I've met exactly three people who have this.

Eyes with four whites occur when the iris is small compared with the rest of the eye. A soul signature trait, it signals exceptional perspective and wisdom. The challenge is lack of peers. Should you meet somebody with this trait, strike up a conversation if you can. You'll find that person's point of view absolutely fascinating… even if you, personally, don't suffer from pedestal-itis.

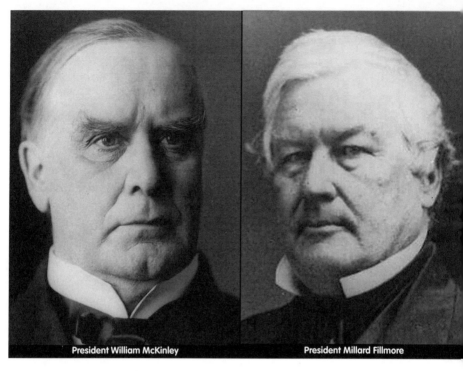

President William McKinley   President Millard Fillmore

Spontaneity

Brow height relates to preferred timing for speech. Highbrows and lowbrows are my face reading terms (not cultural terms) for the varied amounts of distance between the eyebrow and the eye.

The Data

Extreme **highbrows**, like Millard Fillmore's, may appear to be levitating, while **lowbrows**, like William McKinley's, seem at risk for tumbling, splat! into the eyes. **Middlebrows** mean eyebrows positioned exactly where you'd expect them. You can thank Ronald Reagan for not keeping you in suspense about his brow position.

The Meaning

Read your own brow height to appreciate an aspect of communication style that few people understand. You will want to understand it, however, if you care about making the most of yourself.

Highbrows indicate personal reserve, verging on secrecy. If you have that brow position, it's immensely important that you think before you speak. Advance planning will help you to build power as a communicator. The challenge? Because you keep secrets so well, others may find you inscrutable.

Having highbrows doesn't mean that you'll never choose to speak impulsively, just that you'll do it as the result of a deliberate choice. By contrast, owners of **lowbrows** can hardly stop themselves.

Recognize yourself here? With lowbrows, you're at your best speaking off the cuff, not buttoned up beneath a starched shirt and tie. In fact, the more perfectly you prepare your speech, the worse you'll do. Blurting puts you in your power.

Middlebrows don't have issues related to the timing of speech. If you have this brow height, reading about the alternatives may already have caused you to scratch your head (or eyebrows) in disbelief. Automatically timing your speech in a situational manner, you'll be reserved or forthcoming as appropriate. Lucky you, to have no brow height issues greater than that pesky lack of tolerance for the rest of humanity!

Although I have very low brows, I seldom talk about myself, especially when I'm really upset. How do you explain that?

Since your lips are thin, that counterbalances your lowbrows.

Thin? You're being polite. Basically I have no lips.

The combination of **thin lips plus lowbrows** can create chronic conflict. One part of you longs to get things off your chest. Another part recoils from the very idea. So here's the likely outcome: When the topic is personal, your recalcitrant lips will prevail. But when the subject's not personal, blurting will win.

Nixon had the same combo as you. Taping his words for his own amusement (and, it later turned out, for posterity's), Nixon's uncensored stream-of-consciousness exemplifies totally spontaneous speech without the constraints of inner reflection.

I'm no Nixon but often the stuff I want to blurt out is very negative. If I let my tongue loose, I could get myself fired, divorced or God knows what. Any advice?

Souls can orchestrate some very interesting conflicts with lowbrows. Yours are combined with **down-angled eyes**, which make you a problem finder, plus **close-set eyes**, which go with the ability to criticize like crazy. Supplementing lowbrows with either trait, you'd be well equipped to keep up a running commentary of negative observations. Having hit the facial jackpot, it would be great if you could get a job like lawyer, engineer, consumer advocate or ombudsman. Blurting out the difficult truths could make your professional reputation!

Change

Temporary brow shifts are one of the fastest face changes possible. Some singers learn to raise their eyebrows on purpose to enhance vocal quality. And lowering your brows is so quick, it can be done faster than touching your toes. But for brow height to change on a face in repose, that develops in its own sweet time. Decades, usually, so check your old photos. Unbeknownst to you, over the years, your brow height may have moved up or down, shifting as quietly as snowdrifts in a blizzard. Just as it's wise to update your hairstyle periodically, it can be smart to rethink your habits of verbal spontaneity.

An outrageous intellectual bent

Eyebrows can develop certain **unusual hair patterns** that show the evolution of a curmudgeon.

The Data

Wild hairs consists of eyebrow hairs that grow extra long, like the wacky nest-like configuration developed by William McKinley.

Contradictory hairs go beyond being long; they tangle up with other brow hairs; examples include presidential aspirant Pat Buchanan, businessman Donald Trump and that conundrum of an Iraqi leader, Saddam Hussein.

People who develop either unusual eyebrow pattern have three choices:

- You can train the unusual hairs to follow the rest (in the manner of balding men with comb-overs). That's what McKinley did.

- You can deem the maverick hairs unacceptable and trim them. Countless examples exist; they're just hard to find in photos.
- Or you can let the hairy extravagance be, unabashed, untamed and, as in the case of Saddam's contradictory hairs, a law unto themselves.

For your sake, as a face reader, I hope you know some people who dare to let their outrageous eyebrows show. You'll have fun comparing the meaning to what you've seen of that person's behavior.

The Meaning

Could any physical traits be easier to take at face value? **Wild hairs** correspond to wild, unconventional ideas. **Contradictory hairs** are about eccentric or unusual ideas that conflict with the person's chosen lifestyle or public views.

It takes courage to wear one's shadow self on the surface for everyone to see, but people with contradictory hairs do it routinely. Conflict is the challenge, but the mental originality is something to prize; it can make this personal style well worth having.

Change

What if you feel you're eccentric enough without having your eyebrows add to it? Change can be quick, unlike the process of growing these unusual hairs in the first place. But if the distinctive hairs keep returning, consider allowing at least a few of them to stay. Many a midlife would become more interesting.

Decisions, decisions

One of the most revealing face categories is a complete unknown to most people. Honestly, how much attention do you normally pay to **ear position?** If it's enough for you to have your ears attached to your head, you're in for a fascinating surprise. As for you salespeople, I've been told that some of your colleagues have used my system of Face Reading Secrets to become millionaires, and what helped them the most was reading this particular trait. Is that earie or what?

The Data

To orient yourself, check out a face in profile. Your benchmarks are the lowest part of the eyebrow and the bottom of the nose. Then compare where the ear is located relative to these two benchmarks.

Low ears, like Fillmore's and Reagan's, have lobes that hang below the nose.

High ears, like Clinton's and King's, have tops that peak out above eyebrow height.

Middle ears, like Teddy Roosevelt's and Harry Truman's, fit top-to-lobe between eyebrow and nose.

I'm having trouble seeing this category. Any suggestions?

Seeing ear position definitely takes practice. Preferably the face is on the level, not tilted up or down. If your photo is tilted, pick it up and turn it (clockwise or counterclockwise) until the eyebrow is parallel to the floor, relative to where you are sitting.

Doing this helps you to compensate for a head being thrust up or down. Martin Luther King's ear is much higher, for instance, than it first looks in the profile photo shown in Chapter Four. To help myself see it, I held the page with his photo and rotated it from 12 o'clock position to 2 o'clock, which put his eyebrow on the level. Lift up your book and try it.

Also, when viewing ear position, it may help you to draw imaginary parallel lines: one from the eyebrow out to the ear, the other from the lowest part of the nose out to the ear. These lines help you to see if an earlobe shows below the nose or an eartop protrudes above an ear.

The Meaning

Low ears mark a deliberate decision maker, someone who may incur the impatience of others with higher ear positions. By far the most common style with American presidents, it brings a statistical advantage: If you take an extra long time to arrive at decisions, compared to those with other ear positions, you'll make fewer decisions and, probably, fewer mistakes. Incidentally, don't assume that a slow style equates with lack of intelligence. Albert Einstein had *very* low ears.

High ears go with a quick, intuitive style of decision making. If you have them, you think and learn much faster than others. (I know, you've probably figured this out already, extrapolating from the meaning of low ears.) Because your intellectual timing's so fast, you may often feel impatient. Impulsiveness could be a challenge, too.

How about **middle ears?** With ears plugged into that moderate position, you're apt to find intellectual timing a big fat non-issue. Except why can't everyone be moderate, like you? You'll take time when you have it, decide quickly when you don't.

This ear position thing has me freaked out. I just discovered I'm lopsided. My right ear is high but my left ear is low. What does that mean?

Asymmetrical ear position is very common, as faces change over time. And it doesn't mean you're an Al Capone. A gangster's face doesn't just happen to anyone; it takes work. Asymmetrical ear position is more likely to be related to the beauty of your soul. To interpret different ear heights, remember that ear position on the right shows your typical style of making decisions at work, with quick, intuitive decisions producing the best results for you.

Ear position on the left shows how you make personal decisions, like whom to marry, where to live, or which career path to follow. Your low left ear suggests that your style of making these decisions is very thorough.

That's putting it politely. The word is agonizing.

Well, if you suffer a lot from the challenge, it may help to remind yourself of the strength that goes with it. Low ears signal an inner commitment to make decisions that are wise. Be glad that you take the time. It's worth it.

Incidentally, the direction of your ear position asymmetry gives you something in common with Jimmy Carter. Turn back to his photo in the last chapter and take a good look at his ears. The left one is just about as low as a human ear could possibly be, while his right ear lands squarely in the middle position. He's proof that a slower rate of making decisions, in your private life, can be a good thing.

President James Buchanan | Thor Heyerdahl

Change

Do you ever find that ears become higher, or is it always a matter of going downhill?

Depending on the soul's journey, ear position can shift either up or down. I've seen it in clients and you will, too, doing Transformation Readings of people you know. It's fun to show ear changes to those who firmly believe that "gravity" explains everything that can happen to a face.

"Which gravity do you mean?" I ask them. "The gravity weighing on your nose, your eyebrows or your ears?"

Conformity

Many people begin with **out-angled ears** but later achieve a different angle on life, developing ears that grow close to the head. Sometimes the opposite happens, and **in-angled ears** wing out. What's the soul-level reason? **Ear angles** reveal your pattern for handling other people's rules.

The Data

To develop an eye for ear, look at your face from the front. **In-angled ears** show in photos you've seen in this chapter of Teddy Roosevelt and Gerald Ford. Ears like these may seem to be stuck down with chewing gum but they can stay put all by themselves!

If ears stick out, like James Buchanan's, they're **out-angled**. Sometimes you'll find **middle-angled** ears, as on Thor Heyerdahl, the modern-day explorer who wrote *Kon Tiki*.

What if your ears can't decide what the heck they want to be? I have one innie and one outie.

Welcome to a very large club. It's called "Owners of the Most Common Facial Asymmetry." Most adults have a right ear that's more in-angled than the left; for an example, check out that guy with the ultra-moderate face, President Reagan.

The Meaning

In-angled ears mark a person who deeply desires to belong. What a social asset! If your ears are innies, admit it. Don't you have great manners? Your ears are practically radar devices—whatever the social situation, you switch on those ears and know what behavior is considered appropriate. Your related challenge is the need to belong.

Out-angled ears are the sign of an individualist who makes her own rules. Who cares what other people expect? (Hey, who noticed in the first place?) Sure, sometimes your spunky actions may require a little damage control, but to you that's a small price to pay for being yourself.

Middle-angled ears mean that you don't have issues around conforming and belonging. Your only potential challenge with this trait is wondering what makes others so strange: Why are some folks so clueless about manners? What makes others so stuffy?

Thor Heyerdahl is my favorite example of ears that swing both ways. I've seen a documentary of the journey he made from Peru to Polynesia just to prove an archeological theory. Heyerdahl came across as the most straight-laced Norwegian you've ever seen sail 4,000 miles on an imitation aboriginal balsa wood raft.

My whole life, people have called me "Dumbo ears." Why do people make fun of ears that stick out? And what's your perspective as a face reader?

When you consider the significance of out-angled ears, it's understandable that some folks might find them threatening, as in, "What, you don't care about my rules?" As if that wasn't threatening enough (to the insecure), *very* out-angled ears like yours mark pioneers, entrepreneurs and other independent souls who don't care, deep down, whether others approve of them or not.

Are you saying ear angles dictate conformity? Although I have very in-angled ears, I'm proud of my "alternate lifestyle."

Ear angle doesn't dictate your sexual preference, your favorite form of medicine, your politics or diet or, even, your table manners. No face data determines how you live, actually. What in-angled ears *do* show is that you'll agonize before choosing a counter-culture behavior.

Change

Usually change to ear angles happens from out to in. Children often outgrow their spunky, out-angled ears. As an adult, Ulysses S. Grant developed an increasingly in-angled right ear. Prince Charles, as a young man, had a set of *very, very* out-angled ears; although still out-angled, his ears have become less outrageously so. And the highly unconventional prince's behavior has mellowed somewhat, no doubt to the relief of his *very* in-angled mother, Queen Elizabeth.

Evolution can move ears in the opposite direction, though it happens less often. In my case, when I started to teach face reading, I had two *very* in-angled ears and, believe me, I suffered from the challenge about wanting to belong. Most people hadn't heard of physiognomy, and it bothered me that I couldn't belong to a large group of professional physiognomists. (By contrast, a Ross Perot-style, out-angled entrepreneur would have been *delighted* to be a pioneer.)

Over the decades, I've come to terms with my unconventional profession, as well as the need to act like an entrepreneur. And guess what? My right ear has edged halfway between in-angled and out-angled.

What does it mean if you develop a left ear that's more out-angled than your right one?

You're more conservative at work than at home. If your left ear is really far out, your personal life could be wild and crazy.

Does the opposite change ever happen?

Sure. One example is Jimmy Carter. In his photo at the U.S. Naval Academy, the young midshipman had *very* out-angled ears, with the left one more extreme than the right. But by the time of his presidential photo, both ears had settled down considerably, and his right ear angled out more than his left.

The combo means relatively conservative values in private vs. unconventionality in public. Carter demonstrated this his very first day in office. To show disdain for the "imperial presidencies" that preceded him, Carter left his official limo and walked to the White House. The Democrat's refusal to engage in politics as usual quickly won him disdain from Congress, a considerable achievement in the annals of non-conformity since *his own party* held power in Congress at the time. Life is probably easier for people with the more common ear asymmetry, the one opposite to Carter's.

Creature comforts

Conventional wisdom predicts that your earlobes, like your nose tip, will grow as you age.

Part of this stereotype is true. It's *unusual* to encounter a person, like Reagan, whose nose tip actually shrank over the years. It's *unusual* to see earlobes diminish, as we saw in our reading of Colin Powell. More commonly, these face parts grow larger.

But for many faces, there's no significant change. And then there's the ticklish matter of *who* evolves those larger or smaller earlobes or nose tips. So let's put aside the ageist stereotypes and consider what long-term changes, in either direction, could mean.

We'll start with earlobes. **Earlobe size** relates to a soul's deep priorities about being metaphysical or physical.

The Data

View **earlobe size** on one ear at a time. Compare it to the size of the other two parts of ear structure, inner ear circles and outer ear circles. As soul signature traits, these are unlikely to change. (Read more about them in *The Power of Face Reading*, pages 94-101.)

Earlobes come in the three varieties Goldilocks would understand: **Big**, like those on William McKinley; **small,** like those on Franklin Pierce and John Tyler; and **moderate,** the ones Goldilocks would have considered "just right." Like (you guessed it) Ronald Reagan's.

A face reader won't bother to read the moderate size, as it simply denotes a flexible approach. With this, sometimes you act like a person with big earlobes, other times you act like a person with small ones. And at no time are you required, like Goldilocks, to deal with semi-domesticated bears.

The Meaning

Big earlobes symbolize a fascination with physical reality. For instance, can you list all the items of furniture in the room where you are right now, no peeking allowed? If you pride yourself on doing spontaneous furniture inventory (or in other ways proving yourself to be uncommonly observant), you can look forward to a future with bigger earlobes.

Does it mean anything special if the earlobes are puffy as well as large?

Count it as a *very* version of big earlobes. The super-duper groundedness seems to be especially helpful for a military career. I've found **large, puffy earlobes** on Generals Grant, Eisenhower and, more recently, Powell. Demagogues find these super-sized lobes useful too, unfortunately. Slobodan Milosevic has the most extreme set I've seen so far.

Your potential challenge, whether your earlobes are large or puffy or both, is taking life too literally. Ever hear of not seeing the forest for the trees? Huge earlobes can bring on a case of not seeing the forest for the streaks on the window.

Small earlobes relate to a metaphysical orientation. You don't feel your main mission in life is to work out at the gym. No sweat there! It can be a beautiful thing if your soul has set you up to be metaphysical rather than physical. Your related life challenge is getting the folks with big earlobes to think you're credible. Do you seem practical enough to earn their respect?

Change

Could you stretch your earlobes on purpose by wearing heavy earrings? Would that make you more practical?

A metaphysically-minded individual would feel extremely uncomfortable weighting her ears down, long-term. Even if oblivious to the face reading significance, her desire to wear heavy earrings would, most likely, wear off long before her earlobes lengthened.

But what if there was social pressure, a fad led by someone like Britney Spears?

Going along with the crowd can mute inner awareness of soul. So, yes, a short-earlobed woman, caught up in a heavy metal jewelry craze, could alter her earlobes. This would result in her becoming more materialistically oriented.

Keep in mind, there's always a reciprocal relationship between the soul and the face. Usually physical change is based on inner growth, but change can come from the other direction, too.

Speaking of direction, parts of the face further south will be featured in the next chapter. Prepare for another wild ride, as we travel further through time and face.

8. More Facial Changes

If the last chapter surprised you with all that face data you never noticed before, this chapter could really make you feel like a bobblehead. (But only in the nicest possible way, of course. One could do far worse than be a nodder doll.)

Most people focus only on the upper half of a face, supplemented by an occasional peek at the mouth. Spiritual talent scouts don't stop there. What can you learn from the data on the lower face? Nostrils ahoy!

The most controversial face data

Sex works fine, power can do. But to truly turn up the energy when reading a face, no topic works better than money. Think about it. Your best friend probably tells you plenty about power struggles, and even a fair share about sex. But did you ever swap the vital statistics on how much money you earn?

No wonder I recommend discretion when you read this most private part of the face. Be circumspect about what you say out loud, anyway. Even on a physical level, many folks are jittery about nose reading.

Still how can you resist doing research privately? **Nose tips** will clue you into a person's preference for saving money.

Whoa! You can read how much a person has in the bank?

No part of the face shows exact dollar amounts. Otherwise face reading could bring new meaning to terms like "inflation." Still, nose tips can inform you about the nearest thing to net worth: saving style. This is useful to read for business, sorting through sales prospects, even choosing dates if you aim to marry rich.

President George H. Bush   President Bill Clinton

The Data

In Face Reading Secrets, we interpret nose tips along with two other face bits related to money: nostril size and nostril shape. All three categories can change as a person evolves. A **nose tip** is the ball-like structure between the nose roots. Its size is relative, best gauged by comparison. Two methods can help you do this.

Compare your subject's nose tip to her *eyes*. If her nose tip is small enough to fit into one of her eyes, the tip is small. Whereas a nose tip that won't fit into her eye would count as... large. Alternatively compare your subject's nose tip to the width of her *nose* right above the tip. Sometimes the tip is actually narrower.

Using either method, you'll find **petite** nose tips (like the one on George H. Bush), **chunky** nose tips (like Bill Clinton's), and **moderate** nose tips (like the one in last chapter's photo of Jimmy Carter).

The Meaning

Petite nose tips signify prosperity consciousness, a spiritual mindset about money where you expect that you'll always have plenty. Therefore, you tend not to worry about saving.

Chunky nose tips reveal concern over financial security, plus strong appreciation for creature comforts. With advancing years, most people worry about the size of their nest eggs. So usually (though not inevitably) their nose tips grow.

At any age, a chunky nose tip signifies that you have a gift for financial prudence, while your potential challenge is nagging worry, regardless of how much money you have in the bank.

Moderate nose tips correspond to an instinctive balance about saving. Sure a nest egg seems like a good thing, but obsessing over money does not. As you might imagine, opportunities abound to be flabbergasted at the foolish financial foibles of the rest of humanity.

When looking at nose tips, do you count the whole thing? How about the nostril covers?

You mean those fleshy flanges to either side of the tip? I call them **nose roots.** Nose tips do not include them. Nose roots are about gaining financial support from family.

To gauge the size of nose roots, compare them to the size of the nose tip. Of the three previously mentioned presidents, Bush has the largest, then Carter. Clinton has almost none.

This is a soul signature trait. Before incarnating, when they shaped their life plans, each of these men was destined to receive different amounts of financial support from family. Bush was set up to gain most, Carter less, Clinton least.

It's mind-boggling that there's a connection between money, nose tip size and the responsibility to look after yourself. No wonder kids start off with small tips. And seniors, they can't afford to skimp on nose tips, can they?

Face readers see a clear parallel between the relatively carefree financial lives of children and their tiny nose tips versus the solid responsible tips that belong to heads of households.

What if the family's poor?

Even then, children are less likely to worry about money than the head of the household.

Does a big nose tip tell you how rich a person is?

Nose tips only reveal how much a man feels he *needs* to have savings, not his bank balance. Gauging his precise degree of financial solvency will be up to you (and perhaps, your private detective).

Gandhi had a huge nose tip, yet he lived like a monk. Doesn't that disprove your theory?

Mahatma Gandhi applied his financially prudent instincts to his country rather than himself. He urged families to work toward economic self-sufficiency. This was, in fact, one of his major concerns.

Do Republicans have bigger nose tips than Democrats?

Interesting question! If you study the history of presidents' political deeds, in contrast to their campaign promises, nose tips are immensely revealing.

Bush Sr. promised no new taxes, implying that he would not be a "tax and spend" president. Unfortunately he made no promises about being a "borrow and spend" president. His fiscal preferences translated into debt for the nation. Clinton, with the heftiest nose tip of any American president of the 20th century, may have been a Democrat but he left the country with its largest financial surplus ever.

To a face reader, political parties are less meaningful than the festival of meaning that shows in a face. To anticipate what presidential candidates will do with money, in contrast to their campaign promises, don't read their lips. Read their noses.

What's the financial significance of the little chunk of flab beneath my nose tip? Or should I just put my nose on a diet?

Flab? That's a **nose bonus,** indicating a wonderful kind of work behavior. Physically, the bonus is a bit of extra cartilage between your nostrils and below them. Pinch it and you'll feel for sure that it's not flab.

The nose bonus marks a person whose work must involve service. No matter how well a job might pay, you won't stick with it unless you're sure that the work would really help people. Harry Truman developed his nose bonus long before he came to the White House. Later in this chapter, you'll see them on Betty Ford and Ladybird Johnson.

Cosmetic surgeons have a more technical term for this service-oriented trait. They call it a **"hanging columella,"** and consider it one of the many facial "deformities" that people should pay to have fixed. As you may have noticed, vanity surgeons appear to define **deformity** as any facial difference between a human being and a Barbie doll.

Change

At the rate my nose tip has been growing, my whole face is turning into one big schnozz. When you say that nose tips relate to materialism, that makes me feel even worse. Believe it or not, I happen to be a very spiritual person. So how did I get stuck with this huge honker?

Some of the most spiritual people around have chunky nose tips. First, appreciate that the need to earn money is one of the great grounding forces in human life. Have you known many children of millionaires? I have. It's not unusual for them to have trouble taking life seriously. Earning a living forces us to pay attention to life. (Pay, get it?)

Second, concern over financial security doesn't necessarily make you materialistic. Often it's highly spiritual people who are brought down to earth through financial circumstances. Either they'll have a substantial nose tip and the accompanying craving for financial security or they'll have other aspects of life conspire to ground them, like weight gain and a craving for cigarettes. (For a more thorough discussion of grounding, see my book, *Empowered by Empathy,* Chapter 13.)

One way or another, human beings are meant to keep their feet on the ground. It's part of the rules here on The Learning Planet.

What happens when a nose job shrinks the size of your nose tip?

With the corresponding change in personal style, you'll find yourself less apt to save money. I've had the opportunity to ask many women who've had this surgery if they changed in this way. All agreed.

Do you realize how many people have nose jobs? In America, there were 177,000 in 2001 alone. Did any of these consumers have a clue what they were buying, in terms of potentially altering their style with money?

Americans are outraged when we discover that an accounting firm like Arthur Andersen can be tied to an Enron or that pharmaceutical companies influence the FDA. But even worse than a compromised oversight authority is none at all. Except for malpractice cases, vanity surgery goes uninvestigated. When enough people appreciate that faces are spiritual, as well as material, perhaps that will change. In the meantime you'll have to do your own accounting, materially and spiritually.

More about money

Nostril size reveals personal style about spending money. Interpret this along with a related bit of face data, nostril shape.

The Data

Shy about delving into nostrils? Don't be. Simply view the nose in question from the front, at a straight angle. Do you see nostrils or not? Visible air holes count as **large** nostrils; the merest hint of an opening means they are **small**, and **medium** nostrils are moderately visible.

Kennedy had the largest nostrils of any president since World War II. Nixon had the smallest. Most have had medium nostrils, with the most moderate of all belonging to, who else? Ronald Reagan.

The Meaning

Large nostrils mark a free spender. **Small** nostrils indicate frugality. **Medium** nostrils reveal spenders who are willing but wary.

President Herbert Hoover

First Lady Pat Nixon

First Lady Barbara Bush

President George W. Bush

Whereas nostril size relates to a person's comfort zone with amount of spending, **nostril shape** shows the preferred style of spending.

The Data

Admittedly some practice may be required before you feel comfortable scrutinizing nostrils. And useful though the information may be, I don't recommend that you develop your eye for it on a first date. Otherwise there will be no second date. Photos in this book, supplemented by your own personal nose and a mirror, are a better way to practice seeing the shapes of nostrils.

As you'll discover, they can be **round,** with a half-circle shape visible. **Flared** nostrils have a curve at the inner half, near the center of the face; then the shape turns oval toward the outer half of the nostril. A **rectangular** nostril looks like the shallow cover of a box, reminiscent of the lid on a shoebox. Finally, **triangular** nostrils come to a point in the center.

James Madison and Martin Van Buren exemplify round nostrils. The most common shape for nostrils is flared, represented by George W. Bush. Both his parents, George H. and Barbara, have rectangular nostrils, while Pat Nixon and Herbert Hoover display triangular nostrils.

The Meaning

Round nostrils correspond to an enthusiastic style of spending. Nobody enjoys spending more than a person with **large, round nostrils.** Even if your nostril *size* is small, should their *shape* be round, you have a knack for resourceful money management, juggling debts and assets with a skill born of necessity. Proud examples from America's history are Adams (Quincy), McKinley and Kennedy.

Flared nostrils signify adventurous spending. If you belong to this nose-user's group, typically you thinks of yourself as a careful spender (regardless of nostril size). But, when you decide to spend, oh boy! Your purchases can be impulsive and unconventional. Like the round-nostrilled folk, people with flared nostrils get a charge out of spending, in more ways than one. During election 2000, who spoke convincingly of putting Medicare surpluses in a lockbox? It was Vice President Al Gore, with rectangular nostrils punctuating his words, not George W., Mr. Flare.

Rectangular nostrils reveal not much. Oh, I'm kidding. But it's true that nostrils with this shape are almost always small. (Two interesting exceptions from American history are John Adams and Thomas Jefferson, both of whom developed large, rectangular nostrils.) Whether your rectangular nostrils are large or small, your spending style can be summed up in one word: disciplined. Owners of these nostrils are good at drawing up a budget, then sticking to it.

Triangular nostrils show a strong need to control money carefully. Salespeople, run for cover! If it's any consolation to you readers who have developed this face data, triangular nostrils don't just happen. They evolve as a reaction to financial stress. Two examples follow.

Writers, especially, can relate to the story of Russell Baker's nostrils. As a young reporter for *The Baltimore Sun,* he suffered financially along with all his colleagues. "Obsession with money... made it easy to recognize *Sun* people," Baker wrote in his autobiography, *The Good Times.* Although hardship drove other reporters away, Baker "lingered on, grousing, desperate about unpayable bills."

The cover photo for *The Good Times* shows a youthful photo of Baker with large, round nostrils. Photos taken after the period he described reveal that his nostrils turned triangular.

In politics, Herbert Hoover's example is equally poignant. When he campaigned for president, his nostrils were rectangular. The year following his inauguration, the stock market crashed, sending the U.S. economy into the Great Depression. Bam! went his nostril shape into (you guessed it) triangles.

Change

By your logic, shouldn't there be triangular nostrils on everyone who has gone on welfare? How about all the people who lived through the Great Depression?

What causes a face to change is the inner sense of struggle. Stress, like beauty, lies in the eye of the beholder. Therefore, outwardly identical circumstances will impact people differently.

To illustrate this, I'll share a story about my nostrils. As a TM teacher in 1971, I lived in extreme poverty. Every paycheck, I'd miss the cutoff point for a living wage; I even spent three weeks living on cornmeal and tomato paste. Yet the frustration didn't go deep into my soul. My lifestyle was a matter of choice, and I passionately believed in what I was doing. My small, flared nostrils didn't change.

Many decades later, I married a generous man whose income may not have been especially affluent, but I sensed that he would give me anything I wanted. (He has!) During our honeymoon, a honeymoon where I bought more clothes than I had in the previous several years combined, my nostril size grew significantly. Being a face reader, I quickly noticed the difference.

How come my nostrils never changed like that?

Maybe they have. Who but a face reader notices nostril changes, a tissue salesman? Go ahead now. Grab your family album and look old photos of yourself straight in the nose.

After years of financial stress, your nostrils may have grown smaller or even turned triangular. It depends on your inward response to the circumstances. Conversely, a financial windfall may have expanded your nostrils or rounded their shape.

What if your nostrils only change on one side?

Nostril asymmetries are exceedingly common. Do you spend money differently at work than in your personal life? Long-term, your nostrils will show asymmetry. For George H. Bush, for instance, the left nostril is significantly larger.

Influential noses

One of the more intriguing ways that faces can change is **nose angling** to the left or right.

The Data

Usually noses stay put in the middle of a person's face, but not always. There may be a gradual shift; in other cases there's a so-called "accident." To tell if your nose has migrated, take a sheet of paper and use it to cover one side of your face at a time. Does the lower half of your nose lean toward one half more than the other? For more practice, use blank paper to cover up the left and right halves of a photo, or draw an imaginary line. Soon you'll find it easy to spot nose angling.

The Meaning

What are the odds on your becoming famous? Nothing on the face predicts this for sure. But destiny for fame correlates to this bit of face data more than any other.

Left leaning noses develop on people whose work has deep inner significance. Prestigious though their careers may be, they evaluate success in terms of their personal values. Only one clear example emerges from all U.S. presidents, George H. Bush. Nor do other walks of life furnish many famous examples.

Since it's the opposite of a fame-related trait, you'll more likely find it on people in your own neighborhood, maybe even yourself. If your nose angles to the left, congratulations that you relate to work in a relatively deep way. Worldly success matters less to you than knowing you've spent your time meaningfully.

Right leaning noses go with a destiny for work that has great outer impact. With this fame trait, you enjoy more success and status than might otherwise be expected, given factors like your intellect, emotional IQ and ambition. Does it seem fair that some people should lead a charmed work life? Maybe only if you believe in reincarnation!

You'll find significantly right-angled noses in nearly one out of every two U.S. presidents. The roster includes Buchanan, Bush (W.), Carter, Clinton, Eisenhower, Fillmore, Ford, Harding, Harrison (William), Hayes, Hoover, Jackson, Johnson, Monroe, Nixon, Roosevelt (Franklin), Roosevelt (Teddy), Taylor, Truman, Tyler, and Wilson.

You'll also find extreme right-leaning noses on these notorious headline grabbers: Osama Bin Laden, Adolph Hitler, Saddam Hussein, Timothy McVeigh, Slobodan Milosevic and Muammar Qadhafi.

Change

Most people seldom notice noses, aside from short-term acts of personal grooming and long-term attitudes of (unjustified) shame. As a face reader, you can have fun going back over old photos to chart the slow migration of your nose. Has it diverged from being a straight-arrow nose? Usually the shifts are extremely subtle, taking decades to develop.

What if your nose changed because of an accident?

James Madison   **President Dwight Eisenhower**

However it happened, nose angling relates to your agreement with the Universe. Go back over your personal history and see if you can correlate nose angling to your perspective on work (or school, if you were a kid—this is one trait where you could accurately read meaning on a face under the age of 18).

More popularity points

Lip length also impacts your influence on the world, revealing your ideal audience size. Do you prefer to speak to large groups or small ones? Either way, there's scope for greatness.

The Data

Speaking of audiences, when gauging your lip length, I recommend that you do it privately. Otherwise, if there's any ham in you whatsoever, it's hard to stare at your mouth in the mirror without making it do tricks.

But to read lip length, you'll have to tell your mouth to roll over and play dead. Or, at least, to stop grinning. It may help to put the mirror down for a minute, let your mouth relax into a semblance of normalcy, then freeze the non-expression while you hoist up your mirror and stare.

Look on the level, remember. Then compare the length of your lips to the overall width of your face, your eyebrows, eyes and nose. **Short** lips make a brief horizontal journey. **Long** lips really travel. Most mouths have **moderate** lip length. James Madison was a shortie. Ike Eisenhower was long, and Pat Nixon's lip length was moderate.

The Meaning

Short lips imply comfort with talking to one person at a time. Sincerity and truthfulness are your strong points. Maybe you've noticed the challenge, too. People with short lips are usually terrible at lying (as in literally being bad at it, which is not what's generally meant by "a terrible liar.")

Long lips, by contrast, go with a preference for talking with many people. Yes, that can involve stretching the truth, as well as stretching your lips. Being a crowd pleaser, your potential challenge is being so other-directed that you don't examine what *you* really believe, deep down.

Moderate lip length signifies a flexible communication style. You're able to please crowds or share one-on-one, without the compulsion to do either.

Change

A related way to explore mouth length is to study the amount of **change in mouth length with a smile.**

Big change, from short to long, indicates great sociability. Although the person feels most comfortable talking with people one-on-one, he can open up for public speaking. Franklin Delano Roosevelt did this facially, just as his Fireside Chats used an intimate radio format to broadcast his views.

Small change means that the mouth shows moderate or short lip length, even when smiling. This signifies that a person's comfort zone for talking with others doesn't adapt greatly, even if he's invited to address large groups of people, as in the case of Woodrow Wilson. The significance of small change for a long mouth is constant sociability. An example is President George H. Bush. Famous for saying "Read my lips," he had a lot of lengthwise lip to read, no matter how large or small his audience.

How about mouth length changes unrelated to smiles? Can that happen?

Depending on a person's choices and values, mouth length in repose can grow enormously. Once, when a guest on "Jenny Jones," I was asked to comment on how the talk show host had changed since she was a high school beauty queen. The question might have seemed tricky, since she'd altered her face a great deal through cosmetic surgery. But her most significant facial change was all natural, resulting from long-term ambition. Jones' mouth length had grown by leaps and bounds.

Shyness has been a problem all my life. Could that be related to my short mouth, which doesn't widen even when I smile?

When a mouth is consistently short, shyness is the flip side of some enviable qualities, like truthfulness and depth of friendship. Your soul has set you up to be a private person, not Miss Popularity with a mob. Unreasonable expectations may be your real problem, not the shyness.

Self-disclosure

Not everyone feels comfortable discussing intimate secrets about emotions, psychological traumas, religious beliefs and the like. How can you learn in advance who feels comfortable discussing the juicy stuff? It shows in **lipfulness.**

The Data

Extremes in this category are **full lips** and **thin** lips. Most faces show **moderate** lipfulness. Examples are James Madison, Dwight Eisenhower and Lady Bird Johnson, respectively.

First Lady "Lady Bird" Johnson   President Woodrow Wilson

The Meaning

Despite the current craze for artificially inflated lips, in face reading they are *no guarantee whatsoever* of sexiness. Instead, **full lips** reveal a willingness to talk about personal matters. The potential challenge is embarrassing others, as in the famous *Playboy* interview when President Carter revealed that he had lusted for women in his heart, but God had forgiven him.

Thin lips go with greater reserve. Imagine "Read my lips" Bush making a comparable statement!

Moderate lipfulness symbolizes comfort with a moderate amount of self-disclosure. In some situations, you'll feel comfortable discussing deeply personal matters, but if other people don't wish to, you won't mind. Altogether, you feel complete without having to spill your guts.

"Isn't that the best way to be?"

Something can be said for every communication style. Moderate lipfulness makes your life easier but you still face the nasty little problem that occurs whenever an aspect of life comes too easy. You've even implied it with your question. Beware a lack of tolerance for the rest of humanity!

Change

Within the range possible for a particular person's mouth, there's room for more or less lip. The relative fullness of your lips reflects your unconscious choice about self-disclosure.

Don't lips grow thinner with age?

Question that stereotype. Indira Gandhi's upper lip grew fuller, not thinner, remember?

Long-term lipfulness depends on whether you have the habit of "stifling yourself." Does your spouse never want to hear how you feel? Then the long-term consequence for you will be smaller lipfulness.

Over time many people become more expressive, not less, which results in lips actually growing fuller. For instance, one of my clients told me that she'd been in psychotherapy for three years when she was told, "You're ready to graduate from therapy. Now you have lips."

In my opinion, the only interesting part of the ageist stereotype is to ask, "Which seniors develop the thinner lips?"

Go ahead, ask the people you know who have compressed their mouths physically.

- Over the years were they discouraged from talking about their personal feelings?
- Was there selfless devotion to a spiritual ideal, as with Mother Teresa's life of renunciation and ultra-thin lips?

You'll find that, when lips grow thinner, the human story attached to them is about self-effacement, not some inevitable aging process.

Self-censorship

What's the difference between not speaking up and self-censorship? The latter involves considerably more psychological pain. So maybe it's not surprising that these two patterns correspond to different types of face data. For personal reticence, notice if lips grow thinner. But for self-censorship, check out the presence or absence of **mouth puckers.**

The Data

Mouth puckers look like miniature dimples on either side of the lips. To see if you have them, don't smile in front of the mirror. Go back to the bland, unadorned way of holding your mouth that you used when examining lip length. Most people *don't* have them. See if you do.

Are these puckers supposed to look like what happens to the corners of my mouth when I play the oboe?

Exactly. Except after you put the instrument down, do you still keep the puckers? If so, they count as face data. Martin Van Buren provides an example. (In all the portraits I've seen, he posed without an oboe.)

The Meaning

People with **mouth puckers** excel at self-censorship. In particular, they have learned to avoid asking for what they need most. Show me a baby with mouth puckers. Just try!

Change

Personal history is revealed in those puckers. Before they appear on your face, there has been a significant other, such as a parent, sibling, spouse or teacher, who consistently belittled your feelings. Mouth puckers are learned.

Is there any natural way to remove them?

Yes. Practice asking appropriate people for what you need. Behavior is part of this practice, the rest involves healing your stored-up emotional pain. Over time, you'll release the mouth puckers. By then you will have worked through what caused you to clam up in the first place.

Besides the not inconsiderable benefit of emotional healing, you'll receive another bonus after your mouth loses its puckers. You'll remember what you learned earlier about the value of verbal discretion, a kind of knowledge that can be highly useful.

Taking sides

Mouths migrate—not all the way to foreign lands, thank goodness, but as an asymmetrical bent toward one side of the face. **Horizontal mouth changes** relate to taking sides, literally as well as figuratively. Which side matters most to the speaker, public or private?

The Data

Sometimes mouth asymmetry shows only in **smile depth.** With George H. Bush, gums show on the left, revealing that he's a giver in his personal life, not in public.

Aside from smile depth, there's the fascinating matter of **crooked smiles,** where a smile tilts higher on one side than the other. A smile angled toward the **right** has often been displayed by Ronald Reagan. George W. Bush furnishes an example of a smile angled toward the **left.** Either way, a smile with mouth angling is sometimes called a **smirk**.

The Meaning

A **right-angled smile** suggests that you speak to impress others and seldom believe what you're saying. Ironically, this often impresses people favorably. Still, the potential challenge is lying.

A **left-angled smile** implies a secret personal agenda that's more important than the public one. This type of asymmetry can also intrigue people; once again the potential challenge is lying.

If crooked smiles are bad things, what makes them so darned appealing?

Mystery is the main reason, I think. Asymmetry in either direction leaves a subconscious impression that the smiler may be holding back a delicious secret. Also, if the person with the crooked smile is young or attractive, it can seem extra cute.

Baby *anythings* are cute. When a human face shows the sparkle of youth, it's rare for it not to look adorable. Attractiveness really starts to become interesting when it appears on an un-retouched face over thirty. Should a smile become

Experiment with a Crooked Smile

Smile asymmetries happen to be one of the few bits of face data where the negative aspect outweighs the positive. Spiritually it's vitally important to speak on the level. Otherwise you risk losing your integrity. .

Here's an easy way to prove this to yourself. Choose a good long sentence to repeat three times, such as Lincoln's gem, "You can fool some of the people some of the time and all of the people most of the time but you can't fool all of the people all of the time."

Repeat this sentence three times, holding your mouth differently each time. Notice how you feel as you speak, using:

- Your normal mouth position.
- The left side of your mouth raised as high as you can.
- The right side of your mouth raised as high as you can.

increasingly crooked, however, it's less likely to be considered adorable, at least to a face reader.

Change

As personal integrity grows, smiles can straighten out. More often, unfortunately, an adult's crooked smile deepens over the years. This happened with Reagan. Compare Photo A with Photo B in his Transformation Reading.

What can I do on the inside to change my crooked smile on the outside?

First, become aware of when you're doing a crooked smile—not just how it feels physically but what, in that moment, you feel. This will take both courage

President Martin Van Buren

President Warren Harding

and honesty. (Probably you're either manipulating people or feeling contempt for them.)

Changing the pattern will eventually change the facial habit. Gradually, you'll do the smile less and less, provided that you're willing to do the psychological work. Professional help might even be necessary, if you're serious about healing the underlying causes of a crooked smile. And I don't mean the kind of professional help offered by a cosmetic surgeon!

When a mouth freezes over

"Don't hold your face like that, it might freeze," mothers warn their children. In most cases, that's as likely as having the hot place freeze over. But one exception is mouths. Habitually pulling a mouth toward one side more than the other can create results that last. Spiritual talent scouts, don't miss out on reading **mouth pulls.**

Isn't that the same as what we just saw before, crookedness?

No, since raising one side of the mouth higher is an up-and-down thing. Mouth pulls go sideways. They edge toward either the **right** or the **left.**

The Data

All politicians with a mouth pull tend to have it in the same direction: mouth pull toward the right. Examples are Martin Van Buren and Warren Harding.

The Meaning

Mouth pulls mean that much of your speech is intended for public consumption. Concerning integrity, this is not a good sign. It's comparable to having people preface what they're about to say with the disclaimer, "To be honest with you." Why use the preface at all unless you're habitually dishonest?

Similarly, why would an honest person live with a habitual emphasis on saying things only in public?

Martin Van Buren compounded his mouth pull toward the right with a crooked smile angled toward the right. Frankly, I doubt that his inner convictions often matched his official pronouncements.

Warren Harding developed a particularly interesting version of mouth asymmetry. Besides mouth pull toward the right, he developed a **lipfulness asymmetry:** thinner lips on the right side only.

Although every degree of lipfulness has beauty and value, a marked difference between one side of the face and the other is not a good sign. **Markedly thinner lips** on one side shows a habitual lack of honesty. This form of dishonesty relates to restricting the flow of information in the area of life where the lips are thinner. Harding's asymmetry indicates a lack of full disclosure in public.

Even more ominously, Harding developed a killer **sneer**... on the right side of his face only. To sneer, a mouth must first angle upwards, then tilt down at the edge. This corresponds to offering a smile, then retracting it contemptuously. Sneers reveal cruelty.

Harding's presidential portrait clearly catches him sneering at the public. In his personal life he was, undoubtedly, far more congenial.

How about the line that comes off the right side of Harding's mouth? What does that mean?

Line without lip is a secrecy trait. The significance of having it just on the right is lack of full disclosure when in public. More commonly, it shows on both sides, as with Eisenhower and Hoover.

Usually, if you're a spiritual talent scout, this trait will stir your compassion. It's one of the few face traits without a positive side, just a life lesson. Moreover, the meaning can include an emotional component of hopelessness or resentment, as if the mouth sighs, "Why tell you what I'm feeling? What's the use?"

You really think President Warren Harding felt hopeless and helpless when he dealt with the public?

Since his mouth also sneered, definitely not! "What's the use?" can be said in an arrogant tone, too.

Change

Can't someone's mouth pull to the side due to medical reasons, like a stroke?

Although the meaning remains the same, use one more factor to temper your interpretation. Pay attention to **lack of facial mobility.** When a significant portion of the face is held rigidly, as a result of illness, it may open a spiritual talent scout's heart, not only because the person has lost the ability to move freely but because of the underlying emotional pain that caused the illness in the first place.

Metaphysically, illness often relates to inner pain or other prolonged imbalance in the mind-body system. According to medical intuitive Mona Lisa Schultz, M.D., denial is often present as well. Until the patient heals the psychological trauma held in the body, the physical illness will remain or worsen. In *Awakening Intuition*, she cites scientific evidence that shows "the body is the repository of actual physicalized memories of events and emotions that have befallen us and that continue to affect us in the present."

President Franklin Roosevelt in 1932   President Franklin Roosevelt in 1900

First Lady Mamie Eisenhower

One advantage of reading faces is that it can make you more sensitive to nuances of human experience. This, in turn, may help you to pay perceptive attention to your own inner life, so that even a slight degree of inner imbalance sets off warning bells.

By healing yourself of imbalance in its early stages, you may be able to prevent physical problems from surfacing. Medical intuitives consistently uphold the concept of mind-body connection. And holistic physicians like Andrew Weil and Deepak Chopra emphasize the role of inner peace in preventing illness.

Sex appeal

Sex isn't simple, either in life or face reading. Masculine and feminine energy show in many ways, and each face contains a mixture of both. *The Power of Face Reading* devotes an entire chapter to ways that you can read faces for sexiness. Here, we'll consider the part of the face that reflects raw sex appeal.

The Data

Philtrum definition means how clearly one can see the twin ridges that join the nose and mouth. A **chiseled** philtrum appears here on a youthful photo of Franklin Delano Roosevelt. You can see a strong groove, clearly defined. By contrast, an **undefined** philtrum shows in the smooth overlip of First Lady Mamie Eisenhower. **Moderate** philtrum definition shows some contour—not enough to stand out clearly, yet enough to be easily visible. That's what FDR developed in his later years.

When you study your own overlip in the mirror, avoid smiling, which can temporarily flatten out your philtrum definition. As you'll remember from previous discussion, smiles can rearrange more on your face than the mouth. Whatever the changes, all of them symbolize projecting your personality to others... and that persona may be significantly different from who you are in private.

In movies, a *very* chiseled philtrum is practically a job requirement for leading men and ladies.

The Meaning

Regardless of your career, a **chiseled philtrum** brings you the advantage of big sex appeal. When people are with you, your presence turns up their amount of life force energy. There's juice, flirtatiousness or a sense of general attractiveness. One of my students, referring to her own face, has called this trait "upper cleavage."

Philtrum definition helps politicians win elections, attracts groupies to athletes, keeps businesspeople in command. So there's more to having sexual charisma than physical seduction alone. If you're well endowed with it, your challenge is handling the attention. Maybe sometimes you'd prefer that dates would get to know you before they profess their undying lust. Good luck!

An **undefined** philtrum helps you to be taken seriously, rather than sexually. Acquaintances don't respond to you first and foremost as a love object. That's both the advantage and the challenge. For perspective, remember that sex appeal only applies to the drool factor in relationships. With an undefined philtrum, you could still have a great sex life. It's just not likely to be the first thing that strangers associate with you.

Moderate philtrum definition corresponds to having considerable choice about the amount of sex appeal you project. You can dress down or up to amplify your come-hither wattage. And you'll be more versatile than people with either less or more overlip definition. Your only challenge is the usual lack of tolerance. In this case, that means respecting both the apparently mousy personalities and the flaunters.

Change

Usually, but not always, philtrum definition is a soul signature trait. Yet you can see it change in this chapter's paired photos of FDR. His wife, Eleanor, evolved exactly the same change over the years. Philtrum definition decreases because of inner choices and values. It's unlikely to increase, however, short of cosmetic surgery.

Backing up the soul signature dynamics, there's a physical reason. This part of the face is one of the last things to form while you're in the womb. At the same time it develops, you grow a string-like structure inside your mouth, called the **frenum**, located on the gums directly above your front teeth.

British Prime Minister Margaret Thatcher

First Lady Rosalyn Carter

Cesar Chavez

If you didn't grow a frenum, you won't have much philtrum definition. But not to worry. Aside from the many ways sexiness evolves in a face other than sex appeal, there will always be the pursuit of power—which has been called the ultimate aphrodisiac.

Power preferences

Cheek proportions reveal a person's characteristic power dynamics. The ways they change over time are particularly fascinating.

The Data

For insights into power style, examine which part of the face is widest. Use cheek width as a reference point. When the area *under* the cheeks is widest, as in the case of labor organizer Cesar Chavez, that's the **pacifist power style**.

Which American president has shown this style on both sides of his face? There's only one: Chester Arthur.

When the cheeks *themselves* are widest, that's the **leaderlike power style.** So far in American history, Lincoln is the only president to have borne an extreme version of this trait.

When the face is *even*, with cheeks no wider than the rest, that's the **polite power style**. Starting with Founding Father George Washington, many presidents have made use of that style, including FDR and William Taft.

A face with forehead *wider* than cheeks demonstrates the **passion power style.** Among the general populace, the style is uncommon. Among U.S. presidents, however, it's surprisingly popular. Ford, George H. Bush and Clinton each have it on the right side of the face (with the polite power style on the left). In this chapter alone, you'll see the passion power style pictured on both sides of Eisenhower, Harding, Madison, Van Buren and Wilson.

The rarest power style takes the form of a diamond-shaped face. Cheeks are widest, while under-cheeks and over-cheeks both taper. This **survivor power style** is seen on long-time British Prime Minister Margaret Thatcher. America hasn't yet elected a president with this style but you can see it on First Lady Rosalyn Carter.

The Meaning

Does power style correlate with politics? I'll leave that question to the political scientists. To me, what's far more interesting is how the style plays itself out in relationships. Everybody has a favored way of relating to others. Here's what I mean:

Pacifist power style involves caring deeply that everyone around you gets along. You'll do whatever it takes to create harmony.

Typically, having this style means that you gain respect from others gradually, as they discover your bedrock stability. How will they show this wonderful respect? They'll burden you with all their troubles, then saunter away, feeling better.

Handling this dynamic is one challenge with a pacifist power style. Your other challenge is assertiveness, expressing personal discontent before it develops such a big charge that your temper flares out of control. Sustained rage, assertively managed, can lead to protracted, effective leadership. Remember the career of Cesar Chavez? He led the first successful farm workers' union in U.S. history. Robert Kennedy called him "One of the heroic figures of our time."

Leadership ability comes in many guises, at least five of them, as we're seeing. But one variety, the **leaderlike power style,** comes closest to what Americans typically expect in a leader: Someone who takes responsibility, likes making decisions for the group and feels comfortable in the spotlight. Will other people react with jealousy? Sometimes, but owners of leaderlike cheeks grin and bear it.

If Americans admire this leaderlike style, how come it's so rare in our presidents?

Dislike of government runs deep in the American character. After the Revolutionary War, we adopted a system of checks and balances to control it. And in terms of voting patterns, we've resisted giving power to the same party in both the White House and Congress. Given this disinclination to concentrate power in government, it makes perfect sense that we'd feel qualms about electing a leaderlike president.

Who else had it besides Lincoln?

- Kennedy did, but only when he actively mobilized leadership, making an effort to reach out to others (i.e., corresponding to when he smiled).

- Our second president, John Adams, barely fit into the category, and on the right side only. In his personal life, Adams showed an extreme version of the pacifist power style.
- James Garfield's un-emphatic version of the leaderlike style showed on both sides of his face, but he backed off by wearing so much facial hair that his mouth was nearly obliterated.
- Ronald Reagan's version of the leaderlike power style worked well for him. The wide cheeks were hidden beneath so much well-toned padding that you'd have to look carefully to discern his unusual face width proportions. Appropriately, he led the nation with a strong, but casual, leadership style.

For contrast, consider the **polite power style**. Cheekbones that don't stick out correspond to an unobtrusive style of leadership. Instead of feeding your ego, you prefer to get results. No other leadership style shows more skill at working the system (any system). Your challenge is not getting as much credit as people with those bigger egos.

At the opposite extreme come the intense people with the **passion power style**. You're intense about life, intense all the time. And it doesn't turn off. In particular, you're intense about ideas. A goal will seem more real to you than any obstacle. So you sweep past obstacles that would deter other people.

Challenges include impatience with others and a tendency to burn out co-workers. Be kind! Remember that most people don't share your passion power style. It's only found on about 1 in 200 faces—except for American presidents.

Even less common, in everyday life, is the diamond-shaped configuration of **survivor cheeks**. You're a survivor, someone who endures like a great defensive football player. Accepting help is your life lesson.

Being a survivor, you may have developed the habit of coping without outside help. But you don't want too much of this good thing. It's important to accept gifts graciously. Give others the chance to give to you.

Change

Faces move in and out of the leaderlike, polite and pacifist traits. Occasionally people even develop the passion face. Only the survivor style seems to be a soul signature trait, i.e., unlikely to change. It develops, I believe, when a soul sets up a life contract that will involve exceptional physical, social or emotional challenges. This rare cheek structure, with the unique form of courage that accompanies it, gives its owner a fighting chance to get through that tough life contract.

More power surges

Cheek emphasis tells you even more about power specialties

The Data

Emphasis on cheeks means where they stick out most. To see this, look for padding as well as the bones beneath.

Let's use first ladies as examples. In general, they have far more prominent cheeks than most mortals, a fact that's surprising only if you forget that cheek prominence is about wielding power.

High-set cheeks are exemplified by Barbara Bush. **Low-slung** cheeks are common denominators for Senator Clinton and Nancy Reagan. **Close-set** cheeks show on Betty Ford, while Jackie Kennedy and Helen Keller exemplify **far-set** cheeks.

The Meaning

Cheek emphasis symbolizes a special ability to use power in life.

When cheeks stick out most near your eyes, you'll stick up for your ethics whenever you see people try to do something wrong. You'll make a fuss, even if you're otherwise terrified of fighting with people. Acting as a conscience for others can be a thankless job. Many people have told me stories related to their **high-set** cheeks, concluding with, "And that's how I got fired"!

Low-slung cheeks go with exceptional tolerance. If you have this rare face data, you use your strength to support others with unconditional love. Even when they make mistakes, you'll be there for them.

The potential challenge is that if your soul chose those cheeks, at some time you're sure to *need* them. Senator Clinton, for instance, has signed up for a life

First Lady Hillary Clinton

First Lady Nancy Reagan

First Lady Betty Ford

Helen Keller

(and husband) where tolerance might come in handy. Nancy Reagan's need for great tolerance came after her husband developed Alzheimer's.

Close-set cheeks symbolize the ability to work well under pressure. Your only problem is the inner toll. When Betty Ford moved into the White House on very short notice, she coped beautifully but secretly dealt with the stress through substance abuse; later, running the clinic she founded, Ford has continued to deal with other people's emergencies.

Far-set cheeks show a gift for long-term courage, as when Helen Keller raised society's consciousness about disabled persons. Sometimes long-term courage is needed more in private life, as with Jackie Kennedy's private struggles, first with an alcoholic father, later with a philandering husband.

Change

Can cheek emphasis change? Of course. We've already seen it with Eleanor Roosevelt. There is no set pattern; your cheeks evolve to match your inner growth.

What happens when your cheeks really head south? Ugh, jowls!

Jowls are one of the less popular traits of maturity. Their appearance in the mirror can come as a shock. Replacing regular cheeks, mounds of flesh droop off the sides of your face, reminiscent of a slow-motion avalanche. And an avalanche at any speed can be scary. If this hadn't happened to Martin Van Buren and Millard Fillmore, they might have been chosen for Mt. Rushmore over more firm-cheeked presidents.

Doesn't it seem unfair to you that some people get jowls while others don't?

Jowls only develop on the faces of people who previously enjoyed the benefits of well-padded cheeks. If you have jowls now, compare your face in the mirror to earlier photos. Your formerly plump cheeks symbolized your receiving exceptionally generous support from others at work, within the family structure, maybe even politically. Jowls develop to reflect change in your balance of power. Formerly you could rely on the support of others; but now it seems those ingrates have developed wills of their own, and with that, reluctance to lend you support.

How to cope? Maybe you'll push harder to mobilize the troops. Maybe you'll simply decide to do more for yourself. Folks who've lacked cheek padding all along have managed, after all, taking action without expecting to be supported by others. When help comes, it's considered a bonus. This strategy would work well for anyone with jowls.

How about these jowl-like things in the middle, those disgusting double chins?

Double chins relate to groundedness. Do you appreciate creature comforts? Do you value being down to earth? Extra chins are where it will show.

"Grandmother" is all mine means to me. Can you give me one reason not to have it fixed by a cosmetic surgeon?

You can accept the natural framing that has evolved for you, as for many others. Over time, faces soften in many ways. I think it helps to see each of these changes as God's makeup, there for a reason.

The bottom line

Chin bottoms can alter in ways that don't involve double chins. In Chapter Six, we discussed chin bottom changes via beards. Other chinformation can change, too, it just takes longer.

The Data

Chins can become **curved, straight** or **angular**. Remember how Lady Diana's chin went from curved to angular? Elizabeth Taylor's chin did just the opposite.

The Meaning

Chin bottoms reveal a person's basis for making major decisions. When chins become **curved**, they imply greater concern about people's feelings. (Most often, chins change to become more curved.)

Straight chin bottoms relate to making decisions based on "the principle of the thing."

Angled chins reveal the need to stay in control. Decisions are made to strengthen personal power more than to protect the needs of others.

Change

Chins don't change often, do they?

Chin changes are rare, indeed. As a spiritual talent scout, you'll want to notice them. I suspect there's greater inner agony involved in changing chin shape than for any other non-surgical face change—except for the financial pain involved in growing triangular nostrils.

These chin changes seem so abstract. Can you give an example?

Elizabeth Taylor's chin is an interesting example of angle mellowing into curve. Since she's been photographed nearly as much as Diana, the public has had ample opportunity to watch her face evolve. The angular chin bottom she wore for most of her life related to self-will.

Before she married husband #7, I can imagine Liz telling her friends, "Sure, I met him at the Betty Ford Clinic. Sure, he's 20 years my junior. And instead of being in show business like me, he's a construction equipment operator. Who cares? I'll show you I can make this work!"

But Taylor's marriage to Larry Fortensky failed. After their divorce, she became increasingly involved in the fight against AIDS. And, lo and behold, her chin bottom mellowed into a curve.

Life priorities

Did you ever notice that the folks who develop extra chins don't usually get the receding hairlines, and vice versa? These changes show in **Life Priority Areas.** Any of them can be worn with pride.

To see why, imagine that your life is a house, and your face proportions symbolize the rooms where you spend the most time.

The Data

To read your Life Priority Areas, spread your thumb and forefinger apart to form a measuring tool. Then measure each of the three areas. How do their sizes compare? Like rooms in a model home, your facial real estate has ideal proportions—a perfect expression of your personality.

Priority Area I goes from hairline to eyebrow. **Receding hairlines,** like Eisenhower's, show that quality time has been spent in the library. (You may choose to add a balding bonus to the size of Priority Area I.)

Priority Area II goes from eyebrow to the lowest part of the nose. *Lengthening* in the nose, as occurred with Eleanor Roosevelt, suggests more time spent in the home office. Increased *nose tip* size, related to concern over financial security, is another change that can impact the size of Priority Area II. (But only in the land of stereotypes does nose size always increase. Compare the author photos, for instance, and you'll see mine *decreased*, and with it the relative size of Area II.)

Priority Area III goes from the lowest part of the nose to the chin. **Double chins,** like those on James Madison, reveal that you've spent loads of time in the kitchen and bedroom. (When doing Transformation Readings, it's fair to add additional chins to the size of Priority Area III.) Any one of these three areas can be biggest. Or two can share equal length. A rare possibility is **Equal Priority Areas,** where all three areas display equal length.

The Meaning

Priority Area I **biggest,** as with Herbert Hoover, means a fascination with ideas.

Having this area **smallest,** as with George W. Bush, indicates the possible challenge of lacking intellectual curiosity.

Priority Area II **biggest** suggests the desire to make a mark on the world—and be acknowledged for it. My favorite example is Helen Keller. Can you think of anyone who has accomplished more for disabled persons?

Having this ambition area **smallest**, as with Woodrow Wilson, corresponds to reluctance about asking for recognition.

Priority Area III **biggest**, exemplified by Colin Powell, reveals the salty sense of humor and built-in B.S. detector of a truly pragmatic person, resulting in enormous credibility.

- Having this area **smallest**, as with Franklin Pierce, signals potential challenge with getting things done in real life (rather than theory).

Finally, having **equal** Priority Areas, as with Lady Bird Johnson, signifies a natural desire to balance all three areas of life, scheduling plenty of time for ideas, work and play. If that's what you see in the mirror, consider yourself fortunate. You can easily make friends with people who have any of the three facial priorities. Your only potential challenge is that funny lack of tolerance for the rest of humanity—especially when people lose balance in ways that you wouldn't have countenanced, either figuratively or literally.

Change

How could someone's Priority Areas change? Isn't that a set trait, like bone structure?

Look back at our Transformation Readings in Chapter Five. Eleanor Roosevelt shifted from Area III to Area II; Thurgood Marshall went from Area I to equal Priority Areas.

If someone goes to a cosmetic surgeon to clean up the chin line, wouldn't that alter Priority Areas?

Only slightly, because most Priority Areas shifts happen in ways that surgery can't touch. I do invite you to question the language you just used, however. Why should any thinking person believe that a vanity-based surgical procedure would simply "clean up" the face. Soap cleans, not a scalpel.

Vanity surgeons spend obscene amounts of advertising money to persuade the American public that there's something wholesome about operations that are medically unnecessary and sometimes cause disfiguration or death.

"Redraping the skin of your neck" may sound like a fashion statement. But it isn't. No matter how the language is prettied up, vanity surgery comes with a spiritual price: numbed awareness of the soul in everyday life.

Besides, who says that a soft chin line needs to be "cleaned up"? There's nothing dirty or shameful about it. The next chapter questions stereotypes that surgeons promulgate in order to make a vain public more vain than ever.

9. What Wrinkles Really Mean

Face reader or not, you're entitled to obsess over wrinkles. If you're over 45, wrinkles may hold an especially lurid fascination for you. Many of my students come right out and say it:

Honey, I look for the wrinkles.

Actors and models rarely have them these days. Many are too young, most of the others have been "fixed." Between magazines, newspapers, TV, movies and the Internet, you're shown a well-laundered lineup of so many permanent press faces, you might mistake them for normal people. But don't.

The real world can show you plenty of authentic faces over 45. By the year 2000, we represented more than a third of the U.S. population, and our average age continues to climb. Already more than 96 million Americans are middle aged or older. That's a lot of faces for God to paint wrinkles on.

In this chapter, we'll explore just about every kind you've seen, coming or going. Because whether wrinkles are coming or going, they have meaning. The first time I saw wrinkles *disappear* on their own, I was flabbergasted. But doing Transformation Readings, I've seen it happen and you will, too.

I know, we've been taught that wrinkles are permanent, as if time were a one-way street automatically leading every face to the same destination, Wrinkle Land. But my ability to see wrinkles clearly improved once I was willing to question this deterministic belief.

If wrinkles also God's makeup, they have meaning. They're relevant to a soul's most significant learning. And since wrinkles symbolize learning life lessons, it makes sense that, depending on the specific lesson involved, inner evolution could cause those facial markings to be modified.

Sure enough, some forms of anger, fear and pain have facial counterparts that smooth out after the related life lesson has been learned and released.

What, you think my sun damage will fade away because of some happy self-talk?

Sun damage is real, part of biology's true (though incomplete and relatively uninteresting) perspective on faces. A smart face reader still wears sunscreen.

Can't wrinkles be genetic? I have exactly the same lines as my father.

When lines run in families, that's because attitudes do too. The good news is that attitudes can be changed, thus altering your patterns of wrinkles. When wrinkles appear before you are 18 years old, they relate to your destiny, or life contract (discussed in the next chapter). Regardless of how early a wrinkle appears, or how many family members share a similar wrinkle, what matters most is its specific meaning on *your* face.

Like the frown lines that show a disagreeable, angry person?

Wrinkles aren't only about emotions, including those you just mentioned. I've heard people refer to all types of forehead wrinkles as "frown lines." Yet, in my experience, only two types relate directly to anger. Even they are not what you might assume. This chapter gives you a different way to see *all* facial wrinkles, via the perspective of Face Reading Secrets. These interpretations have been tested on hundreds of clients and have a 99 percent accuracy rate.

Frowning in concentration

Why do folks frown, anyway? Literally, "frowning" just means wrinkling the forehead. To many, the word implies anger. Is that true? Let's explore more deeply.

The Data

Horizontal forehead furrows show concentration and come in three varieties. **Right-side furrows** are higher or more numerous on the right side of the forehead, such as the ones you'll find on Franklin Roosevelt. Coming from the opposite direction, **left-side furrows** can be seen on Gerald Ford. Horizontal

Are Wrinkles About Emotions?

Here's good reason to peek into the esoteric academic discipline known as **the history of ideas.** In post-modern America, we take it for granted that wrinkles are about emotions. That's because we assume that *all* of inner life is about emotions. But, according to intellectual history's changing definitions, this assumption turns out to be just a fad. And relatively recent.

It started with the Romantic movement in the 19th century and intensified enormously with the onset of movies in the century that followed. Looking back further, America's Founding Fathers cared little about emotions. What mattered to them was **character**, a person's ethical strength.

They would have been appalled that today we're so focused on **personality**, the set of distinguishing personal characteristics that make a person seem socially appealing. In pop culture, the search for inner life goes no deeper than personality and the emotions it arouses. (Our best known figures are, in fact, known as "personalities.")

But, perhaps, this superficial perspective is changing. Since the events of September 11, I've noticed early signs of a new cultural era in America. Thoughtful people are starting to examine life in terms of ethics, honor and spirituality. In my view, this concept is a welcome change from glorifying either personality or emotions. Inner life transcends both popularity points and transitory moods.

How does this relate to seeing faces? Don't be satisfied with expression reading and what it tells you about moods. Face reading can show you more about character and the soul's journey. Whether you're reading wrinkles or other face data, don't settle for clichés about emotions.

lines that extend the full length of the forehead are **whole brain lines**, like the one on John F. Kennedy.

The Meaning

When push comes to shove, which side of your brain do you lean on? **Right forehead furrows** suggest that you apply your experience analytically, based on what you've learned about objective reality. **Left forehead furrows** disclose the struggle to find meaning related to your inner life.

Whole brain lines reveal that your whole brain is used, intensely and often. The more such lines you'll find, the more extraordinary the intellectual power. Einstein managed to summon up three, plus two partial horizontals above them, working their way inward from the edges of his forehead.

Forehead wrinkles don't usually show unless you scrunch up your face on purpose. Why do people like me form really heavy, deep forehead wrinkles that show all the time?

It's a matter of concentration. Deep down, do you trust your brains to deliver the goods? People who rely on intuition don't wrinkle their foreheads as much, whereas forehead furrowers work hard to get a thinking job done right. Either style is fine. They're just different.

Spiritual magnificence

Worry lines? That's the most common interpretation for **vertical forehead wrinkles.** But they tell a spiritual talent scout about inner *conflict*, more than worry. With interpretations related to the particular wrinkle's position, each one has beauty. In fact, one type of vertical wrinkle is my favorite of all possible face data.

The Data

Most vertical wrinkles on foreheads are **anger flags**. These extend upwards from the start of an eyebrow. George H. Bush grew a huge one on the right, while Rutherford Hayes' big one was on the left. By contrast, the **mark of devotion** is a

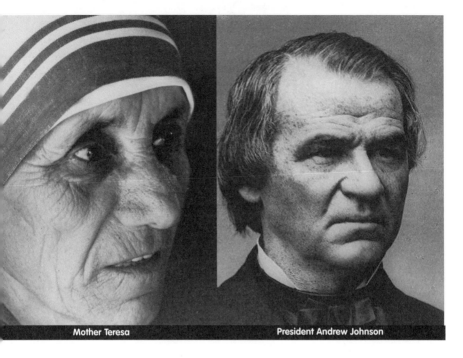

Mother Teresa   President Andrew Johnson

forehead vertical that grows in, or toward, the center of the face. Although the mark can stay at eyebrow level, a *very* version can reach halfway up the forehead. Examples follow. For fun, see if you can remember having seen a president with this fascinating trait.

The Meaning

An **anger flag on the right** reveals stored-up anger related to work. Should you find this wrinkle on your own face, may I offer my compliments as well as my condolences! Yes, you've had cause for anger. But consider the related gift: displaying good manners in public. The first President Bush was, in fact, famous for this.

An **anger flag on the left** reveals stored-up rage related to one's personal life. Some of my clients have found that, following a divorce or psychotherapy (or both), left brow flags disappeared on their own.

Even more fascinating is the **mark of devotion**. This symbolizes an especially intense spiritual vocation, where service to others seems instinctive, inner inner standards exert perpetual pressure and sacrifice may be required. My favorite

Israeli Prime Minister Golda Meir · First Lady Laura Bush

example is a Catholic nun who was one of my students; once she told me that she had a terrible problem with selfishness. I can assure you, the day most people are as selfish as she, earth will have turned into heaven.

In this book, I've pictured a more famous nun, Mother Teresa. Check out her deep mark of devotion. Not all wearers of the mark lead scrupulously virtuous lives. But inwardly they struggle to live in accordance with the highest ideals.

Statistically, I'd estimate that this mark appears on 1 in 200 adults over 40. Unless they're U.S. presidents. Then the odds climb to 1 in 2. Maybe higher. Portraits that predate photos may not show wrinkles adequately.

How many presidents have borne the mark of devotion? It shows on the faces of Carter, Cleveland, Coolidge, Ford, Grant, Harrison (William Henry), Jackson, Jefferson, Johnson (Lyndon), Kennedy, Lincoln, Monroe, Nixon, Reagan, Roosevelt (Franklin), Taft, Truman, Washington, and Wilson.

A bad guy like Nixon had a spiritual vocation? Are you kidding?

Please, resist the temptation to peg people as either good or bad (at least until after you've read Chapter Eleven). Here I'll merely point out the challenge that goes with the mark of devotion. Although everyone faces temptation to do wrong, owners of the mark are less likely to get away with it. As you may remember, Nixon didn't.

Couldn't vertical forehead lines develop that aren't either anger flags or the mark of devotion?

Sure. A testament to intellectual conflict, they're relatively common in presidents. But they're rare in people who don't need to justify their every action to congress, media and popularity polls. If more Americans stood behind our elected executives, rather than stooping down to heckle them, maybe presidents wouldn't develop such rumpled foreheads.

One fascinating variety shows on George H. Bush. His aforementioned deep anger flag on the left turns into a sweeping arch on the opposite side of his face. The meaning? Personal anger is sublimated into plans for taking public action.

Do anger flags mean explosive anger?

Just the opposite. The anger has been stored up rather than expressed. Benjamin Harrison's wrinkles suggest that he was America's angriest president ever. Given his double set of anger flags, he must have done a remarkable job of controlling his rage. (For more insights into how temper shows in a face, see the "Top Ten Temper Traits" in *The Power of Face Reading*, pages 264-66.)

Spiritual signboards

As a people watcher, do you make it a point to notice jewelry that signifies religious orientation? Even these adored symbols are downright boring compared to the jewelry that God places directly on a person's forehead. **Forehead wrinkles** include third eye covers, third eye indents, and eyebrow bulges.

The Data

Third eye covers are rare horizontal lines that bunch up at the third eye, as seen on George H. Bush.

What is the third eye anyway? I've heard about it but have never known what it meant.

Third eye is a term from aura reading that refers to the energy center above and between the eyebrows. Bush Sr. developed horizontal wrinkles in the physical area corresponding to this energy center. Unlike horizontal forehead furrows, his lines form a circular pattern, leaving the rest of his forehead untouched.

Third eye indents look like a depression, right at the third eye area, clearly visible on Andrew Johnson.

Eyebrow bulges are a raised, fleshy area above the eyebrows. A magnificent set has been evolved by Russell Jim, a leader of the Yakama Indian Nation and long-term environmental activist (see his photo in the Online Supplement).

The Meaning

Third eye covers suggest that a person struggles to solve problems intellectually, refusing to accept intuitive assistance.

Sometimes fierce concentration happens to be a person's religious path. Other times, the wrinkles are symptoms of a "me do it" pushiness that blocks the reception of spiritual grace. In either case, and on the bright side, this trait goes with having a really good mind. Maybe the person with third eye covers overuses his mental muscles, but at least he has them in the first place!

Andrew Johnson grew something more problematic: a **third eye indent**, crossed by a whole brain line. This suggests the intellectual process of an atheist, someone who depends on himself rather than God. The gift is taking responsibility for his own life; the downside is missing the benefits of conscious connection with a Higher Power.

Sometimes a face shows a line or shadow above the eyebrow. Examining it closely, you'll find that it's really an **eyebrow bulge**. The meaning is an intellectual gift: exceptional here-and-now awareness of facts and circumstances. Eyebrow bulges as large as Russell Jim's symbolize extraordinary wisdom. You'll see a

Spiritual Life Shows in the Forehead

Face readers can learn a great deal about how people connect to their spiritual source by reading the forehead. Word lovers may be intrigued that the sides of the forehead are known as the **temple**. Actually, the entire forehead has spiritual significance.

After I read Andrew Johnson's third eye cover, it made me so curious that I supplemented his face reading with an aura reading. It confirmed the president's extreme lack of spiritual experience. Even more curious, I followed up with some biographical research.

Did Johnson dare to come out of the closet as an atheist? Not quite. But he came as close as any American president has dared. As noted at www.adherents.com, a website about religious affiliation:

"Of all U.S. presidents, however, many historians consider Johnson the least religious, and the president who was least affiliated with any religious group or identifiable religious philosophy."

less extreme, but still nifty, example on our photo of Golda Meir. Note that the lines above her eyebrow bulges are forehead furrows, in contrast to the shadows cast by Russell Jim's eyebrow bulges.

God's eye makeup

For most people, the first significant wrinkles develop around the eyes. But don't be too quick to dread or despise these Divine doodles.

The Data

Lid puffs appear directly above the eyes. They're not wrinkles, actually, so much as wads of flesh that balloon downward; a *very* version can inflate to cover part of the eye. Witness the prodigious lid puffs on Golda Meir.

Eye deepeners extend eye contours in a downward direction. They circle beneath the eye and, sometimes, run in parallel tracks. FDR developed a *very* version: four-fold eye deepeners on the right side of his face (related to his political life).

The philosopher's circle is a semi-circular line extending from the outer corner of the eye all the way to the inner corner. Not to be confused with eye deepeners or bags, this is a single chiseled line. FDR and Mother Teresa developed it on the right eye only.

Crow's feet, or **eye extenders**, are horizontal wrinkles that fan out from the corners of an eye. These were the most intense wrinkles grown by Ronald Reagan, prominent on the left side of his face (and, thus, related to his personal life).

The Meaning

Lid puffs mark a person who works hard, whether to rule a nation, earn money or simply attend to the needs of others. If you've developed puffs on one or both eyes, you know how it's done. Rather than focus on your personal comfort, each day you challenge yourself to push a little harder in the direction of your prized ambitions. Eventually "inconsequential" personal things—like your physical health—cry out for their share of attention.

Neglecting yourself physically is a challenge that leads to another challenge: losing your temper over little things. Think "cranky baby," only this version is for grownups.

Have you ever wondered how to spot a curmudgeon? Look for puffs. They're often your first clue.

Eye deepeners belong to people who face life with a highly serious intent. When problems arise, they're likely to blame themselves rather than anyone or anything else.

Do you constantly reach within, refusing to take life events at surface value? Do you believe that every situation holds a potential lesson, even when the problem isn't really about you? This can be a beautiful sign of spiritual seeking.

Still, friends may implore you to lighten up. Sometimes it's wise to cut your losses with a particular situation and move on, no more introspection needed. After all, earth is a place for fun, not just lessons.

The philosopher's circle is one mark of a spiritual teacher, someone who makes an exceptionally dedicated effort to seek and communicate wisdom. Usually found on the right eye only, it relates to direct or indirect efforts to share wisdom through one's work. No Ph.D. in philosophy is required, nor is heroic greatness a requirement, which is how this circle could appear on a workhorse like me, after decades of teaching. (See the more recent of the two author photos at the back of this book.)

Eye extenders show a different reaction to life's problems: the attempt to gain perspective by reaching out to others.

I always thought crow's feet were about having a sense of humor. They're not?

Not necessarily. Humor shows more reliably in other bits of face data—most notably a smile followed by laughter. *Affability* is the real message of eye extenders. The potential challenge involves not thinking deeply on one's own.

How come some people don't develop either kind of eye stuff?

They're the people who flow with life, rather than wrestle with it. Flowing may help you to have an inwardly simpler life. According to social standards, you'll look better, too. Laura Bush is an example of a middle-aged woman who lives almost wrinkle free. Eye extenders are more developed for her than eye deepeners, and they're mostly on the right, suggesting that she worries about problems more in her political role than the rest of her life. She also has *very* up-angled eyes, related to extreme optimism. Laura Bush may, in fact, have the most up-angled eyes of any first lady in American history. That pie-in-the sky optimism helps to explain her lack of wrinkles.

Are people like her, without eye wrinkles, better off?

Regarding wrinkles, everyone can be considered well off in one way or another. Having fewer wrinkles outside, and less struggle on the inside—sure, that's great. But when people wrestle with life, they develop an inner beauty born of their struggle, and the corresponding face changes have value, too.

One of the most extraordinary sets of God's makeup around eyes shows on Mother Teresa, the saintly nun who won a Nobel Peace Prize for her work with the poor of Calcutta. She developed *very* versions of eye extenders and deepeners; they went on to merge with additional lines (including the previously mentioned philosopher's circle). These symbols of Divine recognition were drawn all the way down her cheeks.

Since eye extenders vs. deepeners mean reaching out vs. reaching in, how can a person develop both?

Thoughtful people may seek both outward and inward. Still, you're right if you wonder whether most people have a preference for one direction over the other. It's always interesting to compare which is more pronounced.

- Pensive President Benjamin Harrison had **deepeners without extenders**. To get a sense of his personality, read an excerpt from his Inaugural Address at our Online Supplement. Wiser at philosophy than emotional intelligence, he treated his audience to an intensely solemn exegesis of the responsibility involved in taking the oath of office.
- George W. Bush, by contrast, has **extenders without deepeners**. Since his first day in office, he's been more known for affably nicknaming reporters than any serious introspection.

Whichever type of natural eye makeup you have, consider yourself beautifully gift wrapped by spirit.

These circles and lines are outlook traits, you say. So how come they show up in wrinkles around the eyes, instead of changes to the actual structure of the eye itself?

Great question! Here's a major secret about God's makeup. Wrinkles often modify soul signature traits, the face data tied to a life contract and seldom altered. For instance, far-set eyes are unlikely to develop if you don't have them to begin with.

Nor are most people blessed with the corresponding trait related to a broad perspective on life. However, using your free will, you may seek for years to gain broader perspective. Eventually, this will cause your face to develop eye extenders.

Doesn't puffiness around the eyes really have to do with health, not character?

It's true that lid puffs and eye deepeners can follow a night on the town. Long-term health problems also can show around eyes. When we eat, drink or breathe substances that don't agree with us, we literally face the consequences.

Facial diagnosis is used by the venerable holistic healing traditions of acupuncture, Chinese herbal medicine and Ayurveda. Yet health problems don't necessarily show on the face. Why? Face readers find it's the inner component of life that outpictures on the face, rather than a one-size-fits-all disease process.

For instance, many people with food allergies develop eye deepeners. I have them. But my friend, Donna, doesn't. Her allergies are even worse than mine, and we're both in our mid-fifties, yet she has the wrinkle-free eyes of a teenager. Donna is also a lot better at flowing with life. What I have going for me is a relentless search for inner truth; in fact, it began to out-picture as eye deepeners when I was just 15 years old.

Allergies often show in puffs and "allergic shiners" (a.k.a. bags under the eyes). Yet you'll find plenty of people with these health problems who *don't* develop the corresponding face changes. To a face reader, this validates that faces are about spiritual evolution, even more than health or heredity.

Scary earlobes

One application of diagnostic face reading has caught the fancy of the AMA. Since 1973, Western doctors have noticed a correlation between heart disease and **earlobe creases**.

If the appearance of an earlobe crease encourages you to adopt a heart-healthy lifestyle, that's great. But consider the dire predictions strictly optional. Recent research has shown the predictive value is only 16 percent. So let's find out what the data means in the system of Face Reading Secrets.

The Data

An **earlobe crease** is a diagonal wrinkle across an earlobe. James Buchanan developed one on his right ear (perhaps after the onset of his previously-mentioned lid puff). Lyndon Johnson grew an earlobe crease on his left ear (see his photo in Chapter Three).

The Meaning

In the system of Face Reading Secrets, **earlobes** are about appreciating material life. A **diagonal earlobe crease** follows severe disillusionment. "Heartbreak" is generally used to refer to romantic disappointment, but it can also mean wrenching pain over other life events, which is precisely the meaning of an earlobe crease.

Perhaps you'll be in a position to share this interpretation with someone you know who has developed such a crease. Give that person a chance to grieve. By releasing emotional pain, perhaps she'll eliminate the seed of future illness.

Be sure to tell the owner of the crease (especially if it's *you*) that the related talent is perseverance.

Nose anguish

Anguish isn't only expressed on earlobes. It can show up just about anywhere on the face, even the nose. Let's explore how four different types of nose wrinkle can reveal anguish to the inquiring physiognomist.

The Data

A **tip topper** is a horizontal line directly above the nose tip. In medical quarters this line is known as the "allergic salute." According to doctors, food sensitivities or environmental allergies can cause a patient to develop nasal congestion. Frequently she brushes her hand upward against her nose; repeated often enough, the gesture causes a nose wrinkle. Tip toppers are more common in children than adults. No president, for instance, shows a tip topper.

A **burnout line** is located higher than a tip topper. This horizontal wrinkle develops at the bridge of the nose. Many presidents have had them: Benjamin Harrison, Taft, Taylor and Van Buren. George Washington grew the strong start of one. Poor William Henry Harrison developed two, one ringed beneath the other.

Regarding *vertical* nose wrinkles, one variety divides the nose tip itself. Although such a mark is usually subtle, to the wearer, the meaning is anything but. I've named it **the mark of Divine discontent**. You can find one adorning Rutherford Hayes.

Finally, vertical lines can creep across the nostrils on either side. These **nose grooves** set off flanges at either side of the nose from the nostril. You'll find a very clear example on John Quincy Adams. Maya Angelou developed a groove on the right.

The Meaning

A **tip topper** reveals discomfort with your physical surroundings—which can include your own body. With this face data, challenge comes foremost. But the related talent is potentially a blessing: heightened awareness of your physical surroundings.

Burnout lines signify the habit of working too hard. Although there's merit in a strong work ethic, this wrinkle's main message is "Slow down."

Burnout lines don't seem fair to me. Couldn't someone who works just as hard, other things being equal, not acquire the line?

Spiritually, as you may have noticed, other things are never equal. Each individual must find his own balance. When that life lesson is learned, burnout lines can disappear, as I know from personal experience. By my teens I'd developed a *very* deep burnout line. Inwardly, I was well aware that I pushed myself. About the time that I released anxiety over this issue (my forties), the line disappeared.

Speaking of work-related fears, another fascinating variety shows in the **mark of Divine discontent**. This relates to an unusually quick pace for outgrowing jobs. Although you start a new job as enthusiastically as anyone else, soon the inner conflict begins. You worry, "Is this job really right for me?"

Think about what happens to most people by the time a new job has been mastered. Don't most of us hunker down for a long, comfy stay? If we could, we'd stick around long enough to collect a gold watch at retirement. But if you wear the mark of Divine discontent, not so! Soon as you've satisfied yourself that you're capable of doing the new job, you feel bored and start worrying about what your next job should be.

Inconvenient though this pattern is, and counter-culture too (assuming that the worker is over the age of 30), the trait means something spiritually beautiful. Living on The Learning Planet, you have only one important job: spiritual evolution. Someone who's pushed to change jobs extra often is driven to grow extra fast. That's why my name for this face data is *Divine* discontent.

Guilty as charged. Except my mark didn't appear until my mid-life crisis. How come?

Timing for wrinkles like this involves your agreement with the Universe. Whenever you developed this mark, right before it came onto your face, I suspect that you made a choice (either consciously or unconsciously) to sacrifice surface comfort for greater wisdom.

Nose grooves are another example of an inner agreement with profound life consequences. The meaning is "no financial handouts." Material success for that soul must be earned through hard work, and nothing will come easy. A groove on the right relates to career; a groove on the left relates to receiving wealth from family. Even if the groove extends only part-way across the nose roots, it counts, while a complete line should be read as a *very*. The owner of such a wrinkle will have to work extra hard to receive money, status or recognition.

What you're talking about is horrible. I know from experience. Why would a soul choose to make such an agreement?

Over the decades, I've interviewed dozens of people about their nose grooves. Sometimes proudly, sometimes ruefully, all agreed that they lived their lives according

President Lyndon Johnson

President Zachary Taylor

Apache Leader Geronimo

President Andrew Jackson

to a "no handouts" policy. When I asked, "Was it worth it, to aim for self-made success?" the glow that came across their faces was worth a thousand words of gush.

A spiritual glow? Seems to me that a "no handouts" agreement is an awfully tough way to earn a little extra twinkle on your halo.

Admittedly, yes. Few of us would like to swap places with Abe Lincoln, nose grooves and all. Destiny gave him the chance to become one of the greatest men who ever lived. That doesn't mean it was easy. But living the way he did was his soul's choice.

Can nose grooves disappear like the other nose lines you've described?

With face changes, anything is possible. Usually, though, I'd expect nose grooves not to alter. They represent a spiritual agreement that's not easily broken.

Powerfully painful

Although all wrinkles could be interpreted in terms of human suffering, marks to the cheeks signal an especially poignant variety. They relate to conflict over personal power.

The Data

Suffering lines run from the nose to the mouth. In extreme cases, a second segment of **grimness lines** continues from the mouth to the bottom of the chin.

Among presidents who have served during the past 50 years, most have carved out at least one segment of suffering line. An especially deep **suffering + grimness combo** appears in the casual photo of Lyndon Johnson on the previous page.

Powerline dimples are vertical lines or curves that show when a person smiles. Some faces grow multiple sets. Charmers with these dimples include Gerald Ford.

Cheek dents are one of the most unusual forms of God's makeup. Neither scars nor wrinkles, they're more like hollows set into the cheeks, located high up, towards the eye. You'll see one on Dr. Martin Luther King, toward the left. Maya Angelou also developed one on the left.

Courage scores are lines that crisscross the cheekbones, as if Mother Nature decided to play a variation of tic tac toe. In addition to Mother Teresa, Zachary Taylor provides an example.

The Meaning

Cheek wrinkles are so important that, if I could read only one part of the face for wrinkles, it would be cheeks. Why? The theme of cheek wrinkles is courage.

Suffering lines reveal that a person has taken on the pain of others. Growth of compassion is the plus; suffering the minus. When Lyndon Johnson began the War on Poverty, it wasn't done to win popularity in the polls. As with his efforts on behalf of Civil Rights, LBJ genuinely cared.

Is the cause of these lines always suffering for others? How about plain old self-pity?

Sure, self-pity *may* be involved. But suffering is *always* involved, and the circumstances can have been undertaken nobly, out of a sense of duty. Look at the intensely deep suffering lines on Mother Teresa, as you've seen her earlier in this chapter.

Grimness lines relate to compassion that has touched too close to the bone. By the time someone has taken on that much suffering, life has lost its sparkle. But a spiritual talent scout will notice that this price is paid in exchange for something valuable. Sometimes people can learn through joy, but other times learning must come through pain. Grimness lines attest to the very human struggle to learn life lessons of a very difficult kind.

Powerline dimples relate to lessons in humility. All of us fall down sometimes, both literally and figuratively; in the process of getting back up, some of us learn graciousness. Only then do cheeks develop one or more sets of powerline dimples.

The related talent is charm. Although the dimple wearer has wealth, prestige, good looks or other blessings, her good fortune isn't flaunted. In fact, this face data parallels a genuine "Aw, shucks!" attitude that makes others feel like friends instead of competitors.

Gerald Ford, for instance, showed such humility in office that he was often underrated by the media and the public. Although he'd been a star athlete in his youth, he allowed himself to be portrayed by the media as physically awkward. More likely, he was *better* coordinated than other politicians.

Cheek dents are about being treated as though you needed to show more humility. These marks appear after someone important in your life has considered you uppity and tried to cut you down to size. A dent on your right cheek is a souvenir from trauma at work or school; a dent on the left serves as a memento of psychic wounding from a family member or friend.

Without exception, the dent-wearers I've spoken with could remember a time when they were attacked for seeming too big for their britches. What really matters, though, isn't memory but recovery. The dent appears *after* the person has reclaimed a measure of personal invincibility. After the inner bounce-back, the face develops the physical cheek dent.

Courage scores are another trait worthy of respect. They develop in response to exceptionally severe long-term tests of courage. For example, Georgia O'Keeffe pioneered a kind of art that brought her scathing personal criticism. Decades later, her face bore the evidence. And during the course of an eventful life, Texas Governor Ann Richards developed some of the most extreme courage scores I've ever seen.

You can also find a fascinating set of courage scores on Geronimo, the Apache warrior. His were compounded by small cheek padding and jowls, other power-related face data. Small cheek padding, as we've seen, denotes receiving minimum support from others—or *feeling* as if that's all you receive.

Jowls correspond to a personal power base that sags, too. Such jowls were evident on George H. Bush when he campaigned for (and ultimately lost) his second term. On Zachary Taylor, the little cheek padding he had in the first place turned jowly. In that context, his subsequent cheek scoring suggests that he struggled to keep his political power, and the fight took an enormous inner toll.

Have you ever seen the cheek wrinkles on actor Dennis Quaid? I love when he smiles and the crinkles in his eyes go all the way down to his cheeks. What does that mean?

Eye extenders reaching to the cheeks suggest that he has reached out to others for perspective and support, then used what he learned to find courage. Quaid developed his magnificent set of extenders after overcoming a cocaine addiction.

Though not nearly so photogenic as Quaid, Martin Van Buren evolved a similar configuration.

Squelched, stifled or ignored

Mouth wrinkles develop around lips in ways that relate to conflict about communication.

The Data

Lips always have lines; their semi-circular formation is as inevitable as the rings around trees. **Lip scoring** is different; it involves vertical lines, as seen on John F. Kennedy. **Overlip add-ons** are vertical wrinkles between nose and mouth. Mother Teresa developed these. **Lip extenders** look like horizontal parentheses around the mouth. Sometimes they come in pairs, as was the case for Andrew Jackson.

The Meaning

Lip scoring reveals conflict over self-expression. We've already seen that lips may grow thinner if self-disclosure has been discouraged by a significant other. Lip scoring is related. It signifies that the speaker is routinely squelched, even when speaking about things that aren't personal.

And what kind of relationship would that be, where a person is squelched, teased, ridiculed or contradicted? Though wrinkles of this sort are a tribute to endurance, they should, perhaps, also constitute grounds for divorce.

Talk about marital problems, lipstick bleed lines mean something juicy, don't they?

True, but let's call them **overlip add-ons**, so they won't be confused with a lipstick problem.

To read these lines, it helps to remember that the overlip is the part of the face where sexiness shows. Verticals on the overlip symbolize frustrated libido, or creativity, or both. The person doesn't feel she's being taken seriously enough. Biologically there's a pattern where sex drive increases in middle-aged women while it decreases in men, so guess which gender is more likely to develop overlip add-ons?

Keep in mind, however, that overlips are about sexual display, not necessarily a person's overall sexiness. (For initiation into reading the complexities of sexual style, see Chapter Eleven in *The Power of Face Reading*.)

Abundance of audience is the gift related to our next lip-related wrinkle. **Lip extenders** show a gift for charming a far wider audience than would be reached otherwise. Depending on what shows in the rest of the face, charisma traits can be amplified greatly. No doubt this helped President Jackson's political career.

Music lovers might find it interesting to consider the evolution of lip extenders on James Taylor. The singer has always had a very long, very thin mouth, suggesting a gift for reaching a wide audience combined with intense shyness. Over the years he has developed a double set of lip extenders, enhancing his appeal like the aging of a fine wine.

Some of the best dates have wrinkles

No one chapter could do justice to how human faces wrinkle, in all their infinitely creative, crinkly glory. What if you're considering dating someone whose face shows a pattern of wrinkles not discussed here? Figure it out. Here's how:

Say you're looking at a your date's home page photo over the Internet. You see a double score of marks on the left side of his jaw. What would you make of it?

1. Start with location

Location counts, e.g., jaws show patterns for handling conflict. (Need to brush up on the symbolism of the face? Turn back to "If Zits Could Talk" in Chapter Six.)

2. Take sides

Remember the meaning of each side of the face. Right face data tells you about patterns with work life, while the left side of the face whispers information about personal life.

3. Ask with an open heart

In a quiet moment, invite your heart—or intuition—to help you interpret the wrinkle.

4. Request feedback

If you have the benefit of reading a real-live person, share your interpretation and ask for feedback. Sometimes the person can show you photos that pre-date the wrinkle, or pinpoint the precise circumstances right before the wrinkle appeared.

5. Evaluate the accuracy

Interview your face reading subject directly, and ask for feedback. But don't stop there. Interview yourself. Has your reading opened your heart? Do you now view that prospective date with more compassion? Then count your reading as a success.

The *meet* market need not be a *meat* market. Face reading can take away some of the vanity pressure.

Wouldn't you prefer for a prospective date to look for the person who's home inside your physical face? Set a quality conversation in motion, and set an example, with physiognomy. With any luck, that date you're considering just might read your photo, too.

10. Vanity Surgery

There's this story about a middle-aged woman who had a heart attack and was taken to the hospital. While on the operating table, she had an out-of-body experience. Seeing God, she asked, "Is it my time to go?"

God said, "No, you have much longer to live: 43 years, 2 months and 8 days."

Since she had so much longer to live, the woman decided to splurge. She got a nose job, cheek implants, facelift and liposuction, which resulted in her looking absolutely fabulous.

After recovering from all these surgeries, she went to a party. Crossing the street to enter the house, she was run over by a car. When she appeared before God, she gave him a piece of her mind: "I thought you said I had a long time left to live. Why didn't you save me from the path of that car?"

God answered, "I didn't recognize you."

Vanity goes public

Vanity surgery is the art of altering the human body to make it look more attractive. The lucrative specialty originated as **plastic surgery** or **cosmetic surgery**. These humane forms of medicine originated to help patients overcome physical deformities. Today, the lion's share of plastic surgery is performed on people who believe that lack of glamour itself amounts to a deformity.

Hold on. When I had my operations, what I changed wasn't a deformity. But I wanted the breast reduction surgery and the eye lift. If I can look 10 years younger, what's wrong with that?

Each case is different, just as each face is different. Controversial though it is to raise questions about these surgeries, I'm not attacking you or the choices you've made. But I am passionately committed to changing the national conversation about cosmetic surgery.

What does **deformity** mean? Strictly speaking, it means being physically malformed, in an abnormal way. If the sight of your face makes strangers stare or avert their eyes, by all means do what you can to correct the problem surgically. Still, that's a far cry from calling your nose "deformed" because you'd rather have a profile like that of Robert Redford.

The perception of "deformity" can be created by advertising and related social pressures. Americans have already seen this happen over weight obsession. At least 80 percent of American women are dissatisfied with their appearance. According to the National Eating Disorders Association, Americans spend over $40 billion each year on dieting and diet-related products. Yet dieting doesn't work; even 95% of "successful" dieters regain their lost weight within five years and 35% of "normal dieters" progress to pathological dieting. At conservative estimate, 11 million Americans now suffer from anorexia.

Given those statistics, doesn't it make sense to question the national obsession with vanity?

Are you trying to make me feel bad about myself because I had a little work done to make myself look better?

Of course not. You probably had good reason to do what you did. My goal is to help you feel good about the face you have *now*. I'd also like to discourage you from choosing future surgeries—at least without being well informed about the inner consequences.

In this book, we've seen that human faces express the soul, evolving in meaningful ways. Artificial face changes won't destroy your soul, but they sure can numb your conscious connection to it.

Spiritually, awareness of soul is precious. It's indispensable for inner fulfillment, outer harmony. If anything, it's wise to do what you can to *enhance* your awareness of soul, as described compellingly in *Care of the Soul* by Thomas Moore.

Of course, the media don't promote loving the face and body that God gave you. Why? Two words: advertising revenue. Have you noticed that vanity surgeons promote themselves more aggressively with each passing year?

It's working, too. The number of customers for vanity procedures is now 8.5 million a year… and rising faster than the number on those old signs at McDonalds that tracked sales of hamburgers.

Who dares to publicly criticize the fad for fake faces and bodies? You risk being called a spoilsport, a nut or, even worse, someone too socially clueless to understand that nothing in post-modern American life matters more than how you look.

Still, plenty of otherwise well adjusted people have dared to grumble in private. You may have been one of them. When respected broadcaster Greta Van Susteren won acclaim by going plastic, did it repulse you? Have you ever felt that artificially improved faces have lost their soul, in some intangible but very real way? Even on the surface, you may feel that surgically altered faces lose their individuality, that too many actors on TV, for instance, look vapidly interchangeable.

Or perhaps your social conscience has been stirred by the class war implications of vanity surgery. Read it as a sign of the growing economic divide between America's rich and poor. Wealthy women today feel social pressure to look impossibly flawless. When I'm hired to read their faces for party entertainment, women who *don't* go under the knife often apologize to me, as though their reluctance to go plastic made them socially inadequate. Is this nuts or what?

Free will's outer limits

Faces aren't silly putty, to reshape at will and whim. Vanity surgery *changes* people, often in deeper ways than they think. Remember, there's a reciprocal relationship between the physical face and the inner person. Usually we evolve first on the inside, setting off a corresponding physical change. Because the relationship is reciprocal, the reverse is also true:

When we alter the physical face, the inner person must follow.

Robert Redford, After Surgery   **Robert Redford, Before Surgery**

For this to happen, the number of physical procedures need not approach the grotesque levels of alteration done to Michael Jackson and Jocelyne Wildenstein. Even relatively minor vanity surgeries have inner consequences.

Check it out for yourself. Talk with people you know who've had vanity surgery. Ask what they physically changed, then interpret the meaning according to the system of Face Reading Secrets. Don't forget to ask for feedback. Of course, you must tell the tactful version, darling. It's both unkind and unhelpful to tell the truth that hurts. (Though later in this chapter, in case you're curious, you can read about the *full* consequences for the most popular facial surgeries.)

Before then, let's explore one of the dirty little secrets of vanity surgery: *It doesn't always work.* After the swelling subsides and the bills are paid, sometimes the face reverts back to the way it was. In other cases, so-called "accidents" cause faces to return to normal.   How does face reading explain this?

Surgery "mysteriously" fails when the resulting inner change would have exceeded the limits of free will.

Body snatched?

For 30 years, "Looks like Robert Redford" has been synonymous with handsome. But this hunky movie star has resisted the pressures of vanity and stardom better than most. Instead of living in glamour-obsessed Hollywood, he leads a relatively sane life in Utah, where he's founded the Sundance Film Festival. Redford has also been the acting community's most outspoken critic of vanity surgery.

"Everyone in Tinseltown is getting pinched, lifted and pulled," he complained at Sundance in January 2002. "They lose some of their soul when they go under the knife and end up looking body-snatched."

Redford vowed that he would never have cosmetic surgery. Months later, however, oops!

Allegedly the deed was done after a cinematographer complained that bags under Redford's eyes interfered with effective acting. Redford chose a minimum of facial alteration. But was it really an improvement?

Compare his before-and-after photos. Redford has lost mobility in his lower eyelid curve, and the shape has straightened dramatically—from 10 to 1. As a face reader, you can interpret the inner loss. Only he can fathom the degree to which this physical change has numbed his connection to soul.

Vanity surgeons might say that Robert Redford looks "fresher" now. But really! How fresh does someone who's sixty-plus-years-old, like Redford, need to look?

How could this be? As described in books like those by James Hillman and Sylvia Browne (see the Bibliography) each soul signs a **life contract** before beginning an incarnation. Your contract includes a life mission plus major problems that will test your mettle. According to many metaphysical traditions, you have chosen all your significant life events and relationships up to the age of 21 (or in some cases, 28). Call this life contract "fate," if you like. Just remember that you chose it all, your face included.

Yes, I believe that your face represents part of your life contract, selected to help your soul fulfill its mission. Picture it as though, before birth, you packed a suitcase with qualities you'd need, such as courage. Courage could be patience to persevere (showing in far-set cheeks); endurance (showing in a diamond-shaped face); or the ability to physically stick up for yourself (showing in puffy earlobes and a lot of chin thrust).

The gifts in your suitcase take form in your unchanging physical face data, those soul signature traits you've been reading about.

Once your incarnation is underway, of course, you forget that you even brought a suitcase. You play the game of life in earnest, identifying with your life circumstances, seeking clarity about your life mission, and using your free will to do the best you can. By the age of 18, you've made enough choices for your face to become worth reading.

As you continue to use your free will, the consequences come back to you, further shaping your life story, your face and your soul. The older you are, the more these evolve according to your choices, toward the direction of your destiny.

Then why shouldn't cosmetic surgery just be considered an act of free will?

It is, which is why surgery works . . . usually. Still, there will always be consequences, and not necessarily the ones intended. When the side effect of a vanity surgery would alter important attributes of a soul, that operation is destined to fail.

Unknowingly, all surgery customers activate Talent Scout Rule #10: Facial Change = Free Will in Action

That rule holds special meaning when the facial change comes from surgery. Although people use their free will to purchase vanity surgery, they seldom know all that they're buying. So how can they assess the inner consequences? The first step really ought to be investigating (and appreciating) what they already have.

When you read a face in detail—a process that takes a good hour even for a professional physiognomist—you'll find layer upon layer of data, including many apparent contradictions, yielding insights into a soul's major life lessons. In this investigation, patterns will emerge. For example, let's take another look at Ronald Reagan's soul-level gift of moderation, a pattern that permeates his life story.

Back when he worked as an actor, Reagan could have gotten away with adding cheek implants and a more aggressive chin (had the surgeries been available then). The corresponding inner changes might have helped his career. Hey, maybe he would have won roles in A movies.

But given the multiple layers of moderation in his face, I doubt that Reagan would have felt comfortable with a more assertive power style. And consider this. As pointed out in Reagan's Transformation Reading in Chapter Five, a deep (and rather stealthy) level of combativeness shows in his long right canine tooth. Cheek or chin implants would have turned his stealth weapon into an all-too-obvious armament. No longer could Reagan have come across as a great moderate.

See how these vanity surgery changes would have conflicted with the pattern of his soul expression?

When I've talked with people whose surgeries failed, the face data that reverted has always been significant. In fact, one reason why clients seek out my Cosmetic Surgery Consultations is to get advance warning about **spiritually inappropriate surgeries,** procedures that, for spiritual reasons, would bring a high risk of failure. To bring perspective, I describe major soul patterns that show in the face. Afterwards, some clients feel more confident about going ahead with the surgery. Others decide to forego a proposed change. In either case, the client is better informed about the choice.

Smart consumers should realize that a true second opinion about cosmetic surgery won't come from a doctor. An experienced face reader is the professional for this job, because a balanced perspective should consider more than conventional attractiveness.

But surgery makes you look better, which causes people to treat you better. Doesn't that make your soul happier?

Let's not confuse a mood like happiness with the soul. The needs of your soul's purpose transcend the shallow benefits of a mere mood. As James Hillman describes eloquently in *The Soul's Code,* each of us comes to earth with a special **genius**, a mission to find and fulfill.

Face reading affirms the importance of pursuing your soul's mission. Transitory happiness comes second. Was Abraham Lincoln happy? What would have been the fate of our country had he chosen personal ease and happiness over his difficult mission of service? We'll never know his soul's full story. But our Transformation Reading confirmed that his facial evolution was magnificent, indicating that spiritually his life was a great success.

I've never understood why good people don't necessarily look good. Does face reading explain this at all?

Signs of inner greatness do show in the face. And everyone's a potential winner, just not necessarily at the same game.

Pretty or talented? Choose one.

As a spiritual talent scout, you've learned to notice extreme face data, the *verys*. Now's you're ready to consider *verys* in a different context, **the Paradox of Extreme Talent.** Most people would like to be extremely beautiful (or handsome). We'd also like to be extremely talented. In movies, leading men and ladies are often supposed to be both gorgeous and brilliant. In reality, that seldom happens.

Here's why. As we saw in the case of President Reagan, **handsomeness** literally means being average. Ample research on attractiveness documents this (see articles in the Bibliography). Face reading suggests that people with moderately proportioned physical features are doubly fortunate. Besides earning prettiness points, they are relatively easy for others to understand.

Outer data that is statistically average corresponds to inner qualities that are also relatively common, what I call **popularity points.** If your face has few or no *verys*, you'll receive social status for your attractiveness, then gain even more social status because of your popularity points.

For any item of face data you choose, you could imagine a bell curve to show its distribution. Most people will be near the center, fewer people at the extremes. For instance, consider cheek prominence:

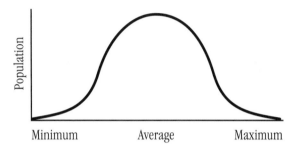

At the left end of this curve is the small number of people with no cheekbone definition whatsoever, like the young Eleanor Roosevelt. At the opposite end is the small number of people with extreme cheekbone definition, like Abraham Lincoln. Toward the center come the vast majority of human beings, who show a moderate degree of cheekbone definition, such as Ronald Reagan.

What's our example about? Cheek prominence signifies personal style regarding power.

- Low-profile cheeks, like the young ER's, signify extreme obedience to others, with the challenge being fear of taking a public stand.
- By contrast, prominent cheeks, like Lincoln's, correspond to a high-profile leadership style, with the risk of attracting criticism from others.
- Most people have moderate cheek prominence. They will show leadership only when provoked by circumstances. Even then, it's not necessarily fun; they'll push themselves forward only when necessary.

You could draw a similar bell curve for any face reading category. Most people clump close to the average, fewer people approach each edge and a very few are positioned at either extreme. The corresponding inner styles are distributed in the same manner.

Babe Didrikson Zaharias

Babe Didrikson Zaharias won more medals and records in more sports than any other 20th-century athlete. You've heard of her, right?

Well, maybe not. Babe Ruth was far more famous. But he was male. Katharine Hepburn starred in a movie loosely based on our Babe's life story, "Pat and Mike." Hepburn was famous. But she was conventionally beautiful. Zaharias wasn't. *Very* extreme face data kept her from being beautiful... but made her great.

What a Babe!

Her *Very* Extreme Face Data	The Corresponding Talents
1. Chin thrust	Aggression when competing.
2. Macho knob	Pride, temper related to proving herself.
3. Huge earlobe (right ear only)	Extremely aware of physical reality (especially when working, i.e., professional sports).
4. Out-angled ear (right ear only)	Makes own rules (especially when working).
5. Eyes small compared to proportions of forehead, eyebrows, ears, nose, mouth, chin	A component of introversion: inward focus when with others, despite pressure to perform.
6. Close-set left eye	Notices nuances. (This trait is often linked to excellence at golf, provided that the person is also physically coordinated!)
7. Left eye higher than right eye	Interacting with people, values her intuition over their expectations.
8. Left eyebrow higher than right eyebrow	Intellectually values intuition over learned procedures.
9. Highbrows	Able to strategize secretly, quietly.
10. Ultra-long eyebrows, especially on right	Strong ability to understand actions in context (especially when working).
11. Priority Area I is longest	Fascinated by learning.
12. Chunky nose tip	Values financial security. Grounded.
13. Long nose	Work talent for planning and strategy.

And what else happens when someone's face data is moderate? You've read about the corresponding challenge plenty of times by now! It's a lack of tolerance for the rest of humanity.

How often has this applied to you? Now you're having the chance to understand this challenge in the deeper context of the Paradox of Extreme Talent.

Super-attractive people, like Reagan, have faces that are mostly average. The majority of people wear a mixture of average data and *verys*, while people considered ugly have faces with a lot of *verys*. For sheer social comfort, pretty people are the winners, and not just because they're considered better looking. People can understand you most easily if your style is like theirs, so your social ease becomes an additional talent, like the icing on a cake.

When it comes to more innovative forms of talent, however, the pretty folk stop being winners, while the un-pretty of the earth have their chance to shine.

Sure, extreme talent means not having conventional attractiveness. Sure, it also means a loss of popularity points. Nonetheless, extreme talent means originality.

Leadership and creativity set a person apart from the norm. Throughout history, most people of significant achievement have had plenty of face data at the extreme end of the bell curve. For evidence, flip through the photos in this book. Presidents don't look like models. You might even come to believe that America's greatest leaders have been the quirkiest looking.

But they've paid the price for it, and not only regarding prettiness. Who's most likely to be lonely or, at least, misunderstood? It's those very same talented people at the edges of the bell curve. The most popular, good looking kids in high school may not achieve as much in later years as high school's social flops, the nerds and outcasts. Yet in the long run, everyone gets something, nobody gets it all. Thus, life is fair—if only in its typically complicated way.

While relatively beautiful people have social advantages, relatively homely people stand a better chance for greatness. Most of us dwell somewhere in the interesting middle ground. And all of us have the chance to change our face data. When we evolve it from the inside out, well and good. But artificial changes cheat the process, which can make it difficult to stay in touch with your soul. (Maybe one in a billion people, like Reagan or Hepburn, beats the odds. Combining conventional attractiveness with extreme talent, they are exceptions that prove the rule.)

Vanity noses

Vanity surgeons say:

- A perfect nose is straight, with a narrow tip. (J. Loftus, M.D., *The Smart Woman's Guide to Plastic Surgery,* Chicago: Contemporary Books, 2000, 91)
- A nose that scoops inward appears unnatural. (Loftus, *Ibid.*,99)
- An arched nose is a "deformity" that can make a person look "obviously disfigured." (J. Wilson, *The American Society of Plastic and Reconstructive Surgeons' Guide to Cosmetic Surgery,* New York: Simon & Schuster, 1992, 91 and 95.)
- Surgery can fix a nose that is "too short" or "too flat." (Wilson, *Ibid.*, 89)
- Rhinoplasty will give you a "more graceful" nose. (E. Morgan, M.D., *The Complete Book of Cosmetic Surgery,* New York: Warner Books, 1988, 208)
- Having a nose job can be considered a status symbol. (Morgan, *Ibid.*, 218)
- Explain your surgery to "nosybodies" by telling them, "I was treated for a congenital anomaly." (Morgan, *Op.cit.*,153)

The surgeons are less likely to tell you:

- So many nose job customers are dissatisfied that 1 in 5 goes back for additional surgery. Even worse, this statistic doesn't include customers so dissatisfied that, though they hate their nose jobs, they don't trust surgeons to go near them again. (Loftus, *Op. cit.,* 102)
- Each subsequent nose job is harder to do successfully. (B. Wyer, *The Unofficial Guide to Cosmetic Surgery,* New York: Macmillan, 1999, 216)
- If an overenthusiastic surgeon takes too much off your nose, you'll need more complicated surgery to enlarge it. And you won't even know there's a problem until swelling from your operation goes down, which takes 1-2 years. (Morgan, *Op. cit.,* 219 and 220)

- Patients over 40 may feel fake when wearing their new noses. (Loftus, *Op. cit.,* 103)
- Rhinoplasty can make your singing voice more nasal. (Wilson, *Op. cit.,* 93)
- You may develop breathing problems, even if you never had them before. (Loftus, *Op. cit.,* 99)
- Nose surgery can also ruin your sense of smell. (Morgan, *Op. cit.,* 219)
- Credentials in this lucrative field are so unregulated that physicians who trained in an unrelated specialty may take just one weekend workshop and then advertise as cosmetic surgeons. (Wilson, *Op. cit.,* 34)

Even the American Society of Plastic and Reconstructive Surgeons has found it necessary to warn consumers against the hype for vanity surgery:

"If you feel you are being talked into a procedure you don't need, or pushed into changing a nose you've lived with all your life simply because you are vulnerable to the promise of looking younger, simply say no."

Buying into stereotypes

As a spiritual talent scout, you've been learning to read the time-hallowed language of the face. Now let's compare it to a trendy new language that's being advertised by the vanity surgeons, interpreting face data according to social stereotypes.

Did you ever wonder how cosmetic surgeons read a face? As explained to me by two surgeons who hired me to instruct them in the art of face reading:

Lowbrows	The person is always angry.
Down-angled eyebrows	The person is always sad.
Down-angled eyes	The person is always sad.
Circles under eyes	The mark of an alcoholic.
Padded cheeks	The person is fat.
Unpadded cheeks	The person is old.
Nose is arched or long or wide	The person is "ethnic."
In-angled chin	The person is weak.

Puhleeze! An intelligent three-year old knows better than to believe that someone with lowbrows is perpetually furious—or buy into any of these pathetic stereotypes. Evidently advertising has its effect, however. I've heard people tell sad stories that involved believing these myths, then suffering until a kindly cosmetic surgeon rescued them. To support self-acceptance instead of surgery, here's how a face reader would interpret that same face data:

Lowbrows	Spontaneous communication is a talent.
Down-angled eyebrows	An intellectual gift enables this person to gain wisdom from the past.
Down-angled eyes	Compassion is a hard-won spiritual gift.
Circles under eyes	The mark of a spiritual seeker.
Padded cheeks	Has an advantage in receiving support from others.
Unpadded cheeks	An independent power style shapes this person's relationships.
Nose is arched	On the job, there's a gift for creative work.
Nose is long	On the job, there's a gift for planning and strategy.
Nose is wide	On the job, there's a gift for teamwork.
In-angled chin	When responding to conflicts, this person values community over personal aggrandizement.

Mislabeled emotions

Another stereotype from vanity surgeons involves mislabeling the emotions connected with wrinkles. For instance, my health club displays an ad for a "Botox Party" with the headline, "Relax your worry lines."

Piling vanity upon vanity, this ad implies that any lines on the face are caused by worry. Actually, different vertical forehead lines have meanings related to a variety of emotions. The one emotion they're *never* about is worry.

Why do advertisers choose worry? It sounds virtuous. You can almost hear the salesman croon, "You don't like your wrinkles, dear? Let's not call that vanity. You just worry a lot, poor thing. It's because you're so responsible and caring. But you don't need to keep those nasty wrinkles. Your new best friend, the plastic surgeon, will take all your troubles away."

What shows an alcoholic?

In the simple land of social stereotypes, the signs of alcoholism are obvious: deep circles under the eyes, a bulbous nose and broken capillaries. But in the land of reality (such as your neighborhood meeting of Alcoholics Anonymous) you'll discover this is nonsense. What does face reading say about the stereotypes?

Eye deepeners are about introspection. If you find them on an alcoholic, it will be an introspective alcoholic.

Chunky nose tips relate to valuing financial security. Sure, some inveterate drunks may develop an extreme attachment to the material world, but they're hardly alone. And with nose tips like those on Mahatma Gandhi and Mother Teresa, the company ain't so bad.

Burst capillaries relate to stress in the area of life symbolized by the location of the rosy display, e.g., cheeks and power, nose tip and money. But why blame alcohol? The causes of burst capillaries range from stress at the office to a side effect of mountain climbing.

Face readers know that, even if your motives are pure, it can be tricky to relate physical face data to emotions. For one thing, emotions are complex. For another, most physical face data expresses the soul, not transitory emotions.

The following chart is provided as a basis for inquiry and introspection, rather than a definitive summary. I group negative emotions into four main categories: anger, fear, sadness and guilt.

Because the emerging field of mind-body medicine associates certain diseases with stuck emotions, I've drawn upon the work of medical intuitives Dr. Mona Lisa Schultz and Louise Hay to add diseases, along with face data, to the chart.

Keep in mind, not every chronic sufferer from negative emotions develops a facial counterpart. Sometimes a disease process emerges instead. Why one and not the other? I don't know, nor am I aware of any scientific research that explains it. But an interesting topic for mind-body medicine would be to track what happens to the health of vanity surgery patients. After the facial expression of toxic emotions is blocked, do related diseases develop?

For research purposes, there's an enormous supply of volunteer guinea pigs, appearance-obsessed people who are eager—make that frantic—to improve their outer packaging, regardless of any health risks. What else explains their willingness to be injected with Botox? The year *before* the Food and Drug Administration (FDA) approved the treatment, close to a million Americans paid to paralyze some of their facial nerves with this vanity treatment.

With Botox the facial equivalent of Viagra, sales are sure to go sky high, but a thoughtful person may still choose to proceed with caution. And the following chart may help. When you read it, note that face changes are different from either temporary expressions or soul signature traits. For instance:

- A deep scowl could make up-angled eyes appear to be down-angled. But, being a temporary expression, this data will disappear when the face is in repose. So the emotional pattern related to the scowl is minor.
- Down-angled eyes usually show as the result of a face change, but sometimes they're a soul signature trait. In the latter case, consider them as part of a person's life contract.

Wrestling to decide whether or not to get cosmetic surgery? Face reading offers a true second opinion. Instead of hearing the party line from vanity surgeons, you can weigh the spiritual consequences. Sometimes they're good! Find out by having a face reader give you a Cosmetic Surgery Consultation. And, yes, **you** can be that face reader, serving as your own consultant!

Emotional Patterns that Shape the Face

Emotional Category	Related Emotions	Related Face Changes	Potential Diseases
Anger	Irritation, resentment, rage, bitterness	Anger flags, puffs above eyes, mouth grows shorter, smaller lipfulness, tight jaws	Bell's palsy, burns, carpal tunnel syndrome, gallstones, gout, high blood pressure, hepatitis, jaw problems
Fear	Worry, anxiety, overwhelm, nervousness, self-criticism	Mouth puckers, nostrils decrease in size, nostril shape turns triangular	Headaches, heartburn, lower back problems, motion sickness, stomach aches, stomach ulcers
Sadness	Suffering, hopelessness, helplessness, hurt, feeling unloved or lonely	Cheek dents, courage scores, down-angled eyes, eye deepeners, lip wrinkles, lips thin, suffering lines at cheeks, grimness lines, diagonal earlobe crease	Arthritis, cancer, cataracts, diabetes, heart disease, lung problems, upper back problems

Emotional Patterns that Shape the Face

Emotional Category	Related Emotions	Related Face Changes	Potential Diseases
Guilt	Blame, shame, conflict, lack of self-esteem, humiliation	Burnout line at nose, front teeth chip or decay, mark of Divine discontent at nose tip	Kidney problems, middle back problems, ringworm, tapeworm, thyroid problems

What evidence do you have to support your grouping of emotions with physical face changes and emotionally-related diseases?

Research by holistic physicians, such as Mona Lisa Schwartz, M.D., has established some connection between the development of diseases and emotional imbalances.

Stay tuned for more research. Links between emotional imbalances, disease and facial characteristics are of interest to holistic healers, notably acupuncturists and homeopaths.

So you have no hard evidence either pro or con?

No, but here's the scary part. Neither do cosmetic surgeons. Holistic health is hardly their specialty.

When it comes to taking responsibility for the overall health consequences of what they sell, how much do you think vanity surgeons care? As the research showing harm trickles in, expect them to demonstrate about as much scientific interest as cigarette manufacturers showed when confronted with evidence that cigarette smoking causes cancer.

A true second opinion

A face reader's Cosmetic Surgery Consultation is a detailed reading designed to provide perspective about facial alterations. Use it even for something as simple as a shot of Botox. Here's how to proceed:

Examine the entire face and look for patterns. Then see if the surgery being considered would contradict a major soul pattern. If so, it's fair to predict that either:

- The surgery will be immediately unsuccessful because the altered face data will revert after the operation; or
- The surgery will be unsuccessful within a few years because a so-called "accident" will move the face back to its old configuration; or
- The surgery, though outwardly successful, will be inwardly traumatic. Adjusting to the facial change will involve enormous inner turmoil.

"I've seen it happen consistently," I was told by one of my students who has worked for years as an assistant to cosmetic surgeons. "With people who are unwilling to change on the inside, their surgery doesn't work on the outside. Mostly I see failed surgeries with women who are getting operations just to please their husbands."

When is cosmetic surgery most likely to be successful? If no major soul pattern is compromised, it's easier for a patient to accept an operation and its corresponding inner change.

Vanity surgery probably works best when the patient places more value on physical attractiveness than the inner self. Otherwise it might be a matter of concern that, inwardly, cosmetic surgery moves patients in just one direction: Mediocrity.

Once, for instance, I was asked to comment on a woman's nose job. "Josie" had traded in a very long, arched nose for a petite, straight nose. The meaning, I told her, was that her soul had given her the opportunity to do significant work during her lifetime: highly original, creative work. By changing her face, she'd declined that opportunity.

Smiling through her red lipstick, Josie told me she didn't care. All that mattered to her was looking good.

What are your values? Would you gladly exchange the rarest gifts of your soul if it meant that, on the attractiveness scale, you could go from being a 4 to a 7?

The tradeoff

Be careful what you wish for. You will surely get it, whether or not you fully under-stand all the consequences. And vanity surgery brings inner consequences that aren't necessarily pretty. For each of the following procedures, I'll share with you both the tactful version of interpretation and the rest of the truth.

As you read through the following list, keep in mind that interpretations of the face data would be different if they were the person's natural endowment. (In that case, they'd develop gradually, from the inside out.) God's makeup is different from vanity choices.

Out-angled ears changed to in-angled ears

Tactful Version: You fit in better, now, socially.

The Rest of the Truth: Distinctive expressions of your personality were lost, along with entrepreneurial talent. You're more apt to take orders from the people in your life, which may cause long-term resentment and stifle your communication.

Lowbrow changed to highbrow

Tactful Version: You're less apt to say things without thinking them through.

The Rest of the Truth: Other people may find you aloof. Inwardly, you may feel a growing detachment between your social façade and your unexpressed feelings.

"Droopy" eyelids changed to small eyelid thickness

Tactful Version: You feel better about yourself and seem more youthful.

The Rest of the Truth: There's blockage to your feelings of intimacy with others; you feel cut off without knowing why.

Puffy upper eyelids "cleaned up" to look smoother

Tactful Version: You feel younger and freer.

The Rest of the Truth: To the extent that your former puffs revealed problems with food allergies or other neglect of the physical body, you have less incentive than ever to improve your lifestyle. To the extent that your puffs were about irritability, your operation hasn't removed the inner component; since irritability can no longer show on the level of your skin, the distress may be driven deeper, into your body's other organs.

Down-angled eyes changed to up-angled eyes

Tactful Version: You feel more youthful and up-beat.

The Rest of the Truth: Much of your hard-won compassion has been lost, to be replaced by a lack of feeling for others.

Single eyelid fold augmented to include extra eyelid thickness

Tactful Version: Your face has a more intense, Western look, and you may feel more sensuous.

The Rest of the Truth: Your habitual degree of feeling connected to others has been doubled, so you now run the risk of becoming excessively social, neglecting your inner self. Sorting out your new identity may take years. Even then, struggles about your personal boundaries may continue for the rest of your life.

Nose profile with an arch made straight

Tactful Version: You're less fussy about work now. It used to be that you couldn't get involved in a job unless you could do it creatively.

The Rest of the Truth: You've lost your gift for creative work. Now you follow procedures without adding the individual spark you once had.

Long nose changed to short nose

Tactful Version: Routine work is easier for you now; you feel better adjusted and take life more easily.

The Rest of the Truth: You sacrificed the chance to create a career based on thinking big. No longer do you bring originality to the workplace.

Well-padded nose changed to narrow nose

Tactful Version: Formerly, interacting with other people brought zest to your work. Now it's easier for you to work alone.

The Rest of the Truth: Your ability to enjoy work has been diminished. Teamwork suffers, and you're more apt to feel lonely while on the job. You also may suffer a loss of physical stamina related to work.

Chunky nose tip changed to small nose tip

Tactful Version: You don't obsess over financial security the way you used to.
The Rest of the Truth: Your desire to do financial planning (also, perhaps, your judgment about money) may be diminished.

Small nostrils changed to large nostrils

(Even if nostril changes occur accidentally, as the result of a nose job designed to correct something other than nostrils, you still must live with the consequences.)
Tactful Version: Since the surgery, you're more apt to spend money freely.
The Rest of the Truth: Living within your means may become harder.

Low-profile cheeks changed to prominent cheeks

Tactful Version: People pay more attention to you now.
The Rest of the Truth: Self-confidence is tested in ways that can make you feel very uncomfortable. You're also more apt to come across to others as phony.

Gaunt cheeks changed to plumper cheeks

Tactful Version: Your personality has changed a lot. You've become more sociable.
The Rest of the Truth: When interacting with others, you're more apt to play a part than to make choices based on what feels right to you. Consequently, your integrity may suffer.

In-angled chin changed to out-angled chin

Tactful Version: It's harder for people to take advantage of you and easier for you to stand up for yourself.
The Rest of the Truth: You've exchanged genuine humility for pushiness. Shortly after receiving the surgery, you may feel a behavior change in the direction of aggression. The good news is, you're likely to interpret that as "more self-respect," since that's how the surgeon has coached you. The bad news is, you'd better not take a survey of people who know you well, because they might give a less flattering interpretation, such as "selfishness."

Flabby jawline "cleaned up" to look like taut jawline.

Tactful Version: You feel a renewed sense of self-discipline.

The Rest of the Truth: Before the surgery, you were developing greater compassion for human frailty, including your own. Now you're more likely to make harsh judgments, push too hard, even wind up making yourself and loved ones miserable.

Botoxically beautiful

Within a week of the FDA's approval of Botox as safe, *The Journal of the American Medical Association* published a highly relevant study. It showed that that the government's nearsighted oversight agency has done its job pretty badly over the past 25 years. How badly? More than 10 percent of the drugs approved by the FDA have turned out to be dangerous.

Wouldn't common sense warn people that there might be long-term problems from injecting faces with a known neurotoxin? Apparently not. But possible medical dangers aside, let's consider the face reading consequences of using Botox.

Removing the mark of devotion

When I read faces, people often tell me they call their vertical forehead wrinkle at the third eye an "anger line." Yet, as you've seen in the cases of Mother Teresa, George Washington and Abe Lincoln, this is the mark of devotion. Symbolizing a spiritual vocation, this mark may be the most beautiful of all God's makeup.

What happens if you nullify it with Botox? You're telling your soul, "Forget that! Why would I agree to grow extra fast spiritually and be of service to others?"

Removing an anger flag

These vertical lines grow upwards from the eyebrows, with the right anger flag relating to work and the left one relating to personal life. Both indicate stored-up anger.

If you remove this mechanism for dealing with anger, who knows where it will show up? Perhaps you'll stop storing up the anger and start expressing it. There's a treat! Or perhaps you'll create deeper mechanisms for storing anger in other organs, like the heart or the gall bladder.

One consequence is certain. When anger flags are removed, it disrespects the body's wisdom. Sure, having no stored-up anger is preferable to having it. The inner work takes more forgiveness, self-awareness and reflection than asking a doctor to zap away a facial symptom.

If you do the psychological work, could anger flags disappear naturally?

At first it surprised even me, but Transformation Readings have taught me that sometimes wrinkles like this *can* disappear.

Forgiveness helps. After resolving stored-up rage, some of my clients have lost their anger flags. Lifestyle changes can also send wrinkles packing. Suffering lines sometimes fade after a divorce. And, as mentioned in Chapter Eight, burnout lines can be reversed. Yet wrinkles are less likely to change than other face data. I think that's because wrinkles are God's most visible makeup, a commendation for major life lessons in progress.

Soul balance

You've heard about the problem with redecorating. Once you buy that $20,000 sofa, the rest of your living room looks dowdy by comparison. So you upgrade the rest of the living room. But then you have to fix up the rest of the house, too.

Similarly, with vanity surgery, more can be involved than your initial purchase. Once you change one feature, it's tempting to go back and "upgrade." Michael Jackson is the most famous example of someone who has become addicted to vanity surgery.

Psychologists have given a name to the form of mental illness where people become obsessed with fixing their real or imagined physical imperfections. It's called **body dysmorphic disorder** and, according to J. Kevin Thompson, Ph.D., co-author of *Exacting Beauty,* this disorder is estimated to affect 1 in 50 Americans. (That's a current estimate. Give the vanity advertisers another decade and see the incidence rise.)

Even for those of us without body dysmorphic disorder, each vanity surgery threatens the inner quality of life. Every change to your physical face causes internal change. At best, you'll adjust easily. At worst, you'll numb awareness of your soul, and others will sense your loss of authenticity.

Surgeons and other surface-oriented people won't notice, of course. They'll talk up the usual clichés: "When you look better, people respect you more. When they treat you better, your life improves. What could be more important than that?"

Expressing your soul is, for one thing—assuming that you care about your spiritual life. It can be deeply confusing to adopt a personal style that's radically different from your soul's pattern. Even without this hurdle, many people don't know who they are, deep inside, until middle age. If you change your face with surgery, you can add both years and difficulty to the process of self-acceptance.

What's a thoughtful person to do, if you still can't resist the lure of a new, improved face? I'd advise you to pay close attention to the inner aspects of that "new you." Before committing to a surgery, research what you're in for. Computer imaging of how you'll look is just the beginning. In terms of soul balance, be especially cautious before you alter **the face's three sites of power:** cheeks, nose and chin.

How can you keep your power sites in balance? Examine the amount of thrust, plus the length, of each of these three parts of your face. Naturally, they're found in perfect balance.

Are you kidding? I have this teensy chin.

Although your power sites may not seem to be in proportion, your soul has balanced them in a way that helps you to learn a major life lesson. You'd be wise to learn that lesson before you "correct" it. Be especially cautious about using vanity surgery to *create* a power mismatch, which can be far more painful than self-judged "unattractiveness."

What do these three face parts have to do with power?

Noses show your power profile at work. **Cheeks** reveal social power, your style of interacting with other people. **Chins** attest to your strength for handling conflict.

What happens when you change them?

Alterations to one or more of your three sites of power can throw off your internal balance of power. Specifically:

If **the nose is minimized,** your career may suffer. Work may not seem as important as it used to. And, despite your being considered "cuter," your job performance may suffer along with your drive to create significant achievement.

Cheek changes relate to your style of interacting with others. Should your cheeks become more prominent than your nose and chin, you may seem overbearing. You also may feel overwhelmed at receiving unaccustomed attention. (Some surgery clients seek to minimize their cheeks, in which case they may lose courage that they'll need in the future.)

Chin implants can result in chronic feelings of not getting enough power, status or fame. When chin thrust overpowers cheeks, in proportion, social skills don't support the drive to compete with others. When chin thrust exceeds nose thrust, the *capacity* to achieve remains tantalizingly less than the desire to achieve.

What if you have your big chin made smaller?

Every face is set up with a well-defined balance of spiritual striving and groundedness. Often an out-thrusting chin helps an otherwise ethereal person to stay down to earth. Examples are author Marianne Williamson and actress Julia Louis-Dreyfus.

Minimizing chin thrust removes this soul-level anchor to the personality. Although a person can always find ways to become more grounded, they're not necessarily pleasant. (See Chapter 13 of my book, *Empowered by Empathy.*)

Even if disrupting my power balance caused these problems, who would know but me? Besides, my doctor says I'll be happier and better adjusted because I look better.

Until a surgery patient adjusts to the inner changes that correspond to the surgical change, she risks giving others mixed messages. For instance, what if Joan's old cheeks say, "I'm part of the crowd," while her new cheeks proclaim, "Pay attention to me. I'm the leader of the pack." Non-face readers receive these messages, even if unconsciously. Should Joan come across as diffident, despite the message of her cheeks, her ambivalence could subconsciously turn off the very people she hoped to impress by getting the surgery.

Bottom line: Expressing your soul is confusing enough without the added problem of adjusting to vanity surgery. My research suggests that, even among people who keep their real faces, it's somewhat rare to express the soul forcefully through your personality: only 1 in 300 people today manages to do this. Yet with greater spiritual insight and a slight shift in lifestyle, this can be remedied within a week (something I've seen happen with many of my clients). Vanity surgery, however, makes it more difficult—not easier—to live in harmony with your soul.

Lip inflation

Nearly every model in today's magazines is wearing fake lips. Could collagen shots just be today's version of lipstick? A thoughtful person says, "God forbid!"

Social stereotypes would have us believe that fuller lips are sexier. Face reading, however, informs us they're about big self-disclosure, not big sexiness.

But isn't sex largely in the head? If I believe pouty lips are sexier, and then I get lip implants, couldn't that become a self-fulfilling prophesy?

Maybe it would. What's sure to happen, regardless of expectations, is that your artificial lips will set in motion specific inner consequences. Thus, if you inflate your lips for social reasons, that doesn't absolve you from the corresponding inner changes. They will last as long as your lip job.

So what do you think lip implants do to the inner self?

Because fuller lips are about self-disclosure, you'll find yourself driven to say more personal things about yourself, especially to strangers.

When lips become fuller naturally (which, as we've seen, can happen as part of God's makeup), it's preceded by a gradual change to your patterns of speech. By contrast, when a doctor injects collagen or fat into your mouth, the change is both sudden and drastic. You could feel an overwhelming urge to blab about your sex life, your feelings, your religion or politics—to the detriment of your relationships.

And what if, before buying your new lips, you had mouth puckers or very thin lips? Then your new lipfulness style will be especially hard to live with. Anyone whose lips are altered may feel great ambivalence, with one part of you wishing to speak up, another part not. Maybe you'll shock yourself with the words that come out of your mouth, feeling a frightening loss of control. Or you may adjust by redoubling your inner reserve, sending others a highly charged mixed message.

Either way, you and your lips could be in for a rough ride.

Lip texture will also change as a result of lip implants. Four talents related to communication show in natural lip texture. These talents are soft lip texture, muscular lips, in-drawn lip texture and puffy lips.

Soft lip texture can be found in people over thirty whose lips maintain a youthful smoothness, as with Gerald Ford and Bill Clinton. It corresponds to a lack of social pretense. If you have these lips, you earned them by refusing to put on a façade to gain popularity. Others respect your genuineness. Oops! Guess what? Collagen shots destroy this mark of integrity.

Muscular lips show in strongly developed muscle tone. Both Israeli Prime Minister Golda Meir and Dr. Martin Luther King, Jr. exemplify this gift of the soul. If you have it, the muscularity shows when you speak about something you care deeply about. Passionate speech, in support of ideals, is your gift. It helps you to move the emotions of an audience—unless, of course, you throw that gift away by buying lip implants.

In-drawn lip texture is the opposite of over-inflated. Sometimes it takes practice to distinguish this trait from thin lips. To develop your eye for it, compare this book's photos of Franklin Roosevelt and Harry Truman. While both had thin lips, Roosevelt also had in-drawn lip texture.

What does it mean if you've got it? Before speaking, you thoughtfully consider what you have to say. Would you be able to shape your words just to please others, when you don't believe them yourself? Unthinkable! Therefore you develop a reputation for verbal integrity—unless this gift is lost by means of, you guessed it, lip implants.

Puffy lip texture (sans collagen) doesn't wear off every few months, requiring extra visits for repeat injections. Different from full lips, this trait is a matter of lip texture. However full or thin the lips are, with puffiness there's an extra ounce of pout, as shown in our first photo of Lady Diana.

Puffy lips relate to a knack for fascinating others, including the ability to switch on flirtatious charm. The conversational lightness is genuine and very appealing—at least if the lips aren't fake. Artificially puffed-up lips don't express this gift of the soul. They scream out for attention, which counters the possibility of artless charm.

234 Wrinkles Are God's Makeup

What's the difference between puffy lips and full lips?

The former have a 3-D rounded contour. One example is the 1981 photo of Lady Diana in Chapter Four. By the photo taken in 1985, Diana's puffy lip texture had gone, although she kept the same amount of lipfulness.

What did that change say about her?

Diana became less flirtatious, more apt to speak her mind without worrying if she was pleasing people. Historically, we know that by this stage in Di's marriage, flirting with her husband, Prince Charles, was a lost cause. As she'd learned, he was having an affair with Mrs. Camilla Parker Bowles. No wonder Diana's lip texture changed. Even without knowing Diana's story, a spiritual talent scout would read a lip change like hers with compassion.

My friend Tiffany is already a blabbermouth. She has medium-sized lips that she plays up with bright red lipstick. Tiffany can't wait to get the heaviest possible collagen treatment. What do you think will happen to her?

A life already out of balance will grow even more out of balance. Based on what you've said about her priorities, Tiffany's mouth would grow longer and fuller without professional help (i.e., from the inside out); she'd see it develop if she'd only have patience. By making a sudden, dramatic change, she is more likely to go overboard in her behavior.

Years from now, the inflated lip craze may seem like just another silly fad. To a historian, however, it will make perfect sense that the magazines enthusiastically referred to **bee-stung lips** as a desirable look. What a disconnect! Have you ever been stung by a bee anywhere, especially a sensitive part of your body like the lips? Then you know that being bee-stung isn't cute, it's painful. Similarly, the bee-stung fad brings the inner self more pain than pleasure.

Face lifts

Unsought, your reflection bounces back at you from a glass storefront. If you're over 50, the shock can be particularly unpleasant. Is that older person really you? How unfair!

Most of the faces in magazines and on TV look so different from a normal mature adult, your real face may not seem real to you. Even if the social pressure were less, it would be human to mourn the loss of your youthful appearance.

Millions of people feel the same way. So they "fix" the problem by buying face lifts. Magazine articles make the choice sound like a no-brainer: What if there were a safe operation that would make you look younger, tighten up sagging skin and get rid of your wrinkles? While you're at it, maybe the doctor could throw in a few other procedures to "clean up" your eyes or jaw line. It wouldn't be major surgery, either (like the violent operation cutely known as a "liposuction"). Wouldn't that be worth the $20,000 or more?

I'm here to urge you to think again. A face lift doesn't just tug away some unwanted facial flab, any more than it can give you a genuine new start at life. Face lifts turn a face into a social mask. If you feel psychologically disconnected from your face now, after vanity surgery you'll be even more disconnected.

What's the difference? Before your outer self reflected your inner self in ways that were hard to accept. Now the bond between inner and outer has been compromised, and your outer image has become, to some degree, fake. Take a good look at the people you know who've had face lifts. At first glance, they seem fine, but could those ultra-youthful faces be stretched just a bit too thin to look real?

So you don't consider it a bad thing that face lifts wear off and have to be repeated?

It gives a person another chance to live in harmony with the soul. Just because you've had face lifts in the past doesn't mean that you need to keep having them.

Do you think face lifts can deaden your soul?

Nothing destroys the soul, not birth nor death nor moving from one incarnation into another. But *awareness* of the soul is another matter. Throughout your life, you have struggled to become more aware of the thought in God's mind that is you.

Spiritual awakening involves getting to know your deepest self. Knowledge of your soul brings lasting rewards, far beyond improving your personality or life circumstances. When you pray, meditate or do other spiritual exercises, you awaken your conscious connection to soul. This helps you to express your soul through your thoughts, words, and actions.

Living with awareness of your soul accelerates spiritual progress, helping you to live the highest ideals of your religion. Meaningful coincidences show up more often, and you feel supported by life. This is the growth of enlightenment. Benefits include more satisfying love relationships and more meaningful friendships. In your business dealings, your reputation can only improve. And besides the personal benefits, you can inspire others by your example.

Are you claiming that a simple face lift takes all your soul awareness away?

No, it takes some of it away. But what in life could be more precious? Why make the sacrifice?

Conscious connection to your soul won't be lost forever, but it may not come back easily. And this could result in delays in fulfilling your life contract.

Let's get real. Actresses have to get face lifts. Otherwise, how could they keep their careers?

This alleged need of actors comes up whenever I speak about the downside of vanity surgery. What makes this question disturbing is that the people who ask about it aren't actors, so they're really asking about themselves. The full question, if spoken aloud, might sound like this:

"Actors need their artificially enhanced faces and bodies. And since there's no higher ideal in life than to look like an actor, all self-respecting Americans must need vanity surgery, too. Don't you agree?"

I don't. I think it's a problem in itself that so many Americans hold actors and actresses higher than any other professionals. Research before election 2000 showed that actors were better known than the presidential candidates. In pop culture, actors are more recognized than people of accomplishment in any other significant field of endeavor. And the pseudo logic is that if Barbara Walters, or other TV personalities, need their face lifts, so do you.

Let me break it to you. Even if you spend hours every day watching TV, that's not going to make you a star. Only so many people can be famous for more than 15 minutes. Besides, there might actually be more important things in life than fame.

But even if your life goal were fame, and you believed your best shot would be acting, guess what? Vanity surgery won't give you talent as an actor. Trading in your face, as a celebrity wannabe, guarantees only one thing: a life that's shallower than it needs to be.

The older you are, the more your face reflects your soul. Unless, out of vanity, you pay to erase it. Doesn't it make sense that a human face could have more to it than Mr. Potato Head? By erasing apparent imperfections, we lose the real perfection—how the physical face mirrors the soul. At least it does until that exquisite mirror is smashed, then reconstituted to have all the individuality of a Pringles potato chip.

The truly frightening alternative to wrinkles

It's your 25th high school reunion. You and your classmates have been preparing for it. Vanity surgery has been the choice for some, Botox for others. At a less extreme level come the tried and true methods of new clothes, better hair and starvation diets. Given the social pressure to look good, it's understandable that otherwise normal people go a little nuts. And preparing to go head-to-head with one's former friends and foes, there is much fretting about how one's face has changed.

As a face reader, of course, you can attend any gathering with aplomb. Bring along your skills as a spiritual talent scout. You'll enjoy discovering how your peers have evolved over time. Having free will, a person can choose not to grow. At a high school reunion, the scariest sight is the classmate who hasn't changed.

Granted, "You haven't changed a bit" usually isn't true. Typically all this expression means is that someone has kept the same hairstyle and weight. Faces get a quick once over. If eyes and the smile seem the same, and there aren't too many wrinkles, the trite accolade is offered up like a supreme compliment. But the only people who really look the same after 25 years are the ones who haven't grown much.

Eternal youth, or sameness, may work for Peter Pan. For humans it represents a loss. Living on this Learning Planet, each of us has a precious gift denied to the angels, the chance to evolve. Each wrinkle on your face, like every other natural change to your face, glows like a badge of achievement. Or, in less secular terms, you're wearing "God's makeup."

The Handshake—Richard Nixon and Spiro Agnew

11. Does Evil Show?

I've saved the hardest question for last. It has no quick, convenient answer. Of course, I wish it did. For one thing, it's the question I'm asked most often:

Does evil show?

Most people try to solve the problem of evil by redoubling their efforts to look where they already look, at expression and body language.

But there is no special, slightly hidden, diabolical twinkle in the eye that could warn an alert expression reader: Bad guy.

Think about it. Have you seen this, even once? You've had better luck picking up loose quarters on the street.

Few facial signs of trouble are both obvious and reliable. They tend to be subtle, too. For instance, you must look closely to notice a **mixed-message handshake,** like the one pictured at the start of this chapter. Sure, it looks fine on the surface. Richard Nixon, the handshaker, is smiling in a charming manner. And Spiro Agnew, the handshakee, is grinning his little heart out. He certainly doesn't seem to notice any problem.

But you can.

Nixon isn't grinning back at the man with whom he's ostensibly shaking hands. Nixon is facing in a completely different direction. Note the distinction. He hasn't twisted around for a quick look at the camera. Nixon is standing, feet firmly planted, not turning. While he goes through the motions of shaking hands with Agnew, Nixon's body and beaming smile are aimed directly at the camera.

So Nixon is posing. So what?

Most people would never pose that way. The handshaker's symbolic message, the hearty public handshake, co-exists along with completely ignoring the smile (and presence) of the handshakee. Try copying Nixon's body position and expression. It feels very peculiar.

Any other examples of expression that can tip you off to a problem?

Mirthless smiles, ones that show in lips but not eyes, can also serve as warning signals.

Sometimes **eye gaze qualities** will give you the creeps, even if you're not seeing something that's definitely physically weird, like the red eye look that pops up on badly lit family photos. Intuition, more than physical sight, may cause you to feel that a person's stare is sinister. You'd be wise to pay attention, even if you can't prove there's something wrong beyond the shadow of a doubt.

Outside of a courtroom, you don't have to prove anything. So keep away from the shadows! (Actually, this kind of caution will give you a better chance of staying outside of a courtroom, too. Testifying as a victim is not a fun way to spend your time.)

Helpful though expression reading can be sometimes, just as often it's wildly inaccurate. Think I'm kidding? According to the FBI, even trained investigators are deceived 50 percent of the time. There's the danger of unwittingly projecting your own fears or prejudice. Another problem is that deceivers can be very accomplished expression manipulators.

According to *Studies in Machiavellianism,* frequent liars use strong eye contact intentionally, seeming more innocent than they really are (R. Christie and F. L. Geis, eds., New York, NY: Academic Press, 1970, 53-75).

Compared to expression reading, face reading is much more reliable. Face data can't be manipulated to mask the lie of the moment. As you've seen, most changes take at least 30 days to develop.

But I still don't see how face reading would show you the bad guys. Where do you look for problems?

Look everywhere on the face. Should you have reason for suspicion, face reading will give you an advantage over people who restrict what they notice to the look of two eyes and a mouth. An entire face-ful of data awaits you. So put on your equivalent of a Superman cape (a Sherlock Holmes cape?) and turn yourself into... **a face detective.**

That's right, you can investigate the entire face for clues to character. In fact, you've been doing that throughout this whole book. The only difference is that so far the emphasis has been on opening your heart, rather than protecting yourself.

But did you ever hear of **situational ethics**? Rather than following one rigid set of rules about how to behave, mature people scope out a particular situation and use flexibility in the way they make their choices.

For instance, children are taught to always cross streets at the green, not in between. Until they get the concept right, parents keep reminding them, "Wait for the traffic light every time. Every time. Every time."

As an adult who has mastered this concept, however, you might survey a quiet intersection, note the complete lack of cars for blocks in every direction and (dare I write this in public?) give yourself permission, on that particular occasion, to cross the street even though the traffic light is red.

In that situation, you've made a smart choice to do things in a way you ordinarily wouldn't. To protect yourself from evil, you can do something comparable. Read faces with **situational suspicion.**

Usually when you meet people, suspicion won't help you at all. You'll risk glumming yourself down, making life grimmer than it needs to be. Why do the spiritual equivalent of tossing perfectly decent human beings into the trash? You wouldn't want people who meet *you* to focus on every flaw and foible.

Ordinarily the best way to deal with strangers is to Golden Rule it. Search their faces appreciatively, as a spiritual talent scout. Even from a thoroughly superficial perspective, relationships generally go better when we can muster up some genuine good will or, failing that, a sense of humor.

Still, there will be times when you feel a need to protect yourself from strangers, and that's when you can turn face reading on its head, as it were.

When a situation warrants suspicion, read faces in a way that emphasizes a person's potential challenges, rather than talents.

Every bit of face data relates to a talent and a potential challenge. When the situation warrants suspicion, turn up your awareness of the possible challenges.

Ordinarily, for instance, I wouldn't feel threatened at meeting someone with large, round nostrils. More likely, I'd admire the person's prosperity consciousness. But screening a new date, I'd notice. Twice it has happened that friends of mine became romantically involved with partners who had large, round nostrils. I warned these friends to be financially wary but both ignored me; each was brought to the brink of bankruptcy by her partner's free-spending ways.

Apart from the useful warnings you'll receive via situational suspicion, a small number of face traits are always more about challenge than talent. If anyone in your life has one of the following, make that person earn your trust:

- **Third eye covers** (those horizontal wrinkles described in Chapter Nine) symbolize going against one's spiritual light, as demonstrated by Slobodan Milosevic.
- Hypocrisy shows in strong **asymmetries of eyelid thickness**. For instance, large eyelid thickness on the right side and none on the left side suggests that someone makes a public show of closeness to others, yet secretly has a highly detached intimacy style. The Ayatollah Khomeini is an example.
- Contempt is proclaimed in a **sneer** like the one Osama Bin Laden developed on the right side of his mouth.
- **Crooked smiles** don't augur well for truthful speech, as demonstrated by the smirks on Al Capone and Mata Hari.
- Cruelty shows when lips are held in a way that shapes a **thin, blade-like mouth,** like that belonging to Joseph Stalin.
- A *very* large **macho knob** relates to pride and temper, as demonstrated by that notorious bully from Iraq, Saddam Hussein. (A more petite and benign version of the doorknob-like chin structure shows on William Henry Harrison.)

Keep in mind, please, that attributes like these don't make a person evil. Wickedness never shows directly in one single item of face data. If it did, don't you think you'd have noticed by now? All of us could have learned to read the (nonexistent) **bogeyman trait** in grade school, along with the ABCs. Unfortunately there's nothing simple about life's huge, sad glossary of evil.

The rest of this chapter is devoted to specific kinds of detective work that you can do with some degree of certainty, culminating in an Integrity Reading of Richard Nixon, plus practical tips that you can use to avoid falling victim to evil.

Pretense

Pretense means a false appearance intended to deceive. When people plan to manipulate or trick you, they'll use pretense to win your trust. Expression reading won't protect you. In fact, staring at expression can actually put you under the spell of an accomplished liar. Use face reading instead:

- Read the face, looking for the person's most *very* significant data. Interpret the meaning.
- Compare that with the person's actual behavior.
- If the person is projecting a strong image through expression, count that, too.
- Pretense shows when someone acts or emotes in precisely the opposite direction of what the face proclaims most strongly.

Usually the *verys* in a face are strongly supported by behavior—just the opposite of pretense. Remember Talent Scout Rule #3? Very = Very. Most people demonstrate **congruence,** rather than pretense. Their actions, speech, expressions, body language and distinctive face data all go together. Mixed messages are minor.

For instance, President Coolidge's highly congruent public image was "Silent Cal." You won't find an American president with thinner lips or a more in-drawn lip texture, and the poor man had mouth puckers, too. Coolidge's mouth data implied that he shrank from self-disclosure, preferring to speak only when guided by inner conviction. On the challenge side, in his personal life he probably found it nearly impossible to advocate for his own happiness. In short, Cal's vaunted taciturnity was undoubtedly genuine.

By contrast, consider double agent Robert Hanssen. When smiling, he projected a choirboy innocence. The problem is that his face had one big *very,* long canine teeth. That's the deepest sign of aggression a face can have, remember? Therefore, a smile that pretended the opposite should have alerted Hanssen's FBI bosses to possible trouble.

Do teeth like that always mean trouble?

Not at all. Look for congruence. Both President Ronald Reagan and First Lady Rosalyn Carter have at least one long canine tooth, but it doesn't show up on either face as the biggest *very*. And, appropriately, Reagan and Carter have more guarded smiles than Hanssen, without pretense of choirboy or choirgirl. When you do find a mixed message, it's up to you to evaluate whether it signifies the intent to deceive or merely a lack of self-knowledge.

Scary people

Reading faces for pretense can be highly useful. But it won't necessarily show you the scary stuff: Who plans to do things that are downright evil?

The reason hinges on a fact well known to psychotherapists. Although neurotics may bumble into wrongdoing, cold-blooded evildoers are different; either they appear to function within the normal range of behavior, masking a significant personality disorder, or else they are psychotic.

Either way, the resulting behavior can be dangerous. If you're on the receiving end, you might think of these forms of mental illness as **character flaws.** Do your best to stay clear of people who have them.

But isn't every human being flawed?

Most of us are merely **neurotic.** Sometimes we'll do wrong, but afterwards we'll feel badly about it and resolve to do better next time. Emotions like guilt and remorse prod us on. Neurotics may seek prayer, psychotherapy or other means to vanquish their inner demons. In that sense, guilt can be a good motivator for personal growth.

Guilt also accelerates changes to the physical face. By contrast, the faces pictured in the Villains Gallery at the Online Supplement show only one thing in common. Each face looks relatively youthful. Wrinkles are few because remorse is lacking. The vast majority of us, the Woody Allens of the world, age very differently.

So you're saying that crazies are less likely to look troubled than people who are actually sane?

Exactly. Severe mental cases aren't neatly locked up and labeled, like animals in the zoo. Walking among the worried well are confident people with hidden illnesses like narcissistic personality disorder.

Sufferers from mental illness are not invariably helped by medication, nor do they necessarily recognize that they have a problem to fix. Perfectly affable some of the time, at other times they may have psychotic breaks they don't remember afterwards.

Won't their faces record that they've done wrong?

No. When the wrongdoer doesn't register pain, or even curiosity about what has happened, there won't be remorse. Therefore, the face won't change. Thus, O.J. Simpson, found liable in civil court for the brutal murder of his ex-wife, isn't only free to walk the streets. He's facially free of evidence.

In fact, sociopaths like pathological liars seldom seek psychotherapy. They won't benefit from it, either, since guilt doesn't prod them to change. People with major character flaws can lie, cheat or kill without compunction.

And if you don't think that such people can be attractive, you've never enjoyed a James Bond film. (If the secret agent wasn't so handsome, suave and *fictional,* he'd be terrifying!)

But craziness and evil ought to show, shouldn't they?

Wishing doesn't make it so, witness the so-called science of **phrenology,** developed during the 19th century. Researchers studied formations of the skull, trying to correlate cranial size with criminal tendencies. Eventually this attempt was discredited.

Phrenology has nothing to do with physiognomy. A thoughtful person will appreciate that the front of the face is vastly more informative than the part usually covered with hair.

By contrast, face reading emphasizes free will. It's an art, not an attempt at science. And instead of phrenology's underlying intent to prove that people are evil, my system of Face Reading Secrets is based on the premise that "God don't make no junk."

Just as no human face carries the label "Junk," there's no facial designer tag for "Evil." Unfortunately, the still prevalent myth that "a bad person's face should look bad" keeps people from recognizing danger when it is really present.

Spotting sociopaths

Another of our society's face-related myths is that a youthful appearance makes a person attractive and, therefore, good. Ironically, this type of attractiveness can represent **arrested development.** It's normal for a face to be tempered by human experience. This shows in asymmetries, faint wrinkles and other face changes. When a thirty-something face looks like a teenager's, that could be the result of wise choices like health food and yoga, or simply being at ease with life.

However, another possible cause is that the person is troubled: either **afraid** to experience life fully, spiritually **programmed** to deny some important aspect of life, **addicted** to substances or behaviors that limit evolution, or **emotionally crippled** to some degree. When that person breaks through to a life with more genuine growth, the face will lose its mask-like youthfulness.

By analogy with handwriting, it's not desirable for a mature person to have the copybook penmanship of a model elementary school student. As graphoanalysis experts will tell you, healthy adults develop quirks in their handwriting that represent inner evolution.

Like handwriting, faces reflect the soul. And a person who never suffers from emotions like guilt or remorse will not evolve facially. An extreme example is the unchanging face of terrorist Timothy McVeigh.

Had you been responsible for the bombing in Oklahoma City, wouldn't you have suffered deeply after the deaths you'd caused? Wouldn't you have suffered even more during the aftermath of the bombing, as heartbreaking stories of pain and loss were reported by the media? Afterwards, being brought to justice, wouldn't you have felt fear? When confessing your crime before a judge, wouldn't you have considered at least the *possibility* that you had done something wrong?

Not McVeigh. Most of us go through more inner turmoil over a hearing in traffic court. But then again, we're not sociopaths.

Since sociopaths and psychotics don't show their problems facially, does that mean there's no way to identify them?

Fortunately, there is. And you've probably been doing it all your life (though not necessarily consciously) by gathering data about the human energy field or aura. Unfortunately most aura reading today is done as a vague vibing out. Or people misguidedly believe that the point is to see colors rather than to gain detailed, dependable information. Anyone can learn to read auras by using gifts that come naturally. My how-to book, *Aura Reading Through All Your Senses,* describes three lie detector techniques, each designed to investigate a different form of deception. Tests like these can warn you when a person has major character flaws.

Dating an image

In today's era of Internet dating, the stakes for reading character have never been higher. It's to a face reader's advantage that photos are often available (the only catch being that photos don't always match the person purported to be shown).

When a prospective date sends you a photo or link to a home page, get busy! That photo has been chosen to convey an image, not merely an appearance. So it's perfect for comparing the expression and body language with what shows in face data. Intentional deception may not be intended when someone pretends to be the opposite of what shows in his face. Maybe he just lacks self-awareness. But is that something you want to hook up with?

Internet dating goes better when you read faces. At services and sites for singles, photos are usually available. If not, ask for one early in your e-dating relationship. Here's how to find out if that face has integrity, not just eligibility:

1. Find two or three *verys* on your date's face. Interpret them according to the system of Face Reading Secrets.
2. Ask questions related to those verys. Dating is an ideal context for doing this because you have every right to ask a date personal questions. (Another advantage of questioning is that if someone is trying to pass off another person's photo as his own, your questions may discourage further deception.)
3. Compare the answers given by your date to what the face tells you. Strong contradictions should set off warning bells. The person is either lying or revealing a lack of mature self-awareness.

For example, Pat has a *very* huge Priority Area II, suggesting that he is highly ambitious. You ask him, "Would you consider yourself ambitious?" He answers, "Not particularly. I'm a very mellow guy." Gong! Hear the warning.

Self-awareness means knowing your own strengths, weaknesses and interests. It's a pre-requisite for meaningful relationships, as well as successful careers. There's nothing wrong with Pat's being ambitious, nor is it necessarily a problem to be "a mellow guy." But there is a problem if Pat's face shows a strong inclination in one direction yet he disowns it. Unless your reading is inaccurate, this man lacks mature self-awareness.

For further insight into a contradiction like this, go on to read his aura. Or get a reading from a professional, just as you'd hire a car expert to check out a used car before buying it.

The handwriting test

People who don't know themselves well may act in ways so clueless that the consequences are similar to those of intentional deceit. Either way, lack of integrity is the common denominator. **Integrity** means being whole, with self-awareness serving as a meaningful link between speech and actions.

Handwriting analysts know where to look for integrity in a signature or handwriting sample: Study the formation of lower case o's and a's.

One extra loop within either of these letters signifies self-deception. **Two** extra loops mean deception of others as well. Examine the handwriting of people you know, particularly your own. If you find a problem, use your free will to fix what's broken. When you overcome challenges to integrity, it shows not only in your handwriting but also in your aura. Your actions, words and inner self become increasingly congruent.

When to read an aura, not a face

What's the best way to audition strangers who'd like to play significant roles in your life, like employer, employee or date? I'd recommend that you supplement face reading by investigating auras. The human energy field contains a variety of databanks, called **chakras**. Aura reading techniques make this data available to you, in depth and detail.

Although some people depend on Kirlian photos to read auras, a special picture isn't necessary. You can learn to do in-depth readings of people and photos (either hard copy or Internet). Eventually these perceptions become effortless. For instance, when reading my morning newspaper, I usually check out the photos of people in the news, reading both faces and auras. Even a simple headshot contains the full hologram of the seven major chakras.

Aura reading is a preferable way to spot liars, spiritual zealots, alcoholics and drug takers, people with a sexual screw loose, plus anyone with a major psychological imbalance. Other information in auras complements what shows in face data about communication, power, life priorities and so forth.

Face reading, I've found, remains a superior method to learn how folks work, handle money, prefer their small talk and set social boundaries.

Another advantage of face reading is that it's so easy to do. Since it works like an alphabet, all you need do is spot the physical data, then interpret it. I've read faces accurately when I felt tired, grumpy or otherwise was in a state of mind where aura reading would be unwise. That's because the quality of an aura reading depends on your inner clarity. Accuracy will be compromised if the aura reader is emotionally or physically out of whack.

A different kind of problem with aura reading occurs for the approximately 1 in 20 people who have at least one strong natural gift as an empath.

Empaths experience directly what it is like to be another person. Until they are skilled, empaths often unconsciously take on pain that doesn't belong to them. Many hypochondriacs, for instance, are really unskilled empaths with a gift for physical empathy.

If you're drawn to face reading, there's a better than average chance that you are a natural empath. Consciously or not, you routinely join with other people energetically. Emotions aren't necessarily involved, incidentally. As explained in my book on this topic, your natural bent may be to pick up data that is physical, intellectual or spiritual, rather than emotional.

If you are a natural empath, until you become very skilled, it's wise to avoid reading either faces or auras of people who are severely disturbed. Tasting the reality of a troubled person isn't like going to the movies, where you can be entertained in a superficial way.

Even highly skilled empaths, if they're wise, select their research subjects carefully. To this end, I've relegated pictures of people with really depressing auras to the "Villains Gallery" at the Online Supplement, protecting you as well as myself.

Reading integrity

When the stakes are high or the deeds are dreadful—or you're simply curious about whether someone is a bit wacky—there's a special kind of reading you can do. Called an **Integrity Reading**, it combines face reading about life challenges with some aura reading.

Richard Nixon makes a fascinating subject for an Integrity Reading. The intense drama of his facial evolution is depicted in the photos on page 251.

Nixon is also intriguing to read because he was such a mixture of good and bad. Hardly a symbol of Everyman (thank goodness!), Nixon wasn't an evil man, delighting in wrongdoing. His imbalances evolved, a fascinating mixture of destiny and poor choices.

"I am not a crook," Nixon once told the American people, although the Watergate investigations suggested otherwise. Undoubtedly he believed in his side of the story, yet more than 30 of his underlings were found guilty of breaking the law.

In his zeal to win a second term as president, Nixon bugged his political opponents in an attempt to discredit them. Then, after the investigations began, Nixon illegally covered up his actions by using the FBI and CIA against his "enemies."

Because RN taped his own meetings, his involvement in the cover-up became undeniable. Equally fascinating to many, the presidential tapes provided a rare opportunity to eavesdrop on presidential power behind the scenes. There was Nixon's scheming, swearing, racism and paranoia, in all its unabashed crudeness.

A. Richard Nixon in 1945

B. President Richard Nixon in 1969

C. President Nixon in 1972

D. President Nixon in 1974

Nevertheless Nixon did good as well as bad. As President he ended the war in Vietnam and improved relations with America's Cold War enemies. Moreover, Nixon did more to help the environment than most presidents, before or after him.

His farewell speech touches on his ethical struggles: "I would say only that if some of my judgments were wrong, and some were wrong, they were made in what I believed at the time to be the best interest of the Nation."

Early challenges

Even by age 32 (Photo A), his face has developed a startling degree of **horizontal asymmetry.**

Compare the two halves of his face and you'll see that most features are higher on the *left* side. There's just one exception, something important. His cheek padding is higher, stronger and altogether much bigger on the *right* side of his face.

All that higher data on the left side represents holding his personal interests higher than public accountability. The aspects of life affected by this aren't trivial, either:

- Thinking patterns (eyebrows)
- Social patterns (eyes)
- How he unconsciously interprets life (ears)
- How he communicates (mouth)
- Handling conflict (jaws)
- Making ethical choices (chin)

Thus, Nixon's life contract has set him up to value his welfare over that of others. As if that weren't tough enough, observe the most extreme *very* on his face, that enormously **padded right cheek** in contrast to his unpadded left cheek. It signifies a gift for attracting power in public life.

What a combo! Much as Nixon might yearn to receive support in his personal life, that's not where it comes. Instead, he receives support only through career. And career success comes so easily and copiously, it's as if he is living out his wildest fantasy. However (and unfortunately), this lifelong blessing compounds his tendency to put himself first. Has he begun to think that the world and its privileges exist just to serve him? Other soul signature data must be viewed in the context of this major life challenge.

- Eyes are **sanpaku** (hidden when he scrunches up his face in a smile), suggesting that, at the soul level, he looks up to others, seeking approval.
- **Lowbrows** mean spontaneous speech while **enders** suggest the gift of thoroughness when carrying out his chosen strategies.
- **Ear proportions** show outer ear circles larger than inner. This boosts Nixon's effectiveness in life. The drawback: He may ignore how other people feel.
- A **nose profile with a scooped shape** suggests the rare work style of being guided by personal feelings, rather than rules and procedures.
- With **blarney lips**, persuasiveness comes easily.

What would I tell Nixon about his **aura**, as portrayed in Photo A? Although generally truthful, he shows a problematic tendency to speak strongly in public, yet hide his personal opinion. Spiritual life is undeveloped. And the biggest part of his aura, by far, relates to power. Not only is this part (the solar plexus chakra) huge, it shows such an extreme lack of emotion, I'd warn Nixon to watch out for ruthlessness.

President at last

By the time of the official White House photo shown here (Photo B), Nixon had survived crushing difficulties. After two terms as Vice President, he ran for president in 1960 and lost. Then he lost his bid to become Governor of California.

Discouraged and disgusted, he announced a retirement from politics. "You won't have Nixon to kick around any more," was the unfortunate way he put it. The press turned him into a laughing stock. (Given Nixon's **lowbrows,** the spontaneous comment was understandable if not wise.)

Amazingly, however, he made a comeback. Photo B shows him in 1969, newly elected President. Here we see that his chin has developed a **macho knob**, symbolizing greater masculine strength. Although he has needed to muster that pushiness to make a comeback, he'd better watch out for pride and temper, potential challenges that go with the macho knob.

Nixon's **nose angling** has become unusual. Near the bridge, the slant is toward the right; halfway down, the direction reverses. Here's what this face data says: "You have strong drive for work that's noticed by the public. But once you establish yourself, you're inclined to use your work for personal ends."

On the positive side, Nixon has developed a faint **mark of devotion,** which shows a bent for spiritual service. Appearing now, it suggests a re-worked agreement with the Universe. From this point on, he won't get away with doing any less than his best. Retribution will be swifter and harsher than for people who haven't signed up for the mark.

Most extraordinary, beneath that incipient mark of devotion, Nixon has begun to grow a **nose bridge notch.** This unusual indentation between the eyebrows symbolizes denial about some aspect of his work. Now that he finally has the power he's dreamed of, could his ethics be taking a turn for the worse?

His **aura** shows that the habit of deception has intensified, so the nickname "Tricky Dick" applies pretty well. Emotionally, he has closed down. Indeed, compared to what shows in Photo A, he's become far more disconnected from his emotions. Spiritually, however, there is good news; more spiritual awareness is available to Nixon, if only he'll *use* the increased energy at his third eye chakra.

Power is the big question raised by RN's aura at this time. The size of his aura at the power chakra has shrunk. Is that because he feels that he can relax his ambitions since he's finally president? Or has he begun to believe that even this much power isn't enough?

Trouble

The year is 1972. While Nixon is campaigning hard for re-election, those obnoxious reporters from *The Washington Post* have started to investigate the break-in at the Democratic National Committee offices in the Watergate Hotel. By this point in Nixon's career, smaller choices have coalesced in the direction of evil; he's broken laws and he knows it. Does it show? Let's examine a wonderful candid photograph from this period in Nixon's life, Photo C.

Eye extenders have grown considerably since President Nixon's last photo. This means that he is now more apt to ask others to help him overcome problems.

But more ominous is the *very* strong **pacifist power style** only on the right side of his face. Way unusual! Chester Arthur is the only other president I've seen with this power style, and he had it on both sides. Nixon's version, on the right side of his face only, suggests that he'll say whatever it takes to placate the public.

Meanwhile, the left side of his face shows the **leaderlike style,** with his cheek widest. This signifies that he prefers the role of "the boss" in his personal life,

Should his face show other integrity problems, Nixon's competing power styles could exacerbate them. And this is exactly what happens:

Rough skin texture around the chin indicates that decision making or ethics, or both, have become problematic. Further, his chin is now punctuated by a horizontal line that angles downward from left to right. Because of the direction of its asymmetry, this skewed **chin line** relates to making ethical choices that hold private interests over his public responsibilities.

Nixon's nose has developed **the mark of Divine discontent** (that vertical line at the tip), which usually relates to frustration at having a job seem too small to fulfill one's ambitions. Being President of the United States is a pretty big job, though. Nixon's frustration may be directed more towards his job's legal limitations.

Most ominous of all, his **nose bridge notch** has added so many extra lines, it's evolved into a **nose bridge star,** suggesting increased denial over what's going on at work. At this point, God's makeup couldn't be much clearer short of having an actual neon sign, like marquee lights, reading "Warning! Danger related to this man's work!"

Aurically, the news isn't good either. At Nixon's throat, rage has been added to the mix of duplicity and secrecy. Regarding power, there's a kind of righteous indignation; deeper, there's self-awareness that he has chosen to do wrong. Compounding this, RN's third eye opening has closed up, the sign of a spiritual invitation not chosen; he has developed a hardened preference for doing whatever it takes to further his personal ends.

Relief

Laws exist to protect people and nations. However, laws ultimately help the very people found guilty of breaking them. Even while Nixon protested his innocence, I believe that part of him was finally relieved when his guilt was exposed. I think you'll see why with my analysis of Photo D, which shows him speaking on television the day before he resigned from office.

What a dramatic change! For the first time in Nixon's adult life, the left side of his face has stopped being higher than the right. It's as if the two sides of the puzzle have finally clicked into place, symbolizing that public and private lives have been re-aligned. I find the data amazing. Look at this!

Cheek width, on both sides of RN's face, has become pronounced at the cheekbone level, smaller below. This symbolizes an unmasked preference for highly visible power.

Simultaneously, his cheek padding has turned into *very* extreme **jowls.** Indicating diminished support from others for power plays, the loose flesh at the sides of his face now extends from ear tops clear down to his chin.

Notice, too, at his chin, the **macho knob** has disappeared and been replaced by an even more **rumpled skin texture**, especially on the left side. Public humiliation, related to ethics, has put him through the wringer.

On the left, President Nixon has suddenly developed a **down-angled eye,** which indicates deep personal sorrow.

In addition, an unusually extensive **suffering line**, again on the left, runs from nose to chin. This is a way that his face documents personal pain.

Yet even these extraordinary changes are less dramatic than the most central fact about Nixon's face when giving his last TV speech as President. **Horizontal symmetry**, from left to right, has clicked into place for his ears, mouth, jaws and chin. His left eye and eyebrow, formerly higher than the right, have lowered, too.

Devastating though the public humiliation has been, RN's personal identity has finally been aligned with his public persona. It's as though the cosmic chiropractor has just cracked his bones. The only question remaining is, will the adjustment take?

Nixon's **aura** is the best place to look for an answer. Only at the level of his energy bodies will we be able to see the immediate impact of trauma, as well as his deepest response to it. And auras always show the truth.

Unfortunately, Tricky Dick's speech chakra has became hollow, now that his "gift" for deception has been undone. His power area appears more bloated than ever. Intellectually, he has drawn a blank. Saddest of all, the spiritual component of Nixon's aura reveals him to be more stuck than ever.

Auras show the deeper side, where free will plays out. As the scandal subsides, will a man like Nixon choose to change, or will he merely cope? His aura suggests the latter. Each person has the ability to heal auric-level problems; I've seen it happen. Positive transformation has one prerequisite, however. The person must choose to start the process in motion. At the time of Photo D, Nixon had the chance to do this but passed on it. To see this, look at his smile in this final photo. For the first time, he has smiled with **lower teeth bared**. This indicates a fierce determination to survive, no matter what. No expression could be farther from repentance.

Real-life face detectives

Now that you've seen how an Integrity Reading is done, relax. Scrutinizing someone that closely, with comparison photos, isn't something you'll have to do on a regular basis. Sure, it's a great way to revisit your ex—assuming that you've kept old snapshots around. And it's an inspiring, yes inspiring, way to revisit *yourself*.

Treat yourself to Integrity Readings of all the people you admire. And remember that, for most relationships, you won't need situational suspicion. Do your detective work to find the talents in people. You know, take time to smell the noses!

But what if I'm still on the paranoid side? Can't you offer any quick tips that I can use in everyday life to avoid people who are evil?

You're not alone in having this concern. Many people imagine that all their problems will be solved by learning to spot evildoers. But that "solution" is overrated. When bad things happen to good people, it's usually not because other people are evil. It's a matter of otherwise good people making mistakes.

The distinction between most wrongdoers and **evil** people is that the latter take pleasure in doing wrong. Like people who make occasional mistakes, people with a long-term pattern of wrongdoing aren't necessarily evil. They can be psychologically unbalanced like Nixon and rationalize their way to making one poor choice after another.

Even if evil did show in a face, it wouldn't show in the faces of most of the people who have done you harm in the past. So how can you protect yourself? Here are my top ten tips:

1. Instinctive wisdom

When a person turns you off for any reason, even if it's just a vague gut reaction, honor your instinct. Avoid that individual if you can.

2. Include yourself in the equation

If the previous experience happens to you a lot, however, maybe it's a signal for you to examine *your* part of the relationship equation: Who owns the problem?

Perhaps your lifestyle needs improvement—either the friends you choose, the neighborhood where you live or your field of work.

Also question your impartiality. Snobbery, prejudice, emotions held in denial and deeper psychological issues—any of these could cause an unjustified sense of danger. Fortunately, problems like these can be overcome. The first step is to acknowledge them, the second to sincerely wish to change. Then professional counselors, healers or support groups can help. Sometimes miracles happen, too. I've seen them happen as the result of one spontaneous heartfelt prayer.

For many people, the seeing-evil-everywhere syndrome may have a ridiculously simple cause that is easily remedied: A foolish habit. Do you start or end your day with "news" about disasters, murders and so forth? What you put your attention on grows stronger in your life. So avoid TV news, especially before going to bed. You can find less psychologically intrusive ways to stay informed about current events.

After you solve the relationship equation, you'll realize that you can be a responsible adult and still trust people.

3. Avoid self-fulfilling judgments

When turned off by people with whom you *must* have business or social dealings, learn about them as fully as possible, rather than dismissing them with a negative judgment. The faster you jump to conclusions, the more likely you are to project our own fears, act upon them and, thus, create a self-fulfilling prophesy.

Face reading can help you to slow down long enough to learn more about people. Even folks who initially seem bad can have their good points as well. Appeal to the good in people whenever you can.

4. Don't trust expressions

When you're attracted to someone as a new friend or business associate, avoid relying on expression as a way to gauge truthfulness.

People with the deepest problems and coldest hearts are master manipulators of expression. No matter how warm a smile, it's still only on the surface.

5. Don't go Hollywood

The movies have taught us well: Heroes are beautiful people. Villains look imperfect. Just one problem: Hollywood's lessons are false.

Conventional good looks and glamour tell you nothing about goodness. But there's another way that faces can attract a spiritual talent scout. Have you noticed? It happens when you learn to love someone—not as a crush or fantasy, but a real-life relationship, which takes time to develop. As love grows, you come to love your friend's looks.

Well, now, as a face reader, you can also appreciate the *meaning* of that face.

Ironically, you may come to especially treasure the face data that keeps your friend from looking conventionally attractive. Related to the Paradox of Extreme Talent, discussed in Chapter Ten, facial quirks correspond to a person's greatest gifts.

6. Use your common sense

When you read faces to do detective work, use physiognomy to supplement (not substitute for!) your common sense. Don't be so busy reading faces that you ignore the obvious. First, pay attention to what a person does. Second, compare it to what that person says. Third, read the face.

7. Notice mixed messages

Human beings are complex, capable of feeling many emotions at once. If you've studied psychology, you've learned the value of spotting **mixed messages**, which happen when a person contradicts his own statements. Mixed messages can be verbal or non-verbal (as in the photo we examined at the start of this chapter).

For self-protection, it's wise to notice when a person gives mixed messages. Although the significance may be minor, it could also be major—as turned out to be the case with Nixon. Important mixed messages can show, in a subtle way, when you investigate faces.

Be alert to lack of congruence between self-presentation and a person's physical face data. To spot problems, you don't need to do a full hour-long face reading. Simply note what is most extreme or unusual about the face, and see if it jibes with

Your facial opposites

Not like somebody's looks? You may have fallen into a sneaky trap which relates to facial *verys*. Having read this far into this book, you've no doubt learned about the *verys* on your own face.

It's common to unconsciously react with dislike when someone behaves in a manner that is opposite from your own *very*. Remember, behavior that corresponds to *very* extreme face data will be strong. Ever hear the expression that a person "pushes your buttons"? Well, those *verys* are some of your buttons!

Thus, when you have extreme tendencies in one direction, your buttons can (and will) be pushed by people with extreme tendencies in the *opposite* direction.

So, what's sneaky about this trap? It operates unconsciously. To escape it, catch the feeling of dislike when it starts surging through your emotions. Look for *verys* on the face of the person involved, interpret what they mean and think about how this might contrast with your personal comfort zone.

Once you become conscious of what's taking place, it's like breaking an evil spell in a fairy tale. For example, if you have *very* large nostrils, you may instinctively mistrust people with *very* small ones, considering them "cheap." If you have a *very* short mouth, you may jump to the conclusion that people with *very* long mouths are "phonies."

Nonsense! Your facial opposites are just the people most apt to push your buttons. Unless you pay attention, you may be wrongly suspicious of them and mistake this for a valid warning.

that person's self-description and body language. Beware, for instance, the man with large, round nostrils who describes himself as frugal.

8. Accept differences in style

More trust is lost on this than most of us would care to admit: A personal style that's radically *different* from your own does not make the person who has it *bad*. (See the sidebar on "Your Facial Opposites.")

9. Stop blaming, start understanding

When life experiences are painful, it's easy to blame other people for being wicked. But don't. Blame can keep you from taking responsibility for your own actions and psychological growth areas.

Human beings are complex. In your entire lifetime, you're likely to meet very few who are simply evil. More often, otherwise good people behave in ways that are confused, selfish, deceptive and so forth.

I'm 54 years old. And only once have I had direct contact with an evil person, a conversation that lasted 10 minutes. Sure, I've met my share of people who treated me in ways that were cruel, irresponsible and so forth, but I have learned to not take their actions personally. The willingness to see people as they are, and not worse than they are, is a mark of spiritual maturity.

10. Use your deeper perception

If you're specifically interested in matters of integrity, learn to read auras in depth and detail. The practice you've had thus far with face reading has prepared you to move in a direction that's even deeper. When you combine reading faces and auras, the possibilities for insight are mind boggling. For examples, see Chapter Twelve, "Integrity Counts," in the Online Supplement.

Conclusion

Hundreds of students have expressed to me that their sole interest in face reading is to help them identify which people might be evil. Time might be better spent if these students would read their own faces to learn about strengths and weaknesses, then choose to lead from their strengths. Ultimately, each of us is responsible for ourself alone.

As meditation master Jack Kornfield writes in *After the Ecstasy, the Laundry,* even enlightened masters aren't perfect:

> "Most teachers will readily admit this truth. Unfortunately, a few West-
> erners have claimed to achieve a perfection and freedom with no shadow.
> Among their communities, things are worse: By their self-inflation they
> have often created the most power-centered and destructive communi-
> ties among us. The wisest express a greater humility." [Kornfield, Jack.
> New York: Bantam Books, 2001, xix-xx]

Reading faces can help in the humility department. I hope that it has also helped you to open your heart to the goodness in people. Each of us has a face-ful of talent, and along with that, the free will to create a life of joy, balance and service to others. When we do that, it will show.

Ultimately what do wrinkles call attention to? Apart from the specific mean-ings you've learned to read, related to facial context, all wrinkles reveal struggle and pain. They're like medals bestowed on the battlefield of life. From a spiritual perspective, the only thing more beautiful than those medals is an upgraded soldier's uniform—physical changes to the face *other than* wrinkles.

By now you appreciate that wrinkles are only the most obvious form of God's makeup. Every human face can evolve in ways that ennoble the physical form. When you interpret these changes as a spiritual talent scout, you will be awed at how much beauty shows in the faces of so-called "ordinary people."

Cowboys ride off into the sunset, in movies at least. Face readers ride on into the sunrise. I wish you a journey with the clear, gentle light of a new day. May your discoveries as a spiritual talent scout bless you and those whose faces you read.

Spiritual talent scouts, share your biggest Aha!s with me. E-mail me at Rosetree@Starpower.net. Or write the old-fashioned way, c/o Women's Intuition Worldwide, P.O. Box 1605, Sterling, VA 20167-1605.

Bibliography
See full Annotated Bibliography at Online Supplement
www.rose-rosetree.com

Cosmetic surgery

At this writing, Amazon.com lists 437 cosmetic surgery titles. Not one, however, questions the value of vanity surgery. Bandwagon books even include so-called consumer-oriented titles, like *The Unofficial Guide to Cosmetic Surgery* by E. Bingo Wyer. So if you're looking for an author who dares to express an anti-cosmetic surgery point of view, *Wrinkles Are God's Makeup* might be your best bet.

Face reading

Khalsa, Narayan Singh, Ph.D. *What's in a Face?* Boulder: Narayan-Singh Publications, 1997. Order at 13808 173rd Ave., N.E., Redmond, WA 98052; 425-885-2286.

Oshawa, George. *You Are All Sanpaku.* New York: Lyle Stuart, 1983.

Rosetree, Rose. *The Power of Face Reading.* Second ed., Sterling: WIW, 2001.

Young, Lailan. *Secrets of the Face.* Boston: Little, Brown, 1984.

Mind-body medicine

Chopra, Deepak M.D. *Perfect Health: The Complete Mind-Body Guide.* Revised Ed. New York, Three Rivers Press, 2001.

Hay, Louise. *Heal Your Body: The Mental Causes for Physical Illness and the Metaphysical Way to Overcome Them.* Santa Monica: Hay House, 1994.

Myss, Caroline, Ph.D. *Why People Don't Heal—and How They Can,* New York: Three Rivers Press, 1998.

Schultz, Mona Lisa,M.D. *Awakening Intuition.* New York: Three Rivers Press, 1998.

Ullman, Robert et al. *Homeopathic Self Care: The Quick and Easy Guide for the Whole Family.* Lava Ridge, CT: Prima Publishing,1997

Psychology

Aron, Elaine N. *The Highly Sensitive Person: How to Thrive When the World Overwhelms You.* New Jersey: Birch Lane Press, 1996.

Laney, Marti Olsen, Psy.D. *The Introvert Advantage: How to Thrive in an Extrovert World.* New York: Workman, 2002.

Soul signature traits
Browne, Sylvia. *Blessings from the Other Side: Wisdom and Comfort from the Afterlife for This Life.* New York: Dutton, 2000.

Hillman, James. *The Soul's Code : In Search of Character and Calling.* New York: Warner Books, 1997.

Vanity pressures
Faludi, Susan. *Backlash: The Undeclared War Against American Women.* New York: Anchor, 1992.

McBryde, Linda, M.D. *The Mass Market Woman: Defining Yourself as a Person in a World That Defines You By Your Appearance.* Anchorage: Crowded Hour Press, 1999.

Wolf, Naomi. *The Beauty Myth: How Images of Beauty Are Used Against Women.* New York: Anchor, 1992.

Articles worth reading
Cashion, Lisa Beth. "Internalization of the 'beauty ideal,' body image satisfaction and willingness to undergo cosmetic surgery." *Dissertation Abstracts International:* Section B: the Sciences & Engineering. 62(3-B) (9/2001)1567.

Epstein, Joseph. "Prozac, with Knife" *Commentary*, 110(7/2000)54.

Gilbert, Susan. "Gauging the Risk Factors in the Search for a Perfect Face" *New York Times.* CXLVII, n 51,194 (1998) 15-18.

Rhodes, Gillian et al. "Attractiveness of facial averageness and symmetry in non-Western cultures: In search of biologically based standards of beauty." *Perception.* 30(2001) 611-625.

Rubenstein, Adam J. et al. "What makes a face attractive and why: The role of averageness in defining facial beauty." *Advances in Visual Cognition,* 1(2000)1-33. Westport, CT: Ablex Publishing. x, 311.

Underwood, Nora. "Body Envy: Thin is in—and people are messing with Mother Nature as never before." *Maclean's.* (8/14, 2000.)36.

Index I: Famous Faces

This index is your shortcut to find all the famous people mentioned in this book. Most are pictured, too. For photos of the rest, check our Online Supplement. Click onto the author's website, http://www.rose-rosetree.com. Then choose the link to the Online Supplement.

In addition to photos and links, you'll find additional readings of famous faces at the Online Supplement.

Index II: Face Data

Use this index like a birdwatcher's guide for people. Look up face data for definitions, references to photographs that illustrate them, plus interpretations of the meaning.

New face readers, use this index to develop your skills quickly. Find just a few new bits of face data each day, look them up here and apply the meanings. Refine and adjust those meanings to custom design *your own system of physiognomy.*

Index III: Behavior

Here's the index to help you fulfill your purpose in investigating faces. Look up the areas of life that interest you most, then use the references to see where in the face you might find the corresponding data. Because the system of Face Reading Secrets® is complex, expect to find a rich variety of face traits and changes, rather than simple, quick answers. Judging people is fast; gaining insight takes longer. Index III also contains topics not directly related to faces, like pets, pests and Internet dating.

Bring These Books Home!

All Rose Rosetree's titles can be special ordered from quality bookstores.
Or use this order form. You can also order securely online at www.Rose-Rosetree.com.

Wrinkles are God's Makeup	**$19.95**
The Power of Face Reading	**$18.95**
Empowered by Empathy:	**$18.95**
25 Ways to Fly in Spirit	
The Roar of the Huntids	**$22.95**
Thrill Your Soul: Inspiration for	**$24.95**
Choosing Your Work & Relationships	
(A how-to video, digitally mastered)	
Aura Reading Through ALL Your Senses	**$14.95**

U.S. shipping: first item - $4.00, addt'l items - $2 each

Sales tax (VA residents only) per item:
Wrinkles $.90, Empathy and Face Reading $.85,
Roar $1.03, Aura Reading $.67, Video $1.13

Total order..

Address _____

Name _____   Telephone _____

[ ] I request an **autographed** copy, signed for: _____

[ ] Enclosed is my check or money order, **payable to** Women's Intuition Worldwide.
Send to: 116 Hillsdale Drive, P.O. Box 1605, Sterling, VA 20167-1605

[ ] Please charge to my credit card number.
Call 703-404-4357.
Or charge by mail. **Choose from Visa, MasterCard or Discover Card:**
Card number: _____   Exp. date: _____
Authorization signature: _____

Thank you for your order.

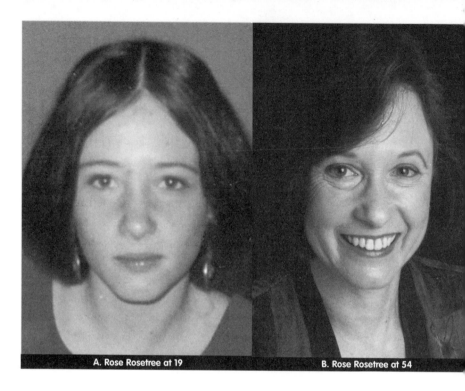

A. Rose Rosetree at 19   B. Rose Rosetree at 54

Since 1971, Rose has taught techniques to develop perception in everyday life, including Face Reading Secrets® and Aura Reading Through ALL Your Senses. The discoveries in this book represent the leading edge of her work.

Media interviews for this award-winning teacher have brought her insights to Europe, Asia, Africa and Australia. In America, Rose's interviews include "The View," "The Diane Rehm Show," *USA Today* and *The Washington Post*. Clients include Long & Foster Real Estate, The Food Marketing Institute and George Washington University.

Rose Rosetree is a graduate of the United Nations International School and Brandeis University. She lives with her husband and son in Sterling, Virginia.

Only a cowardly face reader wouldn't show her photo! See a full Transformation Reading of the author at the Online Supplement to this book at www.Rose-Rosetree.com.

Photo credits: Photo A, Rose's mother, Sue Kramer; Photo B, Jan Kawamoto Jamil